D1410093

The Uniforms of the United States Navy

The Uniforms of the United States Navy

James C. Tily

original illustrations by Marvin H. Pakula

SOUTH BRUNSWICK
NEW YORK • THOMAS YOSELOFF • LONDON

© 1964 by A. S. Barnes and Company, Inc.
Library of Congress Catalog Card Number: 63-18235

Thomas Yoseloff, Publisher
8 East 36th Street
New York 16, New York

Thomas Yoseloff, Publisher
Cranbury, New Jersey

First Printing February, 1964
Second Printing February, 1968

9920
Printed in the United States of America

To the Men and Women of the United States Navy

Foreword

Captain Tily, with enthusiasm and energy, has demonstrated that some of the qualities that make a good naval officer likewise make a good historian—indefatigable application, sincere effort to get at the facts, integrity, and objective evaluation. At least they insure that in the field of his specialty he can produce a work of distinction. Captain Tily has used effectively his naval training in seeking the truth to write this study of the uniforms of the United States Navy.

My able associate, Rear Admiral F. Kent Loomis, USN (Ret.), and I early realized that in assisting Captain Tily we were assisting a man who would produce results of unique value in a study of uniforms.

Those just entering the Navy often consider the "Uniform Regs" as fixed as the Ten Commandments and as enduring as the sea. Experience reveals that change voyages here as in all other affairs of men. It is therefore logical that our uniform today has emerged through a long succession of changes—and a safe bet that it will experience others. This evolutionary process is traceable through uniform regulations, modifications to regulations, general orders, etc.—traceable, that is, with a number of gaps in readily available information until Captain Tily undertook this work.

By extensive research, Captain Tily has succeeded in bringing together a documented, step-by-step history of the Navy's uniforms. His full use of illustrations allows the reader to view changes as they took place, and thereby greatly enhances the value of the book.

The Civil War years and immediately preceding ones marked the effective use of broad innovations in naval warfare—steam propulsion, ironclads, torpedoes, submarines, balloon boats, large caliber rifled guns to name some of the more important. Captain Tily rightly concludes that this same period witnessed the emergence of the essential characteristics of the modern naval uniform. He, therefore, has pivoted his study at the Civil War, but his coverage of the uniform spans our history as a free people.

The need and desire for a naval uniform was frequently expressed during the American Revolution. In 1778 the officers serving on board the Continental frigate *Providence* addressed themselves to their skipper, Captain Abraham Whipple, requesting "that a proper Navy uniform be procured" so that "all may have an opportunity to appear alike as brothers united in one cause."

From the critical days of the War of Independence to the grave crises of our atomic space-age the uniform of the United States Navy has identified men of the sea united in preserving the hard won liberties of our nation and of all men still free across the seas of the world. It is a proud uniform with a proud record that will fire the hearts of men as long as truth and integrity and valor endure. In producing this readable reference on uniforms Captain Tily has made a sound contribution to knowledge of the many faceted Navy.

E.M. Eller
Rear Admiral, USN (Ret.)
Director of Naval History

August 31, 1962
Navy Department
Washington, D.C.

Preface

A study of the uniforms of the United States Navy reveals that the present uniformity in dress dates from the Civil War. Although some progress had been made toward standardization before 1861, the urgencies of a major sea war forced the Navy Department to adopt a common uniform for officers and to prescribe readily identifiable rank and corps devices. Other factors which have had a bearing on Navy dress are Congressional legislation, Naval administration, changes in rank structure, and the changing role played by the staff officers in the ever-changing Navy of the United States.

This present work is concerned not with the role of the United States Navy in every major crisis, but rather with the dress of its officers and men. It is offered in the hope that the many publications issued in the past and which have been or will be released during the Centennial of the Civil War, may be read more intelligently, and that their illustrations will have more meaning.

The Civil War was the first American conflict to be given coverage by photographers and on-the-spot artists. There is a wealth of contemporary material available with which to illustrate the Navy's part in the War between the States. However, it is difficult for most readers to determine from any of this the rank of an officer or the rating of an enlisted man of the United States Navy of 1861-1865. The methods used to show rank, rate, specialty, and corps bear little resemblance to those employed by the Navy today. While the devices used by the Army to show rank and rating were basically the same then as now, in the period from 1861 to 1865 the Navy employed three distinctive systems of gold lace to indicate an officer's rank! Cap devices and shoulder ornaments were frequently changed, and it is difficult not only to identify rank but also to distinguish between line and staff officers.

Contemporary photographs or portraits used to illustrate books about the Navy are often misleading. One photograph may show a group of officers with more than one system of sleeve lace or cap insignia, indicating uniforms authorized under more than one regulation. It was not possible then, nor is it possible today, to have one's insignia changed immediately to conform to new instructions. It has long been the policy of the Navy to permit the wearing of a uniform for a reasonable period of time after a change has been ordered. Uniforms, gold lace, and embroidery have always been expensive. Frequently the new devices are not on hand in shops of military tailors. In selecting illustrations for any work on military matters, it is not always possible for an author to find a portrait or photograph which will show an officer in the dress or rank of the particular period under consideration. This is especially true of the pre-camera era, for even then, portraits were expensive and usually beyond the reach of a junior officer or an enlisted man. Most military portraits are of officers with the rank of a captain in the Navy; or of a colonel or general of the Army, it may be taken for granted that the exception was a man of some means and not entirely dependent on service pay. As a result, there are often discrepancies between the illustrations in military chronicles and the texts they accompany.

For the wars since 1914–1918, it is comparatively simple to determine the rank and specialty of members of the armed services of the United States. Newspapers and periodicals frequently contained such information, often including data on the forces of our allies and opponents. If ever such information were needed, it is to identify Navy rank in 1861–1865! To fill this void and make possible a better understanding of the Navy of the Civil War, tables have been included in this study to show the devices, insignia, and sleeve ornaments of the United States Navy, reflecting the many changes which took place from Fort Sumter to Appomattox.

Some years ago, while on duty in New York, I conceived the idea of assembling all possible information on the insignia of the Civil Engineer Corps of the United States Navy. I was proud to wear the device of the Corps, but had little knowledge of its origin, or of the uniforms on which it had been worn. At first, the assembling of the necessary material seemed to be a simple matter of going to the many excellent libraries, museums, and historical societies in the area. Before long I learned that although the dress of the Army had been the subject of many publications, very little had been published on that of the Navy. Printed uniform regulations do give the basic information as of a specific date, but it is also necessary to have some knowledge of the changes made between the printed regulations. Fortunately, for my particular project the time span was not long. Civil engineers were not permitted to wear the Navy uniform until 1881, even though they had been connected with the Navy since early in the nineteenth century. With the assistance of my parent bureau, that of Yards and Docks, and especially of the Navy Uniform Board, the study was completed and published in the Fall of 1958 *Journal of The Company of Military Collectors and Historians,* with excellent illustrations by Mr. H. Charles McBarron, a Company member and a well-known artist.

The story of the development of the Navy uniform from 1797 to the present fascinated me. I felt it was not proper that the many pieces of information should be scattered in one place and another, unavailable to students of military matters. Since my last tour of duty, prior to retirement, was in Washington, D.C., I had an opportunity to delve into the official archives and to come up with a reasonably complete story. I am obliged to say that it is only "reasonably" complete since the records contain references to orders, changes, and instructions which cannot be located. Let us hope that in time they may come to light.

I was most fortunate in that Rear Admiral E. M. Eller, Director of Naval History, and his assistant, R. Adm. F. Kent Loomis, showed the greatest interest in a study of the Navy's uniform. They gave me not only every assistance, but what is more important, their positive encouragement. Dr. William J. Morgan and his assistants in the History Division provided guidance and assisted in the assembling of material. Mr. Henry A. Vadnais, Jr. and his staff in the Curator's office made available pictures of officers and men and made copies of source material.

Without the use of the facilities of the Navy Library, it would have been impossible to make any study of the Navy's dress. Permission to photograph and otherwise copy books and documents from that inner sanctum, the Rare Book Section, placed me within easy access of information not found in other locations. Mr. W. B. Greenwood, Navy Department librarian, and the assistant librarian, Mr. F. S. Meigs, were most helpful in locating material and in providing books for detailed study. Miss Mary F. Pickens, busy though she always is, managed to find time to dig out answers to telephone inquiries, and, at the library, to guide me to the proper shelf and book, and to suggest approaches to obscure information.

From the first day I began work on my study of the device of the Civil Engineer Corps and the uniforms worn by civil engineers, the Navy Uniform Board has assisted far beyond the call of duty. My article drafts were checked for accuracy and completeness; copies of change orders were provided; my attention was drawn to published material;

and the files of this section of the Bureau of Naval Personnel were always available for study. My first contact with the Uniform Board was by letter with Commander W. S. Edwards, then the Assistant for Uniforms. His successors, Commander D. A. Shonerd and Commander J. R. House, were equally cooperative. The administrative assistant to the Board, Mrs. Ruth Triplett, answered my too many questions—and I fear that some of the queries were answered more than once, for at times I could not read my own notes!

The records of the National Archives helped me to assemble a reasonably complete story of the Navy's uniforms over the years. While there is no one complete collection of information on uniforms, the National Archives does contain a wealth of material not to be found in any other location. Mr. Elbert L. Huber, Archivist in Charge of the Navy Branch, and Mrs. T. G. Goggin, opened the door to a vast store of material and provided me with copies of many, many changes to the uniform regulations. Some of these were not in either the Navy Library or the files of the Uniform Board. The Still Picture Section of the Archives contains a wonderful collection of photographs, including many of the Navy. Through the courtesy of Miss Josephine Cobb, I was able to secure photographs of individual officers and groups of officers and men. The written regulation *describes* a uniform, but one needs a picture to determine how the words were translated by the tailors.

Another valuable source of information was the Smithsonian Institution, where there are many naval uniforms on display and in storage. When I was endeavoring to locate the 1834 device worn by officers of the Medical Department of the Navy, I could not locate any official pattern. Dr. Philip K. Lundeberg located a dress coat worn by Dr. Bailey Washington in the 1830–1840 period, and provided me with photographs of the collar. Here at last was the gold embroidered device described in the uniform change of December 24, 1834 as "a sprig of live oak." It will not now be necessary for any student of military dress to delve in the archives for information on the style of this device, for the Company of Military Collectors and Historians has published a hand-colored print depicting the surgeons of the Navy, 1830–1841, in which the device is shown.

The Naval Historical Foundation collection, now located in the Manuscript Division of the Library of Congress, is an excellent source of information on the Navy in general, and contains some valuable material on the Navy's uniform. The Print and Photographs Division of the Library of Congress has in its Brady Collection many interesting photographs showing naval personnel of the Civil War period. Some of these photographs have been used to illustrate this study. I owe a debt of gratitude to Mr. Marko Zlatich of the Library of Congress staff, who, although not connected with the Prints and Photographs Division, was most helpful in locating material and photographs for this study.

Many fellow collectors have made information available from their personal files and libraries to fill gaps in the information I was able to secure from public collections. Colonel Frederick P. Todd, Director of the Museum at West Point, loaned me a copy of the 1852 Navy Uniform Regulations, as published by Tomes, Son and Melvain of New York. His copy included a pasted-in change issued by the Navy Department on May 23, 1863. This not only altered the sleeve lace of officers of the Navy, but also directed that line officers were to wear a gold-embroidered star on the sleeves, above the stripes. No copy of this order, which established the star as the device of the line of the Navy, has been located in any official file! When I was assembling data on the 1830 Uniform Regulations, I found that while the Navy Department has a copy of the text, it does not have the patterns mentioned in the order. Some of the illustrations were found in the Naval Historical Foundation collection, others at the Archives, and one, showing the device for surgeons, was furnished by Professor George Keester from his own collection of militaria. Mrs. John Nicholas Brown of Providence, Rhode Island has furnished photographs of Navy material from her marvelous private collection.

Appendix A, a reproduction of the 1852 Navy Uniform Regulations, is possible because of the interest and assistance of many people. The Navy Library permitted me to borrow their rare copy of the regulations, and the staffs of the Naval Medical School, Bethesda, Maryland, and of the *Leatherneck,* the Marine Corps magazine, did the photography. When it was discovered that one page was missing, Colonel Frederick P. Tood, Director of the West Point Museum, loaned me his personal copy of the regulation so that Appendix A might be complete.

Mr. Marvin H. Pakula's fine orginal water colors show the various uniforms worn during the Civil War period. His tables of insignia and devices make the many changes of the war period easy to follow. They will be invaluable to all students of military dress.

The office of the Director of the Navy Nurse Corps made available copies of early uniform instructions for the Nurse Corps, and provided some of the illustrations. Thru the assistance of Commander Anna Danyo and her staff at the Philadelphia Naval Hospital, additional photographs were supplied. The assistance of the Nurse Corps is greatly appreciated.

It should be evident that the assembling of material for any study of military dress is not the work of any one person. Without the guidance, interest, and material help of many others, no definitive study would be possible. My heartfelt thanks go to all who were so generous, interested, and helpful.

JAMES C. TILY

Captain, Civil Engineer Corps, U.S. Navy, Retired

Bala Cynwyd, Pa.
April 22, 1962

Contents

Foreword   7

Preface   9

I   Navy Department, 1789–1865: Legislation, Administration, Management   17

II   Uniforms, 1797–1852   55

III   Uniforms, 1852–1862   102

IV   Uniforms, 1862–1866   116

V   Navy Department, 1865–1962: Legislation, Administration, Management   155

VI   Uniforms, 1866–1962   187

Appendix A: Uniform Regulations, United States Navy, 1852   273

Appendix B: Uniform Regulations, United States Navy, 1959   293

Appendix C: Insignia and Devices of the Civil War Period   313

Index   332

U.S. Military Magazine

THE ARMY & NAVY,
Gen! Washington presenting Cap! Barry with his Commission._ 22ⁿᵈ Feb! 1797.

Army & Navy, Vol. 1ˢᵗ. Pl. 8

The Huddy and Duval lithograph shows Captain John Barry in a reasonably accurate facsimile of the dress of a captain of the newly created Navy, as prescribed by the Secretary of War, James McHenry, in 1797. The artist's conception of this historic event is rather fantastic. President Washington, although he was Commander in Chief of the Army and Navy, would hardly have been dressed as a general, nor would this view have been seen from any public building in Philadelphia, then the Capital of the United States. The midshipman is not shown in the "blue and buff" uniform of 1797, but in the "blue and gold" prescribed by the first uniform regulation issued in 1802 by the then four year old Navy Department.

(Courtesy of the Anne S. K. Brown Military Collection.)

I

Navy Department, 1789–1865:

Legislation, Administration, Management

The uniforms of the United States Navy, and the indications of rank and specialty displayed on them, are but outward symbols of Naval organization and military rank or rating. The laws passed by the Congress of the United States, the successive changes in the organization of the Navy Department, the wars in which the Navy played an important part, the changes in technology and weapons, and even those in the styles of civilian clothing, all influenced Navy dress. The naval uniform can be discussed only against a background of administration, with its constant changes to meet the demands of a growing and changing United States.[1]

Since we are concerned primarily with the changes in the dress of the United States Navy in the critical years from 1861 to 1865, it appears logical to divide this study into two major parts—from the creation of a navy in 1794 to 1865, the end of the Civil War; and from 1865 to date—so that the effects on the present dress of the Navy of the major changes in its uniform between 1861 and 1865 can be shown. Matters which modified administration and the uniform itself will be treated within these two general areas.

With the end of the Revolutionary War the few remaining ships of the Continental Navy were sold, for there was no apparent need for a seaborne military force. Even if there had been, the financial condition of the United States under the Continental Congress was such that a navy could not be financed. The major problems facing the newly independent country were the organization of a national government to

17

replace the weak confederation of the several sovereign states, the establishment of a strong national credit, and the protection of the western frontiers. In spite of the lack of stability in either currency or banking facilities, a large merchant marine, flying the new flag, was soon on the high seas. The long tradition of building, manning, and employing ships to carry the products of the New World, which had been interrupted by the Revolution, reasserted itself. Any nation with good harbors, materials, and skills to build ships is not likely to be denied the use of the seas. While the new county was deficient in manufacturing facilities it did have the raw materials and agricultural products which had been the medium of exchange for the manufactured products of Europe prior to 1775.

When the proposed Constitution was being debated, the question as to whether or not the proposed central government should have the power "to provide and maintain a navy" was considered along with all the other powers which were to be surrendered by the states to the Federal government. The Federalists, proponents of a strong central government, believed that if the United States were to emerge as a strong nation and take its proper place in the world, the country would have to be strong enough to maintain order internally and to protect its land frontiers, and also be able to protect its commerce on the high seas. The anti-Federalists (later known as Republicans) favored limiting the powers of the central government, and retaining more power in the individual states. They saw the future of the country chiefly in the west, where new lands could be opened to cultivation to provide for an expanding population. Perhaps at some later date, when the United States had become strong internally, she could look east to the sea.

When, after a long and at times bitter debate, the Constitution was ratified, it contained several provisions with respect to a navy. Congress was given the power "to provide and maintain a Navy," and "to make Rules for the Government and Regulation of land and naval Forces." In addition, the President was made commander in chief of the military forces. The Federal Government was given exclusive legislative authority over such places as were purchased for dockyards and other military depots, and the individual states were not permitted to own vessels of war in time of peace. However, the Constitution did not create a Navy Department, for the executive department were not specifically named. This matter was left to the Congress.

When the Federal Government was organized in 1789, there were no men-of-war and no pressing need for a navy. The War Department was created by an act of Congress of August 7, 1789. The Secretary of War was directed to perform all duties relating to military commissions, or to "the land and naval forces, or warlike stores of the United States, or to such other matters respecting the military or naval affairs, as the President of the United States shall assign to the said department."

The most pressing problems were the maintenance of internal order and protection of the frontiers. While there was no immediate thought of creating a naval force, there were incidents which did affect the expanding American shipping. The Barbary Powers—Algiers, Tripoli, Tunis, and Morocco—and their nominal overlords the Turks, considered the Mediterranean their special domain. Up to the time of the American Revolution, the British fleet had protected all British shipping, including, of course, that of the North American colonies. After independence had been won, there was no force to protect American merchant shipping anywhere in the high seas. In 1785 two vessels had been captured in the Mediterranean—the *Maria* of Boston and the *Dolphin* of Philadelphia— and their crews enslaved.[2] Internal problems and trouble on the western frontiers overshadowed the fate of the captives. Nothing was done for their relief nor to assert the power of the new republic. When the situation worsened, and the actions of the Algerians became more threatening, it was evident that more positive actions had to be taken. On March 27, 1794 a bill "to provide a Naval Armament" was signed into law. Thus our first naval force under the Constitution came into being. The act was specifically directed against Algiers, and the last section of the law showed it was not the intention of the Congress to create a permanent navy. Section 9 of the act read: "Provided always, and be it further enacted, that if peace shall take place between the United States and the Regency of Algiers, that no further proceeding be had under this Act."

The legislation provided for the procurement or construction of four 44-gun and two 36-gun frigates; established the numbers and ranks of officers, the number of enlisted men and marines for the vessels; and set forth in detail the pay and rations of officers.

Commissioned officers were to be appointed by the President and approved by the Senate. Warrant officers were to hold their authority from the President. The following tabulation lists the ranks authorized, and shows their pay and rations.

RANK	PAY	RATIONS
Commissioned		
Captain	$75 per month	6
Lieutenant	40 per month	3
Lieutenant of Marines	26 per month	2

Chaplain	40 per month	2
Surgeon	50 per month	2
Surgeon's Mate	30 per month	2

Warranted

Sailing Master	40 per month	2
Purser	40 per month	2
Boatswain	14 per month	2
Gunner	14 per month	2
Carpenter	14 per month	2
Sailmaker	14 per month	2
Midshipman		—

Petty officers were to be appointed by the captain of the ship. The ratings authorized were:

Master's Mate	Quarter Gunner's Mate
Captain's Mate	Carpenter's Mate
Boatswain's Mate	Armourer
Cockswain	Steward
Sailmaker's Mate	Cook
Gunner's Mate	Master at Arms
Gunner of the Gun Room	Cooper

The non-commissioned officers of the Marine detachment were sergeants and corporals. Each frigate was permitted to have one fife and one drum; the first music of the United States Navy! The President was to set the pay of all petty officers, seamen, marines, and midshipmen.

For a comparison of the newly established naval ranks with those of the Army, it is necessary to go back to a "Resolve" of the Continental Congress of November 15, 1776, which established the relative rank of Army and Navy officers as follows:

ARMY	NAVY
General	Admiral
Lieutenant General	Vice Admiral
Major General	Rear Admiral
Brigadier General	Commodore
Colonel	Captain of a ship of 40 guns or more
Lieutenant Colonel	Captain of a ship of from 20 to 40 guns
Major	Captain of a ship of from 10 to 20 guns
Captain	Lieutenant

This is still the basic correspondence between Army and Navy ranks. Additional grades have been added to both services, and the titles of naval officers for the grades between lieutenant and the senior captain have been modified.

It is to be noted that the act of 1794 made provision for both combatant and non-combatant officers. The three groups of "civil" or, as they are known today, staff officers, were chaplains, surgeons and surgeon's mates, and pursers (the present-day Supply Officers). In the early days of the United States Navy, these three classes of civil officers were adequate to support the seagoing, or, in present-day terminology, line officers. As changes in vessels and administration, and improvements in science and technology, occurred, it was necessary to increase the staff specialists of the Navy. These changes in the Staff, and the creation of additional ranks of line officers, brought about frequent changes in the uniform to permit the identification of an officer's rank and specialty or corps. For this reason, it is necessary to review the many changes in naval administration and the development of the various staff corps.

The act of 1794 gave the President authority to procure the six frigates by purchase, to have them built by contract, or to arrange to have them built by the Government. The decision was made to have them built by Government forces. Six sites were leased, one for each vessel, distributing the work from New Hampshire to Virginia. Captains were appointed to oversee the construction, naval constructors were appointed to take immediate charge of the work, and Naval Agents were selected to procure such materials as were not purchased directly by the Treasury Department. The following table shows the vessels, the ports where they were to be built, the captains who were to act as superintendents, the naval constructors, and the agents.[3]

VESSEL	PORT	SUPERINTENDENT
Congress 36 guns	Portsmouth, N. H.	James Sever
Constitution 44 guns	Boston, Mass.	Samuel Nicholson
President 44 guns	New York, N. Y.	Silas Talbot
United States 44 guns	Philadelphia, Pa.	John Barry
Constellation 36 guns	Baltimore, Md.	Thomas Truxton
Chesapeake 44 guns	Gosport (Norfolk), Virginia	Richard Dale

NAVAL CONSTRUCTOR	NAVAL AGENT
James Hackett	Jacob Sheafe
George Claghorne	Henry Jackson

Forman Cheeseman   John Blagge
Joshua Humphreys   Gurney and Smith
David Stodder   Samuel and Joseph
Josiah Fox   Sterett
                           William Pennock

In addition to his duties as naval constructor for the *United States,* Joshua Humphreys was designated "Principal Naval Constructor of the Navy" at a salary of $2,000 a year.[4] Captain Thomas Truxtun, who was detailed to supervise the construction of the *Constellation,* was to be a key figure in the development of the newly created Navy. This efficient officer played a major role in the establishment of "Regulations for the Government of the Navy," and in the creation of a signal system.

On September 5, 1795, before any appreciable work had been done on the six frigates, a treaty of peace was concluded with Algiers. Under the stipulations of the Naval Armament Act of 1794, work on the vessels was suspended. However, the times were still most unsettled, for the treaty with Algiers did not solve the problems with the other Barbary Powers. In addition, world conditions were most critical owing to the recent French Revolution and the wars which had grown out of it. After much debate a compromise was reached, and Congress, by an act of April 20, 1796, authorized the completion of the three frigates whose construction had been most advanced when the treaty with Algiers was concluded. These were the *Constitution,* the *United States,* and the *Constellation.* The perishable materials which had been secured for the other three vessels and which were not now required, were to be sold, and the non-perishable supplies were to be stored for future shipbuilding. The three frigates, whose names are famous in the history of the United States Navy, were launched between May and October 1797.

Congress on July 1, 1797 authorized the employment and manning of the three vessels then nearing completion. The ranks and ratings listed in the 1794 legislation were repeated. A few changes in pay were made—a Lieutenant of Marines was to receive $30 a month, an increase of $4, and boatswains, gunners, carpenters, and sailmakers had their pay raised from $14 a month to $20. Section 8 of the 1797 act stated that the Navy should be governed by the laws of the Continental Congress of November 28, 1775 in so far as these regulations were applicable under the Constitution and laws of the United States.

Tension in relations with Republican France, then under the Directory, increased, and an all-out war with our former ally appeared imminent. French privateers were capturing American merchant shipping in the Caribbean and off the coast of the United States. To meet this threat, an Act of April 27, 1798, "To provide additional armament for the further protection of the trade of the United States," authorized the purchase, building, or hire of twelve additional vessels of not more than 22 guns each. The Navy was expanding as a result of congressional appropriations and also by the addition of vessels built by private subscription and presented to the Government. The need for a military force afloat had finally been recognized!

With a growing Navy, and a threat of serious war, it was evident that a better arrangement for managing naval affairs was necessary. The War Department's small staff was busy with matters concerning the regular Army, the militias of the various States, land defenses, and protection of the frontiers. Then, too, the construction program for the first frigates had been severely criticized for its cost and slowness. By an act of April 30, 1798, the Navy Department was created. The act provided that "there shall be an executive department under the denomination of the Department of the Navy, the chief officer of which shall be called the Secretary of the Navy." The duty of the secretary "shall be to execute such orders as he shall receive from the President of the United States, relative to the procurement of naval stores and materials, and the construction, armament, equipment, and employment of vessels of war, as well as all other matters connected with the naval establishment of the United States." It is to be noted that the Secretary was specifically charged with the "employment of the vessels of war. . . . " This responsibility was later to be challenged, when the Board of Navy Commissioners was established to assist the Secretary in 1815. Provision was made for a principal clerk and such other clerks as might be necessary. All records pertaining to the Navy were to be turned over to the new department by the Secretary of War.

President Adams nominated George Cabot of Massachusetts to be the first Secretary of the Navy. The Senate confirmed the nomination on May 3, just three days after the act had been approved.[5] Cabot declined the post on the grounds that he did not consider himself sufficiently qualified to handle naval affairs. On May 18, the President nominated Benjamin Stoddert, a merchant of Georgetown, Maryland, who was confirmed on May 21. Although technically Cabot was the first Secretary of the Navy, it was Stoddert who, during his term of office from 1798 to his retirement in 1801, laid the foundations of the American Navy.

Under Stoddert the Navy Department consisted of two offices, those of the Secretary and of the accountant of the Navy. Their combined staff numbered approximately a dozen people. Stoddert was most fortunate in having the services of Joshua Humphreys, who was not only a skilled naval constructor but a man of marked ability in many fields. He was the chief technical adviser to the Secretary, and made studies and recommendations for sites for permanent navy yards to replace those rented for the first shipbuilding program. The Government acquired sites for permanent navy yards at the locations selected for the building of the six frigates, but substituted one at the new capital, Washington, for the original building yard in Baltimore. During the "Quasi-War" with France the size of the Navy grew from the three frigates of 1797 to a total of fifty vessels: five 44's, four 36's, seven 32's, three 24's seven 20's, four 18's, three 14's, nine galleys, and eight revenue cutters secured from the Treasury Department.[6] The undeclared war with France was ended by a treaty signed in September 1800, but an opportunity was nevertheless provided for the new Navy to show its worth. The actions against the *Insurgent* and the *Vengeance* by the *Constellation,* under the command of Captain Truxtun, and those of the schooner *Enterprise,* commanded by Lieutenant John Shaw, against French privateers did much to establish the reputation and to lay the foundations of the traditions of the United States Navy.[7]

The increase in the number of naval vessels and the employment of ships of varying numbers of guns in the 1798–1800 period is reflected in legislation. An Act of Congress of February 25, 1799, to "Fix the Pay of Captains and Commanders of the Navy," provided that ships of more than 20 guns were to be commanded by captains, and those of less than 20 guns by masters or lieutenants. It is to be remembered that the acts of 1794 and 1797 to provide "a naval armament" had listed only captains and lieutenants as commissioned officers. Masters were listed under the heading of warrant officers. The section of the 1799 act covering pay established the following schedule for the senior combatant officers:

Captains of vessels of 32 guns and up $100 a month and 8 rations
Captains of vessels of from 20 to 32   75 a month and 6 rations
   guns
Masters Commandant   60 a month and 5 rations
Lieutenants   50 a month and 4 rations

A new rank was created, that of master commandant, in other words, a "master in command," and placed between those of captain and lieutenant. With an expanded Navy, it was possible to operate ships in squadrons, under the senior officer's command. Congress, while still reluctant to create the ranks of admiral, vice admiral, rear admiral, and commodore—for the American public regarded such titles as smacking of monarchies and royalty—made provision for an officer in over-all command. The recognition thus made did not take the form of a new title, but was monetary! Section 2 of the 1799 act provided that "officers commanding a squadron" should receive double rations, that is, sixteen instead of the eight of a captain. The senior captain of the Navy was also to receive double rations. Since rations over and above those consumed aboard ship were commuted to cash, the increase in pay was rather substantial, especially considering that the basic pay of a senior captain was $100 a month. This same practice is current in the present-day Navy, for all officers receive a "Basic Allowance for Subsistence" in addition to their pay. If an officer is subsisted on board ship or eats regularly in a Navy-operated mess ashore, he loses the allowance, but must still pay a mess bill. If he lives ashore, or off station, he draws the allowance, for he must provide food at his own expense.

When a treaty of peace with France was ratified early in 1801, the Navy was put on a peacetime footing although most of the world was at war. An act of March 3, 1801 authorized the President to sell all but thirteen ships. Six were to be kept in commission and the remaining seven in "ordinary"—that is, in reduced status, with the expectation that they could speedily be put back into service if needed. This policy is in effect today: many of the ships which served in World War II were placed in "mothballs" at the end of the war, and some have been reactivated as emergencies have arisen. The officer force was reduced to 9 captains, 36 lieutenants, and 150 midshipmen. The rank of master commandant was abolished, only to be re-established in 1806. During the "Quasi-War" the number of officers employed, according to Goldsborough's *Naval Chronical*, were 28 captains, 7 masters commandant, 110 lieutenants, and 354 midshimen. The total strength of the Navy was approximately 5,600 officers and men.[8]

It was not long, however, before it became necessary to strengthen the Navy. Trouble developed in the Mediterranean, where the seagoing bandits of the Barbary Powers renewed their attacks against U. S. shipping. Our payment of tribute for protection against attack was very properly considered weakness. A blackmailer is never satisfied; and in May 1801 the Bashaw of Tripoli, who was not pleased with the amount of his annual tribute, declared war against the United States. The sending of a squadron to the area kept the other Barbary Powers in line and led to a peace with Tripoli in 1805. The highlights of this at times unsuccessful war were the stranding and loss of the frigate *Philadelphia* near Tripoli harbor on October 31, 1803, and the subsequent burning of the vessel, on February 14, 1804 by an intrepid party under the command of Lieutenant Stephen

This excellent tinted engraving by William and Thomas Birch, published in 1800, not only shows how ships were built at that time, but also gives an indication of naval dress. This fine forty-four–gun frigate was built at the expense of the merchants of Philadelphia, and presented to the United States. Although not completed in time to be employed in the war with France, the *Philadelphia* served against the Barbary Powers until she grounded at Tripoli, and later was burned by an intrepid crew under command of Lieutenant Stephen Decatur to prevent her being used against the United States.

In spite of the smallness of the figure of the officer in the foreground, one can see the blue coat with buff lapels and cuffs, and the buff vest and breeches of 1797. Several of the workmen are wearing full trousers, jackets, and hats, the dress of seamen of the period.

(Courtesy of the Atwater Kent Museum.)

Decatur. As American strength in the Mediterranean increased, peace was negotiated. Under the treaty no further tribute was to be given, but the United States did in fact pay $60,000 for the release of the officers and men held prisoner since the capture of the *Philadelphia*. Not a glorious solution, but perhaps the best that could be secured by a nation still comparatively weak at sea.[9]

The war in the Mediterranean had shown that the American eagle was a fighting sea bird. Officers and men had received excellent training, which would serve the United States in good stead when in 1812 the country went to war against the British. Many young officers who had served under Commodore Edward Preble in the fighting against Tripoli would add further glory to their names when they were called upon to meet a stronger foe. "Preble's Boys" had learned their lessons under a tough, outstanding leader.

The war with Tripoli had shown the need for a rank between those of captain and lieutenant. This time, the rank of master commandant would not be dropped as it had been after the French war. An act of Congress on April 21, 1806 set the officer strength of the Navy at 13 captains, 9 masters commandant, 72 lieutenants, and 150 midshipmen. An act of March 30, 1812, which made appropriations for the naval service, directed that thereafter pursers were to be appointed by the President and confirmed by the Senate. Under this proviso, pursers joined the ranks of the commissioned civil or staff officers of the Navy.

Although the need for a strong Navy had been shown in our troubles with France and Tripoli, the usual reaction took place. The Navy was permitted to decline in strength and effectiveness. The policy of Jefferson's administration was one of defense, not offense. Instead of a strong fleet capable of carrying the fight out to sea or to enemy shores, gunboats and fortifications were provided merely to protect the coasts of the United States from possible attack. This was the period of the gunboat Navy. During this period of almost continual war involving the major powers of Europe, no shipping was considered neutral by Great Britain, France, or their allies. When American seamen were being impressed to serve in British men-of-war, there was no Navy strong enough to protect the seaborne commerce so vital to the growth and very existence of the United States. When war was finally declared against Great Britain on June 18, 1812, the American fleet consisted of but seventeen vessels, about one-third of them not ready for sea! [10]

The War of 1812, with more victories at sea than on land, brought the Navy into public favor and made the country aware that a navy was always necessary for its protection. It would be many years before the theory that a navy could be used only to protect the coasts from invasion was discarded, although the error of this thinking should have been evident in 1812–1815. The British fleet blockaded the coast, permitting British troops to be landed almost at will. With commerce raiders, and in occasional ship-to-ship engagements, the Navy showed its strength. Ships were built, outfitted, manned, and sent to sea rapidly, filling the gaps due to losses to the enemy. This ability to turn out satisfactory men-of-war speedily in times of national emergency has been of vital importance in every war since that of 1812.

BOARD OF NAVY COMMISSIONERS

A major war showed the inadequacy of the administrative organization of the Navy Department. From the creation of the department in 1798, the Secretary, with a very limited staff, had been responsible for all naval matters: shipbuilding, operation of the shore facilities, appointment and assignment of officers, procurement of supplies and materials, and instructions for commanders of squadrons or captains of vessels acting singly. This last responsibility was perhaps the most difficult to handle at a time when communications were all by mail, carried by horse or ship. The commanding officer was practically a free agent as soon as he cleared his home port. The only way to modify orders, or to secure reports of progress on the seas, was by fast dispatch boats! One detail not handled directly by the Secretary was the recruiting and signing on of seamen. This authority was in the hands of the individual captains. The need for a better system of management had long been recognized, and had been the subject of recommendations to the Congress. A major sea war was necessary to bring the matter to a head. By an act of February 7, 1815, "to alter and amend the several acts establishing a Navy Department, by adding thereto a Board of Navy Commissioners," a definite step in the right direction was taken.

Under this legislation, the Board of Navy Commissioners was to be composed of three post captains (appointed by the President and approved by the Senate), a secretary to the Board, and a staff of clerks. That Congress was concerned with maintaining civilian control of the military is evidenced by the language directing that nothing in the act was to be construed so as "to take from the Secretary of the Navy his control and direction of the naval forces of the United States, as now by law possessed." The Board was to "discharge all the ministerial duties of the said office, relative to procurement of naval stores and materials, and the construction, armament, equipment, and employment of vessels of war, as well as all other matters connected with the naval establishment of the United States."

President Madison nominated Captains John Rodgers, Isaac Hull, and David Porter to be Navy commissioners on February 15, 1815. The Senate confirmed the nominations the following day. Rodgers, the senior of the three captains, was President of the Board. The principal clerk was Charles W. Goldsborough, later to become the first Chief of the Bureau of Provisions and Clothing (the ancestor of the present Bureau of Supplies and Accounts) when the bureau system of management was introduced in 1842. The secretary to the Board was James K. Paulding, who was to serve as Secretary of the Navy from 1838 to 1841.

Shortly after the Board was formed, friction developed between the commissioners and Secretary of the Navy Crowninshield over their respective duties. The original act establishing the Navy Department had made the Secretary responsible for the "employment of vessels of war," and the 1815 act had given this responsibility to the commissioners. Of course, the 1815 act had stated that the Secretary was to retain "control and direction of the naval forces of the United States, as now by law possessed." As a result of this rather poorly written legislation, a referee was needed! The dispute was referred to President Madison, who ruled that the commissioners were responsible to the Secretary for such matters as the building, repairing, and equipping of ships and the management of the navy yards, or what today are termed the matériel functions. The Secretary was responsible for the appointment of officers, the assignment of officers to duty, the discipline of the Navy, and the movement and employment of ships.[11] As a result, the Secretary of the Navy, an appointed civilian, exercised military command, while the commissioners, the three senior officers of the Navy, were in charge of logistics. The wheel has turned somewhat since that day. Now the Chief of Naval Operations— the senior officer of the Navy—is responsible, under the Secretary, for command functions as directed by the Department of Defense and the Joint Chiefs of Staff. Logistics activities are the responsibility of the Secretary's principal civilian assistants and of the naval technical assistants, the chiefs of the various bureaus. In the final analysis, the Navy is still under civilian control.

Until the end of the War of 1812, the navy yards had been poorly equipped, but with a new building program authorized after the war, many steps were taken to improve facilities. The commissioners, who had served in command during the war, were well aware of the inadequacy of the Navy's shore establishment. Under their direction, many changes and improvements were made to provide the badly needed facilities for both new construction and repair.

Not all the improvements were in the yards, however. As administration of the Navy became more complicated with the rise of the United States as a world power, more and more use was made of trained civilian employees. Many of these non-uniformed specialists were eventually given officers' status, and were the predecessors of the officers of the present day staff corps. Naval constructors were employed to design and build the first frigates authorized in 1794. One of them, Joshua Humphreys, was named "Principal Constructor of the Navy." The same procedure was followed under the Navy Board system: naval constructors designed and oversaw the construction of the men-of-war at the various navy yards. Up until Samuel Humphreys was appointed "Chief Constructor" in 1826, the individual constructors had reported directly to the Board. Now the resident naval constructors reported to the Board through Humphreys. The need for some form of centralized control of technical matters had become evident. For many years, the fine qualities of the ships built by the United States Navy had been an example for other maritime powers. The civilian constructors were anxious to introduce new features in design. They were well aware of improvements being made in the design and construction of foreign men-of-war and merchant vessels. The Navy Board, made up of captains who during the War of 1812 had served with distinction in the frigates which were then the finest examples of this class of ship, was reluctant to accept anything new. The story of the Navy's sailing ship construction program, its successes and failures, has been told in excellent fashion (in The History of the American Sailing Navy) by Howard I. Chappel.[12]

Civil engineers, another professional group, later to become commissioned officers, were employed first in 1802. At that time President Thomas Jefferson requested Benjamin Henry Latrobe to submit plans for a drydock to berth twelve 44-gun frigates at one time. This request was based on Jefferson's plans to reduce the Navy and at the same time to have ships readily available in the event of emergency. This proposal, although it was never carried out, was the forerunner of the present practice of "mothballing" ships which were in excess of the needs of the fleet after World War II. Latrobe was connected with the Navy until 1813. He was employed principally at the Washington Navy Yard, but also prepared reports, designs, and estimates for shore facilities at New York and Norfolk, the two most active yards.

Civil engineers were also employed under the Board of Navy Commissioners. When after land had been acquired for permanent shore

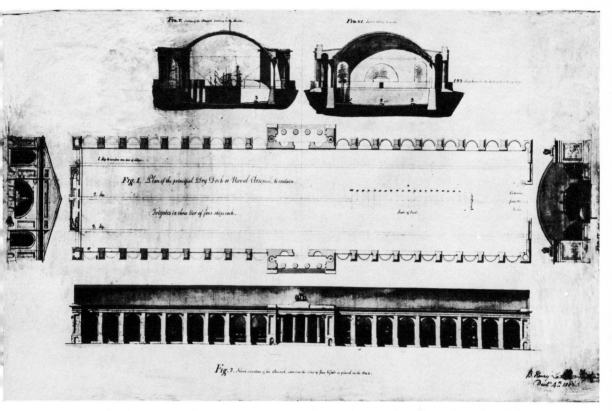

Fig. I. Plan of the principal Dry Dock or Naval Arsenal, to contain

Frigates in three tier of four ships each.

Fig. 2. Front elevation of the Arsenal, shewing the vessels of four tiers as placed in the Dock.

On the basis of a Congressional appropriation of $50,000 for two drydocks in 1799, President Jefferson directed Benjamin Henry Latrobe, an outstanding architect of the time, to prepare plans for a drydock to store twelve frigates. Jefferson, a man of remarkable mechanical ability, believed that if ships were stored in the dry in times of peace, they could be made ready rapidly in any emergency. This drawing by Latrobe, dated December 4, 1802, was intended to be the answer to the problem. The "principal Dry Dock or Naval Arsenal" was to be wide enough to place three frigates abreast, and long enough to have four vessels in each row. The basin of the dock scales 800 feet long, and 175 feet wide. To get the dismasted frigates into the dock, it was proposed to build a series of locks, like those on a canal, to raise the ship from the harbor, and then float it into the dock. When all the vessels were placed in rows on the blocking marked 1, 2, and 3 on the plan, the water would be discharged, leaving the vessels high and dry.

The dock was never built for several good reasons. The cost was estimated at approximately $500,000, and in 1802 it was difficult to secure any funds for the Navy. Ships "in ordinary" and tied up to a pier were subject to attacks by marine borers and wet rot, but in the dry, the seams would open up, and there was always the possibility of dry rot. In addition, there would have been construction problems. The clear span from one row of columns to the other, across the dock, was 175 feet. To build the roof as Latrobe showed it would have been a major problem.

(Courtesy of the Bureau of Yards and Docks.)

facilities, the yards were developed, technical assistance was needed. An Act of Congress of February 25, 1799 had provided $50,000 for two dry-docks. No action was taken under this authority, probably for the reason that at that time the Navy had no permanent shore facilities. The original ship construction of 1794 had been done at rented yards. A "Resolution" of May 22, 1826 directed that an accurate survey be made for the location of two drydocks, by a "skilful" engineer. Latrobe had died in 1820 and the man chosen for this assignment was Loammi Baldwin. As a result of the study, Congress, in an act for "The Gradual Increase in the Navy" on March 3, 1827, provided funds for two drydocks, one south of the Potomac and the other north of Washington. Construction of the docks was begun in 1827, and those at Boston and Norfolk were completed in 1833. The *Delaware* was docked on June 17 in Norfolk, and the *Constitution* at Boston on June 25.[13] Since communication between the two widely separated sites was difficult, Baldwin employed resident engineers at each location. His deputy at Norfolk was William P. S. Sanger, who in 1836 was appointed Civil Engineer for the Navy, reporting to the Navy Board.[14] Sanger is regarded as the "Father" of the Civil Engineer Corps of the Navy.

As the Navy grew and advances were made in science and technology, it was inevitable that legislation would cause changes in Navy dress and insignia of rank. Congress on May 24, 1828 provided for a better organization of the Medical Department of the Navy, in line with current civilian practices. All candidates for appointment were required to pass an examination before a board of senior medical officers. Assistant surgeons, formerly "surgeon's mates," had to pass an examination for promotion to surgeon. Those medical officers who qualified for promotion were called "passed assistant surgeons" during the period of waiting to be commissioned as surgeons. This could be a matter of years, for no system of retirement had as yet been established. With a larger navy, and the more general use of squadrons, many based in foreign locations, it was necessary to make some provision for over-all medical supervision. A hospital ship, carrying a surgeon appointed to oversee the medical work on his own ship and to supervise the medical facilities of the accompanying vessels, at times accompanied a squadron. If the squadron did not have a hospital ship attached, a senior medical officer could be assigned to oversee the work of the surgeons of the various vessels. At times, temporary hospitals were established ashore at an overseas base, with a surgeon in charge. The 1828 act directed that a surgeon performing such duties as have been outlined above be designated a "Fleet Surgeon." The rank structure of the Medical Department thus became:

Fleet Surgeon   (rank and pay only when so designated by the Sec-
Surgeon   retary, and only for the duration of such duty)
Passed Assistant Sur-
  geon
Assistant Surgeon

This change in titles of officers of the Medical Department was reflected in the uniform regulations issued in 1830.

"An Act to regulate the pay of the Navy of the United States," approved March 3, 1835, prescribed the pay of two classes of civil officers, secretaries and professors of mathematics. In addition, clerks were to be paid on an annual basis. Previously they had been selected by the captain from the crew and paid monthly, as were other petty officers. Secretaries to "commanders of squadrons when commanding in chief" were to be paid $1,000 a year. Secretaries to "commanders of squadrons," other than those "in chief," were to be paid $900. This is the first official indication of a recognition by Congress that the commander of a group of vessels required an administrative assistant of sorts, not simply a man from the crew who could read and write.

The need for trained personnel over and above those in the Navy Department, or from the crew on board ship was also recognized. Clerks of a navy yard were to be paid $900 annually. The first clerk to the Commandant of a yard received $900; second clerks to a Commandant, $750; clerks to commanders of squadrons and to captains of individual vessels, $500. The Navy was becoming "big business."

The establishment of the position of professor of mathematics indicated that the educational procedures of the Navy needed modernization and strengthening. The initial attempts to provide some form of education for midshipmen and members of the crew had been unsatisfactory, but were at least steps in the right direction. Since the youngsters and members of the crew had to stand watch and help work the ship, no regular schedule of instruction could be established. The main responsibility for teaching fell on the chaplains, many of whom had been appointed not because of their training as ministers, but for their ability as educators. Since the number of chaplains was never large, this method of education was never very effective. The Naval Regulations of January 25, 1802 prescribed the duties of a chaplain. One section covered his spiritual duties, the other his responsibilities as a teacher. He was to ". . . perform the duty of schoolmaster; and to that end he shall instruct the midshipmen and volunteers in writing, arithmetic, and navigation, and in whatsoever may contribute to make them proficients. He is likewise to teach the other youths of the ship, according to such orders as he shall receive from the captain. He is to be diligent in his office, and such as are idle must be represented to the captain, who shall take due notice thereof."[15]

The employment of schoolmasters under an act of June 2, 1813 was some measure of help to the chaplains and to the over-all instruction program of the Navy. The rate of pay, established by Congress, of $25 a month and two rations could not possibly attract well-educated men as schoolteachers.

In order to improve the Navy's educational system, a school was established in 1802 on board the *Congress,* which was in ordinary, at the Washington Navy Yard.[16] From time to time, other such schools ashore were established for the training of midshipmen who were on duty at a navy yard or station and could be spared from other duties. Three schools were in operation in 1833 at Boston, New York, and Norfolk. A similar school was opened in 1838 at the Naval Asylum in Philadelphia. Education at sea continued whenever a proper instructor, chaplain, or schoolteacher could be found. After professors of mathematics had been authorized and appointed, chaplains were relieved of most of their educatitonal duties.

Legislation of March 3, 1837 made changes in the titles of officers. The rank of "master commandant" was changed to that of "commander," the present grade below captain. The title of "sailing master" was changed to "master," and the latter continued to indicate the rank below a lieutenant until 1883, when the present title of "lieutenant, junior grade" was established. Masters continued to be warrant officers until 1837, when those "in line of promotion" became commissioned officers. Naval Registers after 1837 list "masters in line of promotion," commissioned officers and "masters," warrant officers.

In the middle thirties, during the period of administration by the Navy Commissioners as matériel assistants to the Secretary of the Navy, a new concept in naval warfare appeared—that of steam power. Congress had recognized much earlier the possibility of using the steam engine for the propulsion of men-of-war. An act of March 9, 1814 authorized the construction of one or more steam-powered floating batteries for harbor defense. The United States Congress' concept of a navy was one basically limited to shore defense. Since steam was still in its infancy, there was no idea that a steam-powered vessel could be used as a cruiser. Robert Fulton was employed to design and supervise the building of the *Demologos* or *Fulton,* the first steam man-of-war authorized by any nation.[17] Not having been completed in time to serve against the British fleet that had blockaded New York, the vessel, after tests, was moored at the Brooklyn Navy Yard. In 1829, a magazine explosion destroyed the *Fulton,* ending the short career of the first steam vessel of the United States Navy.

Congress, by an act of April 29, 1816, made provision for additional steam men-of-war, although steam had yet to prove itself as a reliable means of propulsion. Section 3 of this act, "For the General Increase in the Navy of the United States" provided "that for the defense of the ports and harbours of the United States, the President shall be and he is hereby authorized to cause to be procured three steam engines and imperishable materials for building and equipping three steam batteries, on the most improved plan and best calculated for the waters in which they are to act . . ." The country was at peace, and no action was taken under this authority; but we shall later hear more of this 1816 legislation.

During the campaigns to suppress piracy in the West Indies, a 100-ton steam galliot, the *Sea Gull,* was purchased, to be used as a dispatch boat from 1823 until 1825, when she was laid up. Official records do not indicate whether the boilers and machinery were operated by naval or civilian personnel.[18]

The progress being made in the use of steam afloat had not gone unnoticed. In a letter of June 26, 1835, Secretary of the Navy Dickerson called the attention of the Board of Commissioners to the act of April 29, 1816, and directed them to proceed with the construction of a steam vessel.[19] The Board advised the Secretary that while they considered themselves qualified to proceed with the design and construction of the hull, they knew nothing of machinery. They requested permission to employ an engineer experienced in the design and construction of boilers and machinery. As a result, C. H. Haswell, who was well qualified in steam engineering, was employed in February 1836 to assist the Board with the problem of procuring the steam equipment. On July 12, 1836 Haswell was appointed chief engineer of a second *Fulton,* which was then in the process of construction. Haswell thus became the first person employed as a steam engineer in the United States Navy.[20]

The choice of the officer to command this innovation was both logical and fortunate. Captain M. C. Perry, brother of Commodore Oliver Hazard Perry, who had won fame on Lake Erie in the War of 1812, was one of the younger officers who favored the introduction of steam into the United States Navy. Older officers were naturally prejudiced, for sailing ships had proved their reliability, and steam vessels were still experimental. No seagoing vessel of the period was dependent on steam alone. All such vessels were rigged with masts and sails. Large amounts of fuel were required; machinery could and did break down. Perry was farsighted,

The *Demologos* (Voice of the People), later called the *Fulton*, the first steam powered man-of-war of any country, was launched in October, 1814, too late to see action in the War of 1812. This unusual vessel was a type of catamaran, for there were two hulls ,joined together at the ends, with the paddle wheel in the open center of the hull. The steamer was not designed for seagoing service, but as a floating battery, a water supported gun platform. It was a product of the "Navy for coast defense" school of thought.

The men in the small boats are wearing the seamen's clothing of the period, full trousers, large-sleeve shirts, vests, stiff hats, and vests. A few men appear to be in the short sailor's jacket. All these items made up the clothing required by enlisted men, and listed in the Navy Regulations. The officer in charge of the launch at the end of the pier is shown in a "round" hat, the Navy's equivalent of the civilian hat of the day. The officer in the pinnance in the lower right is in full uniform, with cocked hat and epaulets.

(*Official Navy Photo.*)

Steam, not generally accepted in the Navy in 1847, provided the power needed to move a squadron up the Tabasco River against Mexican opposition. The engraving by Lieutenant Walke shows the steamer *Scorpion*, with Commodore M. C. Perry aboard, towing the *Vesuvius*, *Washington*, and boats of the *Mississippi* and *John Adams*; the *Spitfire* towing the *Stomboli*, the *Bonita*, and boats of the *Albany*; the *Scourge* towing the merchant schooner *Spitfire*; and the *Vixen* towing the *Etna* and the boats of the *Raritan*, the *Decatur*, and the *Germantown*. This operation would have been impossible under sail, for the river was winding and bordered by enemy troops. Steam engines and the engineers who manned them had proved their worth.

(*Courtesy of the Library of Congress.*)

for he appreciated the role that steam propulsion was eventually to play in naval warfare. He recognized the need for competent engineers if the United States were to stay abreast of the navies of foreign powers. To man his new command, Perry was authorized, by an order of October 31, 1837, to appoint assistant engineers and to recruit firemen and coal passers. A new day was dawning, and steam was here to stay! It is to be noted that the *Fulton's* captain was authorized to appoint assistant engineers, and that the Secretary of the Navy had appointed the chief engineer. It was not until 1842 however that engineers became an official part of the Navy.

The foundation of the steam Navy was really laid when Congress, by an Act of March 3, 1839, made provision for "three steam vessels of war." Under this authority two wooden-hulled side-wheelers, the *Mississippi* and the *Missouri,* and the iron-hulled frigate *Michigan* were built. Although sailing ships were built by the United States for a few years longer, the day of the sailing Navy was drawing to a close.

In the closing years of the administration of the Board of Navy Commissioners, a major step forward was taken in the Navy's educational program. The "General Regulations of the Navy and the Marine Corps of the United States, 1841" divided the educational responsibilities between chaplains and professors of mathematics. Article 378, describing a portion of the duties of chaplains, read, "When a person is appointed to instruct the boys of the vessel, he [the chaplain] shall frequently attend, to see that he [the person instructed to "instruct the boys"] performs his duties properly, and that the boys attend regularly. He shall report to the commander those who may be particularly deserving, and all who may be idle or negligent." The duties of a professor of mathematics are covered by Articles 379 and 380. The first reads: "He is to give his attendance regularly, and at such times as shall be directed by his commanding officer, and to instruct the midshipmen and others, who may be directed to attend; and report weekly to the commanding officer the attendance they may give, and the proficiency they may make." Article 380 directs: "He shall also make, and present to his commanding officer, similar reports, made up to the last day of March, June, September, and December, for transmission to the Secretary of the Navy," This latter article set up a form of "fitness report" for midshipmen, the future commanding officers of the Navy.

Education was being provided not only for midshipmen, the future commanders, but for the enlisted "boys" of the ship. It must be remembered that the literacy rate was low and that many of the midshipmen had gone to sea at an early age, without the benefit of much formal education. Although the Navy Regulations stress the duties of chaplains and professors afloat, makeshift schools were in operation ashore, and the instructions were equally applicable there. In 1841, schools ashore were located in Boston, New York, and Philadelphia, employing six professors of mathematics and one teacher of languages. In addition, eight professors were aboard ships of the Navy, and three were awaiting assignment.[21] It would be a few years before the Navy's educational facilities were established at Annapolis.

BUREAU SYSTEM OF MANAGEMENT

As the Navy expanded, afloat and ashore, things pertaining to it became more technical and complicated. It was apparent that the system of management required improvement. The creation in 1815 of the Board of Navy Commissioners to serve as advisers to the Secretary had been a step forward. By its very nature this setup, which made the members of the Board assistants and advisers to the Secretary, but without clear-cut lines of authority and responsibility, was not adequate to provide the sort of management now required. Members of the Board were criticized for poor performance in areas in which they had no authority. At other times, the Secretary was censured for matters which were more properly the responsibility of the Board. That responsibility could not always be fixed on any individual. The administrative machinery that had worked reasonably well in the days of simple short establishments and a small fleet of sailing ships had been outgrown.

The Act of Congress of August 31, 1842, which reorganized the Navy, was predicated on a functional distribution of the work of the Department. Five bureaus were established:

1. Bureau of Navy-Yards and Docks
2. Bureau of Construction, Equipment and Repairs
3. Bureau of Provisions and Clothing
4. Bureau of Ordinance and Hydrography
5. Bureau of Medicine and Surgery

The collective responsibility under which the Board of Navy Commissioners had operated was abolished. The chief of each bureau was individually responsible to the Secretary of the Navy. The act specified that ". . . the Secretary of the Navy shall assign and distribute among the said bureaus such duties as he shall judge expedient and proper . . ." This authority has been exercised from time to time. Functions have been shifted from one bureau to another. The bureau system of management is still the basic framework of the Navy's administrative and functional structure. Various offices and boards have now been added for handling functions which do not fit properly into any of the designated bureaus.

The law specified that the chiefs of the Bureaus of Navy-Yards and Docks, and of Ordnance and Hydrography, should be captains of the Navy; that the chief of the Bureau of Construction, Equipment and Repairs be a "skilful" naval constructor; and that the chief of the Bureau of Medicine and Surgery be a surgeon of the Navy. Since no such stipulation was made concerning the head of the Bureau of Provisions and Clothing, this office could be filled by either an officer or civilian.

While the titles of the five bureaus are generally descriptive of their responsibilities, it may be well to see what duties were assigned. The Bureau of Navy-Yards and Docks was responsible for the operation of the navy yards, the construction and maintenance of the docks, wharves, and buildings. The original six yards—at Portsmouth, New Hampshire, Boston, New York, Philadelphia, Washington and Norfolk (Gosport)—had been increased to seven with the establishment in 1826 of a yard at Pensacola, Florida. As the territory of the United States had expanded, so had the Navy's shore facilities, and this bureau was thus originally the largest and most powerful.

The Bureau of Construction, Equipment and Repairs was charged with the design, construction, and repair of the vessels of the Navy, and the equipping of the ships with sails, anchors, cables, and the like to make a vessel ready for sea.

The Bureau of Provisions and Clothing paid the officers and men, provided clothing, consumable supplies, food, and "small stores" for sale to the crews. Ashore, the representatives of this bureau were the navy agents and storekeepers; afloat, the pursers.

The duties of the Bureau of Ordnance and Hydrography included the maintenance of magazines, the manufacture and provision of guns and ammunition, the collection and distribution of hydrographic information, and the issuance of charts.

The Bureau of Medicine and Surgery, the only bureau which still bears its original name, procured medical supplies and superintended the Medical Department of the Navy, the hospitals, the dispensaries, and laboratories.

The replacement of the Board of Navy Commissioners by the Bureau system had little immediate effect on the administration of the Navy Department. Four of the new chiefs of bureaus were, respectively, the three Navy Commissioners and the Board Secretary! The fifth was a Navy surgeon, Dr. W. P. C. Barton. Captain Lewis Warrington, who had been President of the Board, was made Chief of the Bureau of Navy-Yards and Docks; Captain William M. Crane, head of Ordnance and Hydrography; Captain David Conner, Chief of the Bureau of Construction, Equipment and Repairs; and Charles W. Goldsborough, who had been secretary to the Board, Chief of Provisions and Clothing. It is to be noted that in spite of the specific language of the reorganization act, a naval captain—David Conner—instead of a civilian naval constructor, became the head of the Bureau of Construction, Equipment and Repairs. Since the Senate approved the nominations by the President on September 1, 1842, it would appear that this violation of the law was condoned. However, in an appropriations act of March 3, 1853, Congress again specified that the head of this bureau was to be a naval constructor. This time the Navy complied, and Samuel Hartt, who had long served with the Navy in such a capacity, became chief of the Bureau in July 1853.

Several other pieces of legislation approved on the same day—August 31, 1842—concerned the Navy. One of these gave some official status to professors of mathematics, directing that aboard ship they were to live and mess with lieutenants receiving the same rations. Another bill concerned engineers, who, though part of the Navy since 1837, were not specifically covered by law. Secretary of the Navy Abel P. Upshur, in a report to Congress in February 1842, had stated that there was no authority to appoint engineers and that ". . . they can be employed only under some other name. Their pay is unascertained and dependent on private contract, and their rank in the service and position in the ship are equally undetermined."[22] The bill to create an Engineer Corps of the Navy was approved on August 31, 1842. This "Act to regulate the appointment and pay of Engineers of the United States Navy" authorized the Secretary to appoint a chief engineer, two first assistant engineers, two 2nd assistant engineers, and three 3rd assistant engineers for each steamship. Rates of pay were established for each class of engineer for actual service and for periods while awaiting orders. Section 4 of the act provided that the Secretary should appoint a "skilful and scientific" engineer as Engineer in Chief at a salary of $300 a month. Congress was evidently aware that no uniform for engineers had been authorized by the Navy Department in the same manner as that prescribing uniforms for other officers. The act in Section 5 directed the Secretary to "prescribe a uniform for the Engineer Corps." This is the first time the word *corps* was used in connection with any group of officers of the Navy. Surgeons and their assistants were simply members of the Medical Department of the Navy, pursers of the Purser Department. Section 5 also directed that chief engineers were to be appointed by commission, and the other engineers by warrant. To provide for ratings for enlisted personnel attached to the Engineering Department aboard ship, ratings of firemen and coal passers were established by Congress. A new day was dawning!

That Congress was aware of the need for technical specialists is reflected by the language of the Appropriations Act of June 17, 1844. The pay of the "Chief Naval Constructor" was set at $3,000 and subordinate constructors at $2,300 per annum. An act of March 3, 1847 directed that the enlisted men of the Engineering Department were to be given the same pay as other petty officers and seamen of the Navy. This same act directed that naval constructors required to perform duty at a navy yard or station were to be given the same rations and travel allowances as other officers. While not giving naval constructors military status, the act did indicate that they performed duties comparable to commissioned officers.

THE NAVAL ACADEMY

The various steps taken by the Navy to provide for the education of midshipmen and others has already been discussed briefly. It was not until 1845 that a permanent school was established. The Navy Secretary, George Bancroft, a man of letters, historian, and associate of Washington Irving as well as of other authors and scholars of the day, took matters into his own hands. At Annapolis, Maryland he established the school that is now the Naval Academy. With the approval of President Franklin Buchanan, the unused Army facilities of Fort Severn were transferred to the Navy Department.[23] Since Congress had made no funds specifically available for this purpose, it was necessary to use general operational funds. To save money, Bancroft placed many of the language teachers and professors of mathematics in an "awaiting orders" status. When officers were not specifically assigned to a ship or station, the rate of pay while awaiting orders was considerably less than when on active assignment. The 1845 Navy Register shows twenty-one professors drawing full pay at the makeshift Navy schools, at sea, or on special duty, and only two awaiting assignment. In the 1846 Register, eleven are listed as on full pay status, and eleven as awaiting orders! In 1845, three teachers of languages were on duty, one each at Boston, New York, and Norfolk. In 1846, all three were on reduced pay!

The actual transfer of Fort Severn was effective on August 15, 1845,

LANDING OF THE AMERICAN FORCES UNDER GEN! SCOTT

AT VERA CRUZ MARCH 9th 1847

This lithograph by Currier of the landing of American forces at Vera Cruz on March 9, 1847, shows the Navy in a now typical role—putting the Army ashore under a cover of naval gun-fire. The same operation was repeated time after time in World War II. The landing force included Marine and naval contingents, as well as approximately forty-five hundred soldiers.

(Official Navy Photo.)

and on October 10 the school was opened formally, with fifty midshipmen and seven instructors. Commander Franklin Buchanan was the first superintendent and Lieutenant John H. Ward the executive officer, with additional duties as instructor in gunnery and steam. A Navy surgeon, John A. Lockwood, was instructor in chemistry. Chaplain George Jones was instructor in English. Passed Midshipman S. Marcy taught mathematics. Three instructors completed the staff: Henry H. Lockwood, in natural philosophy; Arsene N. Girault, in French; and William Chauvenet, in mathematics and navigation.

The first acknowlegment by Congress that a naval school existed is found in the Naval Appropriations Act of March 3, 1847. The sum of $28,200 was made available to provide for badly needed repairs and for the purchase of additional land. The institution was renamed the Naval Academy on July 1, 1850. From these small beginnings has grown the large and excellent institution which provides the education and training of officers for the United States Navy.[24]

RANK AND ASSIMILATED OR RELATIVE RANK

Congress from time to time had provided the officers considered necessary to man the ships and shore facilities of the Navy. The officers fell into two broad categories: combatant, or in today's terminology, line officers; and non-combatant or staff officers. Each group was broken down into those who held their offices by commission—that is, by appointment by the President and approval by the Senate—and warrant officers, those who held their authority from the Secretary of the Navy. The relative position or rank of the combatant officers was well defined and accepted. It was also understood that a surgeon was superior to a surgeon's mate. However, the position of the non-combatant officers in relation to the combatant officers had not been defined. This matter was brought to a head in the 1840's.

The original legislation which in 1794 had established the United States Navy had set the rank or order of precedence of combatant officers—captain, then lieutenant, followed by the warrant officers who could exercise command at sea, namely masters and midshipmen. As the Navy grew and as new classes of vessels were placed in service, the rank of master commandant was introduced between those of captain and lieutenant, and provision was made for commanders of squadrons to be superior to captains of individual ships. The non-combatant officers originally authorized were surgeons and surgeon's mates, chaplains, and pursers. The latter originally were warranted, but in 1812 became commissioned officers.

By 1840 the list of civil officers had grown. The two classes of medical officers were increased to four—fleet surgeons, surgeons, passed assistant surgeons, and assistant surgeons. In addition, professors of mathematics, secretaries to commanders of squadrons, and clerks had been authorized to provide additional support to officers of the line. Since the possession of rank in any military society entitles the holder to certain privileges in both his official and his social life, it is understandable that the non-combatant officers desired rank comparable to that of their combatant associates.

The first official indication that there was a relative position between line and staff is found in the "General Regulations for the Navy and Marine Corps of the United States, 1841." The following rank structure for line officers was set forth:

Commissioned	1.	Admirals
	2.	Vice Admirals
	3.	Rear Admirals
	4.	Captains
	5.	Commanders
	6.	Lieutenants
Warranted	7.	Masters
	8.	Second Masters
	9.	Passed Midshipmen
	10.	Master's Mates, if warranted as such
	11.	Boatswains
	12.	Gunners
	13.	Midshipmen
	14.	Carpenters
	15.	Sailmakers

Article 4 of the 1841 Navy Regulations established the relative positions of civil officers and line officers as follows:

> The civil officers of the navy shall have assimilated rank with the sea-officers of the navy as follows: surgeons, pursers, chaplains, and secretaries with lieutenants of the navy; passed assistant surgeons, with masters; other assistant surgeons and professors of mathematics, with passed midshipmen; and clerks, with midshipmen . . .

The first attempt to establish a relation between civil and sea officers appears a bit odd. Passed assistant and assistant surgeons were both commissioned, but they were to have the assimilated ranks of warrant officers. Secretaries, who were not commissioned, ranked with lieutenants! This matter of assimilated or relative rank would not be ironed out finally until late in the nineteenth century.

Line officers considered that rank belonged only to the military corps of the Navy, those officers whose basic duty was to fight the enemy and to have naval command. They considered that the only function of staff officers was to support the line. Led by the surgeons, the civil officers were desirous of securing rank, with its accompanying benefits and privileges. An officer's place at the wardroom table, the cabin in which he slept, his relative position when entering or leaving a ship, and even the uniform he wore, were all based on rank.[25]

Officers of the newly created Engineer Corps soon joined the surgeons and pursers in presenting their case and urging their claims. Under the new bureau system, the various classes of staff officers had representatives in Washington. The chiefs of the bureaus had direct access to the Secretary of the Navy and could present their case to him. The pressure for assimilated rank proved to be too strong for the line. Medical officers, who had spearheaded the fight for recognition, were the first to be given rank. On August 31, 1846, Secretary of the Navy George Bancroft issued a General Order which read:

> Surgeons of the Fleet and Surgeons of more than twelve years will rank with Commanders.
> Surgeons of less than twelve years with Lieutenants.
> Passed Assistant Surgeons, next after Lieutenants.
> Assistant Surgeons, not passed, next after Masters.
> Commanding and Executive Officers of what ever grade, when on duty, will take precedence of All Medical Officers. This order confers no authority to exercise military command and no additional right to quarters.

It is to be noted that senior surgeons were to "rank with Commanders," but without holding the *rank* of commander. The rank was relative or assimilated. While staff officers could not exercise military command, they could command within their own departments. Although officers of the staff corps of the Navy now have true rank—and not the relative rank established in 1846—their authority is still limited, and properly so, to their own departments and specialties.

As a result of the August 1846 order, we find that surgeons ranked with commissioned officers, commanders or lieutenants; and that assistant surgeons, also commissioned, ranked with warrant officers. Passed assistants were to rank "next after Lieutenants," which meant with masters; assistant surgeons "next after Masters," or with second masters. This rather unusual situation would not be changed until additional grades of commissioned officers were created during the Civil War.

The next group of staff officers to be granted relative rank were pursers. On May 27, 1847 Secretary J. T. Mason issued a General Order under which pursers of more than twelve years in grade ranked with commanders, and those of less than twelve years with lieutenants. Pursers were to rank with surgeons according to the dates of their commissions, and were subject to the same restrictions as to command and quarters as set forth in the 1846 order concerning medical officers. Some years would elapse before the other two large groups of civil officers—chaplains and engineers—were assigned relative rank.

Congress, in the Naval Appropriations Act of August 5, 1854, confirmed the actions of the Navy which granted relative rank to surgeons and pursers. Section 4 of the act read: "And be it further enacted that the two 'General Orders' of the Secretary of the Navy, dated August thirty-one, eighteen hundred and forty-six, and May twenty-seven, eighteen hundred and forty-seven, upon relative rank, shall have the force and effect of law." We shall hear more about the role of Congress in the matter of granting relative rank to officers of the staff.

The status of professors of mathematics was clarified by an act of Congress of August 3, 1848. The legislation limited the number of professors of mathematics to twelve and instructed the Secretary to assign them to duty at the Naval School, at the Observatory, or aboard ships of war, for the purpose of instructing midshipmen. While the Naval School had been in operation since 1845, the practice of sending midshipmen to school before assigning them to the fleet had not yet been established. The act contained one proviso of special importance to professors. Hereafter, professors would be appointed by the President and confirmed by the Senate. Now they had attained the status of commissioned officers.

For many years there had been a proved need for rank above that of captain, and Congress had recognized such a need when in 1799 it had authorized double rations for officers commanding squadrons. It was not until 1857, however, that "flag" rank was authorized. An act of January 16, 1857, "to promote the efficiency of the Navy," directed "that captains in command of a squadron shall be denominated flag officers." It would appear that Congress was still reluctant to use the time-honored titles of admiral, vice admiral, rear admiral, and commodore, which served to designate the senior officers of navies of foreign powers. "Flag officer" is a generic title. The flying of one's flag is an indication of over-all command, not of rank. Unofficially, since the rank was not authorized by Congress until 1862, the title of commodore had been applied for years to officers in command of squadrons of the United States Navy. Herman Melville in *White Jacket* makes frequent reference to "the Commodore."

Today, the senior officers of the Navy, from commodore (in time of war) through Admiral of the Navy, are known collectively as "Flag Officers." That Congress did not intend to give a rank which an officer would retain indefinitely is evident. The act provided that only so long as a captain commanded the squadron was he to be known as "Flag Officer." When relieved of his command, he reverted to the rank of captain.

Relative rank for engineers was finally granted in 1859, although the number of engineering officers in the United States Navy had increased by leaps and bounds since the Corps was established in 1842. Secretary Isaac Toucey, by an order of January 13, directed that

> Chief Engineers of more than twelve years service will rank with Commanders.
> Chief Engineers of less than twelve years, with Lieutenants.
> First Assistant Engineers next after Lieutenants.
> Second Assistant Engineers next after Masters.
> Third Assistant Engineers with Midshipmen.

The same general basis for the assignment of relative rank was used as in the earlier orders covering surgeons and pursers. However, the unusual situation of having commissioned staff officers rank with warrant officers was not created as it had been for medical officers. Only chief engineers were commissioned, and they ranked with commanders or lieutenants, on the basis of years in grade. Assistant engineers were all appointed by warrant, and ranked with line warrant officers. This assignment of relative rank was approved by Congress on March 3, 1859, as a section of the Appropriations Act.

The last piece of legislation prior to the Civil War which has bearing on this study (and that only indirectly) was the Appropiations Act of June 22, 1860. Section 3 provided "that pursers in the Navy of the United States shall hereafter be styled paymasters." This designation more accurately described the duties of those officers who were responsible for paying the crew, providing clothing and sundries for the crew, and procuring naval supplies and materials. The 1860 title of paymaster was perhaps more descriptive of the duties to be performed than the present one of supply officer.

During the Civil War, Congress passed bill after bill in an attempt to place the Navy on a wartime basis. Some of this legislation affected dress and management. The peacetime Navy was woefully inadequate to maintain a blockade of the Confederate ports, to support amphibious operations, or to assist the Army in closing the Mississippi Valley to the South and by so doing to open a road to the heart of the Confederacy.

As the Navy grew in strength, it is but natural that there should have been many changes in management, in the assignment of rank, and finally in the uniform.

An act of July 17, 1861 established the grade of assistant paymaster, directing that the number so appointed not exceed thirty-six, and that "at the end of the insurrection . . ." the total number of paymasters and assistants be reduced to seventy-five. It became evident that trained personnel were needed to meet the demands of the increased work load of a wartime Navy. The transition from sail to steam, which began in the forty's, had made the business of the Navy Department more complicated, and required more and more personnel. The establishment of the rank of assistant paymaster brought the Pay Department into line with the organizations of both the Medical and Engineering departments, where assistants had been authorized for years.

An act for a "Temporary Increase in the Navy" authorized the procurement of additional vessels, the recruitment of additional men, and the commissioning of officers for temporary service. There was no such thing as a Naval Reserve in 1861. To provide the needed top-level administrative assistance, Congress on July 31, 1861 created the position of .Assistant Secretary of the Navy.

MODIFICATION OF THE BUREAU SYSTEM OF MANAGEMENT

The advances in science and technology, the rapid transition from sail to steam, the development of armored vessels, the introduction of the gun turret, the improvements in ordnance, and the increasing complexity of management called for more specialization than could be provided by the five bureaus created in 1842. Accordingly, on July 5, 1862, Congress established eight bureaus: Yards and Docks (note the change in name) , Equipment and Recruiting, Navigation, Ordnance, Construction and Repairs, Steam Engineering, Provisions and Clothing, and Medicine and Surgery. In effect the former Bureau of Construction, Equipment and Repairs was separated into three distinct bureaus: Construction and Repairs, Steam Engineering, and Equipment and Recruiting.[26]

Dividing the responsibility for ship construction between the bureaus of Steam Engineering and Construction and Repairs may have seemed logical in 1862. But this separation of responsibility for the vessel and its motive power was never completely satisfactory. The matter was not corrected until the Bureau of Ships was established in 1940. Now the responsibility both for the vessel and for its propulsion machinery are in one bureau.

The creation of a central management facility to recruit seamen for the growing fleet was a very definite step forward. The original system of having the captain assemble a crew for his vessel was outmoded and certainly would not have met wartime needs. The "Equipment" side of this new bureau was concerned with the many things that must be provided before a ship is ready for sea: sails, cables, and the like. At the time, the manning of the ship was, in a measure, considered part of the equipment.

The Bureau of Navigation was intended to be the scientific bureau of the Navy, and took over the hydrographic work formerly under the Bureau of Ordnance and Hydrography. This new bureau was assigned responsibility for the Naval Observatory, the Hydrographic Office, the Naval Almanac Office, and the Naval Academy. It did not take over the handling of personnel until later.

As the United States Navy expanded and was employed in widespread areas of operations, the need for a better rank structure was recognized. Squadrons of large numbers of ships, and vessels of many sizes, could not be officered effectively by the chain of command established in 1797.

An act of July 16, 1862 "to establish and equalize the Grades of Line Officers of the United States Navy," established a new rank structure and set the number of officers in each grade.

Rear Admiral	9
Commodore	18
Captain	36
Commander	72
Lieutenant Commander	144
Lieutenant	144
Master	144
Ensign	144

Now officers in command of squadrons had proper naval titles.

The Navy Department took prompt action to provide identifying insignia for the expanded grades of officers. The Navy had gone into the Civil War with the frequently changed uniform instructions of 1852. A General Order issued on July 31, 1862 merely modified the 1852 order, and brought it up to date in so far as the dress of an officer of the line was concerned. It is to be noted that the legislation of July 31, 1862 concerned seagoing officers only. There was no modification of the relative rank of staff officers as previously established by Congress. As a result, the 1862 uniform instruction contained very little reference to the staff. In effect, the uniform in use in 1861 was to be worn by staff officers, but with the sleeve lace as prescribed for the line officers with whom they had corresponding rank.

The next major change in the uniform and insignia of officers of the Navy was brought about by a General Order issued by Secretary of the Navy Gideon Welles on March 13, 1863. Officers of the Medical, Pay, and Engineer Departments; naval constructors, chaplains, professors of mathematics, secretaries, clerks, carpenters, and sailmakers were to be considered Staff Officers. All other officers were to be regarded as of the Line. This appears to be the first time that officers of the United States Navy were specifically classed as either line or staff.

In addition to separating officers into Line and Staff, the order established the relationship between the two groups.

MEDICAL DEPARTMENT
    Fleet Surgeons with Captains
    Surgeons, after 15 years as such, with Captains
    Surgeons, after the first 5 years, with Commanders
    Surgeons, first 5 years, with Lieutenant Commanders
    Passed Assistant Surgeons with Lieutenants
    Assistant Surgeons with Masters
PAY DEPARTMENT
    Fleet Paymasters with Captains
    Paymasters, after 15 years, with Captains
    Paymasters, after 5 years, with Commanders
    Paymasters, first 5 years, with Lieutenant Commanders
    Assistant Paymasters with Masters
ENGINEER DEPARTMENT
    Fleet Engineers with Captains
    Chief Engineers, after 15 years, with Captains
    Chief Engineers, after 5 years, with Commanders
    Chief Engineers, first 5 years, with Lieutenant Commanders
    First Assistant Engineers with Masters
    Second Assistant Engineers with Ensigns
    Third Assistant Engineers with Midshipmen
NAVAL CONSTRUCTORS
    Naval Constructors, after 20 years, with Captains
    Naval Constructors, after 12 years, with Commanders
    Naval Constructors, first 12 years, with Lieutenant Commanders
    Assistant Naval Constructors with Masters
CHAPLAINS AND PROFESSORS OF MATHEMATICS
    Those of more than 12 years standing in grade, with Commanders
    Those of less than 12 years standing in grade, with Lieutenant Commanders

SECRETARIES, with Lieutenants
CLERKS, with Midshipmen
CARPENTERS AND SAILMAKERS, with Gunners

The chiefs of the various bureaus of the Staff Corps were to rank with commodores, and to take precedence over one another according to their dates of commissions as surgeons, paymasters, engineers, and naval constructors, and not according to the dates of their appointments as bureau chiefs. The order specified in detail the cabins aboard ship to be occupied by officers of both Line and Staff. Line officers were to have cabins on the port side, staff officers on the starboard. Among the Staff, the assignment of relative rank brought with it certain privileges, which were guarded jealously. Over the years, various Secretaries of the Navy have received letters from officers who were not assigned the cabins to which they considered themselves entitled!

Chaplains, naval constructors, professors of mathematics, secretaries, and clerks had long been employed by the Navy, and rated as "civil officers." None of these groups had ever been given relative rank, either by the Secretary or by Congress, until 1863. Of these new groups of officers to whom the secretary had given relative rank, only two were commissioned, namely chaplains and professors. It is also to be recalled that prior to 1863, the highest rank authorized for surgeons, paymasters and engineers was that of commander. The action of the Secretary in granting increased relative rank to surgeons, paymasters, and engineers, and giving relative rank to the other staff officers, listed in the 1863 order, seems at that time to have gone unquestioned by Congress. It was not until 1869 that the question as to who had the authority to grant relative rank was raised. In a later chapter this matter will be discussed, for in 1869 it did modify the uniform of the Navy.

One additional piece of legislation was approved during the Civil War which made necessary a change in the uniform instructions. Congress, by an act of December 21, 1864, created the rank of vice admiral and empowered the President, with the advice and consent of the Senate, to appoint one vice admiral from the active list of rear admirals. The Vice Admiral was to be the senior officer of the Navy and to rank with a lieutenant general of the Army. The first officer to hold the rank of vice admiral was David Glasgow Farragut, famous for his services in command of the Western Gulf Blockading Squadron at New Orleans and Mobile, and on the Mississippi. Farragut entered the Navy as a midshipman in 1810, and saw action in both the War of 1812 and the

Mexican War. When he was selected to be the Navy's first Vice Admiral, he had served his country well for fifty-four years. He had reported for duty in the Navy before he was ten!

NOTES

[1] The following works are invaluable for an understanding of the administration of the United States Navy from 1794 to the end of World War II.

Paullin, Charles Oscar. "Early Naval Administration Under the Constitution," *U.S. Naval Institute Proceedings,* Vol. 32 (Sept. 1906), pp. 1001–1030.

—— "Naval Administration Under Secretaries of the Navy Smith, Hamilton and Jones, 1801–1814," *Ibid.,* Vol. 32 (Dec 1906), pp. 1289–1328.

—— "Naval Administration Under the Navy Commissioners, 1815–1842," *Ibid.,* Vol. 33 (June 1907), pp. 590–641.

—— "Naval Administration, 1842–1861," *Ibid.,* Vol. 33 (Dec. 1907), pp. 1435–1477.

—— "A Half Century of Naval Administration in America, 1861–1911," *Ibid.,* Vol. 38 (Dec. 1912); Vol. 39 (March, June, Sept., Dec. 1913); Vol. 40 (Jan., March, May, July 1914).

Paullin's writings are an authoritative documentary treatment of the history of U.S. naval administration and organization.

Smelser, Marshall, *The Congress Founds the Navy,* 1787–1879 (Notre Dame, University of Notre Dame Press, 959). An excellent, well documented study of the creation of the United States Navy, from the ratification debates of 1787–1788 to the creation of the Navy Department by Congress in 1798.

Furer, Julius Augustus, *Administration of the Navy Department in World War II* (Washington, Navy Department, 1959 [G.P.O., 1960]). While Admiral Furer's exhaustive study, is concerned primarily with the period of World War II, it also contains much excellent material on the organization and administration of the Navy Department from its creation.

Sprout, Harold and Margaret, *The Rise of American Naval Power,* 1776–1918 Princeton, Princeton University Press, 1939). While not an operational history, this is an excellent review of the development of American naval policy and the growth of American sea power.

[2] Cooper, James Fenimore, *The History of the Navy of the United States of America* (Philadelphia, Lea & Blanchard, 1839), 2 Vols. An interesting general history of the Navy. Cooper served as a midshipman from 1808 to 1811, when he resigned.

[3] Paullin, Charles Oscar, "Early Naval Administration Under the Constitution," *Naval Institute Proceedings,* Vol. 32 (Sept. 1906), p. 1008.

[4] *Ibid.,* p. 1008.

[5] *Ibid.,* p. 1014.

[6] *Ibid.,* p. 1021.

[7] Frost, Holloway H., *We Build a Navy* (Annapolis, U.S. Naval Institute, 1940).

[8] Paullin, *op. cit.,* p. 1022.

[9] Knox, Dudley W., *A History of the United States Navy,* rev. ed. (New York, Putnam 1948).

[10] Frost, op. cit., pp. 213–214.

[11] Paullin, Charles Oscar, "Naval Administration Under the Navy Commissioners, 1815–1842," *U.S. Naval Institute Proceedings,* Vol. 33 (June 1907), pp. 609–611.

[12] Chappel, Howard P., *History of the American Sailing Navy* (New York, Norton, 1949).

13 Roberts, William P., *History of the Construction Corps of the United States Navy*, Washington, G.P.O., 1937.

14 Tily, James C., "The Civil Engineer Corps, U.S. Navy and the Corps Device," *Military Collector and Historian*, Vol. X No. 2 (1958).

15 Drury, Clifford M., *The History of the Chaplains Corps, United States Navy*, NAVPERS 15807, Vol. 1, p. 17 (Washington, Bureau of Naval Personnel),

16 *Ibid.*, p. 18.

17 Bennett, Frank M., *Steam Navy of the United States* (Pittsburgh, Warren, 1896), p. 8–15.

18 *Ibid.*, p. 16.

19 *Ibid.*, p. 17.

20 *Ibid.*, p. 19.

21 Solvey, James Russell, *Historical Sketches of the United States Naval Academy* (Washington, G.P.O., 1876), p. 40.

22 Madden, Robert B., "The Bureau of Ships and Its E. D. Officers," *Journal of the American Society of Naval Engineers*, February 1954, p. 12.

23 Benjamin, Park, *The United States Naval Academy* (New York, Putnam, 1900), pp. 151–154.

24 Lovette, Leland P., *The School of the Sea, The Annapolis Tradition In American Life* (New York, Stokes, 1941), p. 51; Alden, Carroll S. ed., *A Short History of the United States Navy* (Phildadelphia, Lippincott, rev. ed. 1927), pp. 218–219.

25 Paullin, Charles Oscar, "Naval Administration, 1842–1861," *U.S. Naval Instttuie Proceedings*, Vol. 33 (Dec. 1907), pp. 1465–1468; Roberts, *op. cit.*, pp. 31–34.

26 Furer, *op. cit.*, p. 200.

II

Uniforms, 1797–1852

In order to have a better understanding of the rank and classes of officers shown in the many photographs taken of officers and men of the United States Navy during the Civil War, it is necessary to have some knowledge of the various methods used to show rank and specialty. During the period from 1861 to 1865, three distinct systems of showing rank by means of gold lace on the sleeves were employed, none of which has much resemblance to the lace arrangement of today. On the other hand, it is comparatively easy to determine the rank of Army officers during the War between the States, for the insignia used by them then is fundamentally the same today.

The Navy had taken some steps toward prescribing a common uniform for all officers prior to the Civil War, with distinctive devices to show an officer's specialty. (Today this would be called corps affiliation.) However, it was not until the Navy had a major war on its hands that real and lasting progress was made. And from 1861 to 1865 the Navy was entirely too busy to think about elaborate uniforms! The need was for a serviceable dress to clothe the officers of a greatly expanded Navy, and a simple system for rank identification. As has been true in most wars, the wearing of full dress was suspended, and the current service dress uniform was worn on all occasions.

To set the stage for a detailed study of the dress of the United States Navy during the war years of 1861 to 1865, it is necessary that the uniform instructions issued previously be reviewed. Since the first steps toward prescribing a common uniform for all officers occurred during the life of the 1852 Naval Uniform Regulations, it is advisable that the period from 1797, when the first uniform order was issued, to 1852 be discussed separately.

FIRST UNIFORM INSTRUCTIONS—AUGUST 24, 1797

When Congress authorized the manning and employment of the first frigates of the United States Navy in 1797, naval affairs were under the cognizance of the War Department. It was thus only natural that the uniform instructions issued by the Secretary of War, James McHenry, on August 24, 1797, should reflect the current dress of officers of the Army. This first uniform was not the "blue and gold" now associated with the Navy of the United States, but the "blue and buff" now associated with the American Revolution. Actually, blue uniforms with buff facings were the exception rather than the rule during the Revolution. While many contemporary paintings show officers and men in blue and buff, the army as a whole was never so dressed. Brown was in fact the color first approved, when on November 4, 1775 the Continental Congress selected it as the standard coat color, with different colored facings to distinguish the various regiments.[1]

Blue, however, was the color preferred by officers for their coats, and it was prescribed for the entire army by Washington's General Order of October 2, 1779.[2] Under this order only troops from New York and New Jersey were to display buff facings. Troops from New England were to have white facings, those from Pennsylvania, Delaware, Maryland, and Virginia, red; while those from North Carolina, South Carolina, and Georgia were to wear blue facings, the buttonholes to be edged with white tape. Since the procurement of cloth sufficient to clothe the army was a constantly recurring problem, blue was never actually the standard color. Officers and men wore whatever clothing they could find. Protection from the elements and warmth in winter were much more important than the color!

The Navy's first uniform coat was similar in cut to that of the Army of 1797—a standing turnover collar, buttoned back lapels, and turned—up cuffs. Breeches with stockings and buckled shoes, vests, and cocked hats completed the uniform. Certain features of this first uniform were carried forward for many years, although the style of the uniform itself was changed. Commissioned officers, with some exceptions, continued to have rows of nine buttons on the coats until the Navy's special full-dress coat was abolished after World War I. The number of buttons around the cuffs and the presence of buttons at other locations on the coat, remained an indication of rank until the Civil War.

The two senior commissioned officers allowed by the acts of 1794 and 1797—captains and lieutenants—were ordered to wear blue coats with buff standing collars, lapels, and cuffs. A captain's coat was to have

The original of this portrait of Captain Thomas Truxtun, by Bass Otis, is in the Long Island Historical Society building in Brooklyn. Truxtun, a privateer captain in the Revolution, was one of the six captains selected in 1794 to oversee the construction of the frigates authorized by Congress. The uniform is that of the 1797 instruction. The decoration is that of the Society of the Cincinnati, formed by officers who had served in the Revolution.

(Official Navy Photo.)

long lapels, with nine buttons in a row on either side of the breast. A lieutenant's coat was to have half lapels, with six buttons at the lapels, three buttons below the lapel on the right side, and three buttonholes on the left. As one indication of rank, a captain was to wear four buttons around the cuffs, and a lieutenant three. This use of buttons to show rank was also used at the pockets. A captain had four at the pocket flaps, and a lieutenant but three. This "rank by buttons" was employed for many years.

The Continental Congress, frowning on anything that smacked of monarchy, had forbidden the wearing of gold lace and epaulets by officers of the Continental Navy. But in spite of the regulations, many officers adorned themselves in much the same fashion as officers of the British Navy of the period. The 1797 Navy uniform regulations were somewhat more liberal in that a captain was directed to wear gold epaulets on either shoulder, and a lieutenant one on the right shoulder only. Both officers were permitted to wear "full dressed"—that is, gold-lace-trimmed —cocked hats. The hats worn by all other officers listed in 1794 and 1797 legislation were plain. In full dress, captains and lieutenants carried "small swords (yellow mounted)"; in undress "such swords as may be here-after fixed on, or ordered": a decorative sword for full dress and a more serviceable weapon for action.

Seagoing officers appointed by warrant were assigned uniforms which distinguished them from their commissioned seniors. Sailing masters wore blue coats with blue lapels, edged with buff on the collar and lapels. Their breeches were blue and their vests buff. Midshipmen wore blue coats without lapels, but with buff collars and cuffs, with buff edging on the coats, and buff breeches. Neither of these warrant officers were permitted to have buttons around the cuffs or at the pocket flaps.

The complements authorized for the frigates included four classes of non-combatant, or, as they would be rated today, staff officers—surgeons, surgeon's mates, chaplains, and pursers. The first three were commissioned; pursers were warranted. Medical officers were not permitted to wear the blue and buff of seagoing officers. Instead, they were ordered to wear dark green coats, with black velvet facings, collars, and cuffs; red vests, and green breeches. One could hardly mistake a surgeon for an officer who could command at sea. Surgeons' coats had long lapels, with nine buttons on each breast, similar to the coats worn by captains, whereas their mates had short-lapelled coats like those of lieutenants. Both medical officers were permitted to display three buttons around the cuffs, but none at the pockets. The permission to wear buttons on the cuffs was perhaps intended to be an indication of their status as commissioned officers, but certainly not an indication of rank. The giving of rank to non-combatant officers—even rank of an "assimilated" or "relative" sort —was many years in the future.

Although chaplains were commissioned officers, no uniform was prescribed for them. It is evident that they were expected to wear the conventional black clothing of civilian clergymen. Over the years, chaplains were in and out of the Navy uniform. One order would prescribe for them a uniform similar to that worn by other officers of the Navy, and the next would put them into the black of clergymen. Only comparatively recently have chaplains been uniformed as the rest of the Navy.

Pursers, who in 1797 were warrant officers, were assigned a coat which clearly indicated their status both as non-combatants and as warrants: "Plain frock, blue coat, with proper naval buttons. No lappels." Since they were allowed to wear buff vests and breeches, they did at least conform to the basic "blue and buff." Actually, their association with the United States Navy was indicated only by the "proper naval buttons": ". . . yellow metal, and to have a foul anchor and American eagle on same." The eagle and anchor are still proudly displayed on the buttons of the United States Navy.

The uniform instructions of 1797 were silent on the dress of the other four warrant officers, and it was not until 1813 that uniforms were prescribed for boatswains, gunners, carpenters, and sailmakers. While the dress of petty officers and seamen is not described in this first instruction, records elsewhere show that there was a certain uniformity in the dress of enlisted men. Clothing was procured under contract, and made according to the samples on view in the office of the commandants of the various navy yards. Stocks of clothing for the men were maintained aboard ship in "slop stores", under control of the purser. The "slop stores" were the forerunners of the "ships' stores" of today. In many instances, men made their own clothing, patterned after the articles stocked in "slops." Early Naval Regulations list the clothing to be kept in stock and in the possession of the men. There was undoubtedly some variation in the dress of seamen. Many times they wore what ever clothing they had on their backs when they enlisted; or a certain captain might order his men to be clothed according to his personal whim.

While illustrations of enlisted men's dress in the early United States Navy are few, the "slop store" listings show that the basic articles of clothing were full-bottomed trousers, frocks (jumpers), short jackets, vests, and low-crowned round hats. This was sufficiently similar to the dress of the British Navy, that contemporary paintings and sketches of British seamen can be used as an indication of the dress of the American seamen.

UNIFORM INSTRUCTIONS OF 1802

Although the Navy Department had been established in 1798, it was not until 1802, after minor wars with Republican France and the Barbary Powers, that a uniform instruction was issued by the Department. An order of August 27, 1802, signed by Secretary of the Navy Robert Smith, introduced the "blue and gold" uniform standard for the United States Navy: coats of blue cloth, with blue linings, collars and cuffs, and decorations of gold lace.

A captain's coat was liberally decorated with lace—around the standing collar, on the cuffs and pocket flaps, on the edges of the lapels, and even down the folds of the skirts of the coat. This was a far cry from the plain uniforms of the Continental Navy and the blue and buff of the instruction issued by Secretary of War McHenry in 1797. Even the buttonholes were worked with gold thread. A lieutenant's coat was without lace, with decoration only at the buttonholes. This matter of the buttonholes is a bit confusing. The instructions for a captain's coat call for "the button-holes to be worked with gold thread," while the instructions for a lieutenant's call for "the button-holes laced with such lace as is directed for a captain's." The trimming prescribed for a captain's collar, lapel edges, pocket flaps, and coat skirts was to be "gold lace, not exceeding one half inch in breadth, nor less than three eighths of an inch." From this it would appear that a captain's buttonholes were to be worked with thread, and those of a lieutenant trimmed with half-inch lace. However, contemporary portraits show lace at the buttonholes of captains' coats. It would be some years before the uniform instructions were easily read and understood. The first uniform regulation to contain patterns for insignia was that of 1830. After that, the instructions were more easily interpreted.

Captains and lieutenants wore identical coats except for the embroidery and lace—of blue cloth, lined with blue; standing collar; long lapels, with nine buttons on each breast; cut to the waist in front and with tails behind. The button system for indicating rank was continued. A captain had four buttons on his cuffs and at the pockets, while a lieutenant had but three in each of these locations. Captains continued to wear two epaulets, and lieutenants one. The single epaulet of a lieutenant was worn on the right shoulder when in command, and on the left when second in command to a captain.

A midshipman's full-dress coat was described as "of blue cloth, with lining and lappels of the same; the lappels to be short, with six buttons; standing collar, with a diamond formed of gold lace on each side, not exceeding two inches square; a slash sleeve, with three small buttons; all

Captain Thomas Tingey in the uniform of 1802.

(*Official Navy Photo.*)

Dr. William P. C. Barton, Surgeon, U. S. Navy, shown in the dress uniform of 1802, sat for this painting by Thomas Sully in 1807. The portrait is now in the Philadelphia Museum of Art. Dr. Barton became the first Chief of the Bureau of Medicine and Surgery when the bureau system of management was introduced in 1842. Only surgeons wore the gold embroidered frogs at the buttons of the collar, lapels, and cuffs. A captain's coat was lavishly trimmed with gold lace on the collar, lapels, and cuffs; the button holes were worked with gold thread.

(*Courtesy of the National Library of Medicine.*)

button holes to be worked with gold thread." This short-lapelled coat was very similar to that prescribed for lieutenants in 1797, except for the modification in the collar. The diamond formed of lace was the first distinctive collar device to be used by the Navy, and began the practice of showing rank or class by means of collar insignia. The Navy still uses this system in the metal rank and corps devices worn on the collars of the khaki working shirt. In contrast to the short lapels of a midshipman, those of a sailing master were long and nine-buttoned. The device for sailing masters was a slip of gold lace on either side of the standing collar. The coat sleeves were the same as those worn by midshipmen—cuffless, but open at the outer seam, with three small buttons as a fastening.

Medical officers were permitted to wear blue coats; thus ended the practice, except for chaplains, of prescribing coats of different colors to indicate classes of officers. Chaplains would alternate between clerical black and navy blue for many years to come. A surgeon's coat was cut like a captain's, but was without the elaborate trimming of gold lace. In lieu of a captain's laced buttonholes, a surgeon was directed to have gold lace frogs at each of the nine buttons on the lapels and the three on the pocket flaps and cuffs. A surgeon's mate's coat was blue, cut like that of a surgeon, but less elaborately trimmed than that of his senior: instead of the lace frogs, all buttonholes were worked with gold thread. A purser's coat was similar to that of a captain, but the cuffs were not turned back. The ends of the sleeves were like those of the other warrant officers, midshipmen, and sailing masters—slashed, with small buttons in the openings. All decoration was omitted except that in full dress the top of a purser's standing collar was bordered with a band of gold embroidery.

Aside from the relatively small difference in cuffs, the slash sleeves of pursers, midshipmen, and sailing masters, and the turned back cuffs of the commissioned officers, the Navy had adopted a reasonably standard coat for all officers. The rank and class distinctions were indicated by the amount, type, and location of gold lace or embroidery, and by the number and position of buttons. A standard system of rank indications and specialty or corps devices would not be in effect for many years to come.

All officers wore white breeches and vests, and cocked hats. Only captains, lieutenants, and midshipmen were permitted to wear gold-laced hats in full dress; plain cocked hats were prescribed for all other officers, and for undress. For the first time, an undress uniform was authorized: the same coat as in dress, without lace or embroidery, except for that of a midshipman, who was directed to wear a short coat, in effect a jacket, with a slip of lace on the standing collar. Midshipmen were, for the most part, mere boys, and presumably more at ease in jackets than in long-tailed military coats.

The operations against France and the Barbary pirates had employed small squadrons of men-of-war, under command of a senior captain. Provision was made for the identification of a squadron commander in the 1802 regulations almost as an afterthought. The last line of the order prescribed that "A COMMODORE" have a silver star on each strap of his epaulets. The rank of commodore would not be established by Congress until 1862, though the title was an old and honored one in the navies of the world, and had been used in the American Navy from the period of the Revolution.

The Navy button of 1802 reflected the growth of the United States. Now the eagle and anchor were surrounded by a circle of fifteen stars. The circle of stars was reduced to the original thirteen when the uniform instructions of June 10, 1820 were issued, since legislation approved by President Madison on April 4, 1818 prescribed that the American flag have thirteen stripes, with a star for every state in the field.

UNIFORM INSTRUCTIONS OF 1813

The War of 1812 with Great Britain, in which the Navy played such an important role, brought about a large increase in the number of ships, officers, and men. With a larger officer corps, it is understandable that there should have been many suggestions concerning the uniform to be worn. This is reflected in a letter issued with the new uniform instructions of November 1813 by Secretary of the Navy William Jones:

Navy Department
November 23, 1813

SIR,

A NUMBER of the senior officers of the Navy of the United States, having suggested certain alterations in the established "Uniform Dress," which, in their opinion, would greatly conduce to the convenience and comfort of the officers, and still retain an appearance equally elegant and consistent; the following description of the "Uniform Dress," for the officers of the Navy of the United States, is substituted for that hitherto established; and is to take effect on the first day of January, 1814, to which all officers therein designated, are ordered to conform.

W. JONES

The order of November 23, 1813 is basically the same as that for

1802, with comparatively few changes but with uniforms for masters commandant (this rank having been restored in 1806) and, at last, a dress for boatswains, gunners, carpenters, and sailmakers.

Under the description of a captain's full-dress coat, lace was specified for the top of the standing collar, the edges of the lapels, the tops of the cuffs, the edges of the pocket flaps, and the folds of the skirts of the coat. No lace was prescribed for the buttonholes. Portraits of some of the officers who served with distinction in the War of 1812 depict them in uniforms with decorated buttonholes; in other portraits the buttonholes are plain. This is understandable since the 1802 order had prescribed decorated buttonholes, and this new order was not effective until 1814.

As an officer's rank diminished, so did the amount of lace he was entitled to wear. That for a master commandant was the same as for a captain, except that none was authorized for the pocket flaps. A lieutenant's dress coat was to be "laced with such lace as is directed for the captain's, round the collar and cuffs."—in other words, with no lace around the lapels, on the pocket flaps, or down the folds of the skirts. The number of buttons still continued to be one of the indications of rank. The three senior sea officers had nine buttons on each lapel, with varying numbers at other locations. A captain had four buttons on the cuffs and at the pockets, and one on either side of the standing collar. A master commandant displayed the same buttons except for those on the collar. For a lieutenant the number on the cuffs and pockets was reduced to three, but he did have a single button on each side of the collar. This rather complicated method of indicating rank required good eyesight! As for epaulets, a captain wore two; a master commandant one on the right shoulder; and a lieutenant one on the left shoulder, unless he was in command, when it was shifted to the right.

The 1813 instructions which refer to cocked hats seem to be in error when they read "Captains and lieutenants, when in full dress to wear . . . gold laced cocked hats . . ." This appears to be a direct copy of the 1802 uniform instruction, which was issued when the rank of master commandant had been abolished. It is safe to assume that masters commandant, who were senior to lieutenants, were also permitted to wear cocked hats. Under the 1813 order, midshipmen were denied the privilege of wearing laced cocked hats in full dress, and had to be content with the plain hats of other officers.

The changes in the dress uniforms of civil officers were much more extensive than those which affected sea officers. The 1813 order described a uniform for a new class of surgeon, a "HOSPITAL SURGEON, or NAVAL

Commodore Thomas MacDonough, 1814.

(*Official Navy Photo.*)

Captain James Lawrence, whose dying words, "Don't give up the ship," became the watchword of the Navy, is shown in this painting by Alonzo Chappel, in the insignia of a master commandant. This was the rank Lawrence held when in command of the *Hornet*. The uniform of a master commandant was the same as that of a captain except that there was no lace around the pocket flaps and the button was omitted from the standing collar. The artist has shown the pocket properly, but has added a button and slip of lace to the collar.

(*Official Navy Photo.*)

SURGEON, or acting as such by order of the Secretary of the Navy." The title of Hospital Surgeon would seem to indicate that such an officer was in charge of or assigned to a naval hospital; but since at this period the Navy had not as yet established hospitals in any real sense of the word, we must look for another explanation. From time to time makeshift facilities in the small navy yards had been used to care for the sick and wounded. The first establishment set up as a hospital, at Norfolk, was not placed in service until 1830.[3] It was not until May 24, 1828 that an act provided for a surgeon to be appointed to serve with a squadron as "Surgeon of the Fleet," although surgeons had previously been assigned to the staffs of commanders of squadrons. They were in charge of the medical facilities of a hospital ship if one were attached to the squadron, or in charge of the facilities of the flagship if no vessels had been assigned solely for medical purposes. In addition, during operations in the Mediterranean, temporary hospital facilities had sometimes been established ashore in a friendly port. As in many other cases, special duties were performed by surgeons before Congress actually established a military title to cover them.

All surgeons wore the same full-dress body coat as the senior sea officers, but with differences in lace to indicate their status and grades. In lieu of the gold frogging of the previous order a hospital surgeon had a strip of gold lace around the standing collar and two strips of lace a quarter of an inch wide on the cuffs. There was a single button on either side of the collar, with a laced buttonhole. Other surgeons displayed two buttons and ornamented buttonholes on either side of the collar, but did not have lace on either collars or cuffs. A surgeon's mate's coat was like that of a surgeon, with but one button on the collar and only two buttons on the cuffs. More rank by button!

The width of the gold lace remained an indication of rank or grade. The three-quarter-inch lace worn around the collar by pursers under the 1802 order was superseded in 1813 by lace half an inch wide. This matter of using the amount, width, or location of lace to indicate rank and grade is still a feature in the identification of naval rank. Fortunately the present system, developed during the Civil War, is much easier to follow!

For the first time, the Navy prescribed for undress wear a coat of different style from that of the dress coat. The "rolling cape," the ancestor of the much more casual turnover collar of today, was introduced, following the changing styles in civilian clothing. The new undress coat was certainly more comfortable than that with the standing collar. It was normally worn with several of the top buttons undone so that more freedom of movement was provided. As is normal, all lace of the dress coat was omitted from the service garment. Also in line with changing fashions, pantaloons with half boots were prescribed to replace the knee breeches, stockings, and buckled shoes of the earlier orders. The pantaloons were white for full dress or in warm weather, and blue for undress. Although cocked hats continued to be worn with full dress, the changing times were reflected in permission to wear a round hat for undress. This was an early form of the top hat which finally became the headpiece for formal civilian wear. Military dress follows the trend in civilian clothing, but is generally some years behind. Some items of military dress remain in use long after their counterparts in the civilian mode of the day have passed. Witness the Navy's cocked hat, which did not disappear until after World War II.

Now at last boatswains, gunners, carpenters, and sailmakers, the forward officers of the Navy, were assigned a uniform by official order. Their coat was to be short, with six buttons on each lapel, and with a "rolling cape" (like the undress coat of the senior officers), and was to be worn with blue pantaloons, a white vest, a round hat, and no side arms. This practice of ordering warrant officers of the United States Navy to wear what was in effect the undress uniform of commissioned officers lasted for many years.

UNIFORM REGULATIONS OF 1820

The uniform was again modified by an order of the Secretary of the Navy, Smith Thompson, on May 10, 1820, the changes to become effective May 1, 1821. The dress remained basically that of 1802 and 1813, but with more elaborate gold lace for captains. It would seem that the Navy was decorating its senior officers for the part they had played in the recent war with Great Britain! Another change was the introduction of a means of identifying three more officers in addition to those included in the rank structure approved by Congress. Distinctive uniforms were prescribed for "Captains of Five Years Standing", as well as other captains; for "Lieutenants Commandant," and for "Lieutenants of Line of Battleships."

Congress had as yet made no provision for a rank above that of captain, and all captains drew the same pay and rations. All lieutenants—whether in command of a small vessel, or executive officer in one of the Navy's mighty 74-gun ships of the line, or second in command to a master commandant—were paid identical sums per moth. However, it was nec-

Samuel Chester Reid was a naval officer in command of the New York privateer *General Armstrong* in the War of 1812. In this painting, by John Wesley Jarvis, he is wearing the "round" hat the Navy used in undress in the early part of the nineteenth century. The high hat was gradually replaced by the blue-cloth cap during the 1830's.

(Official Navy Photo.)

Lieutenant David Connor, circa 1817.

(*Official Navy Photo.*)

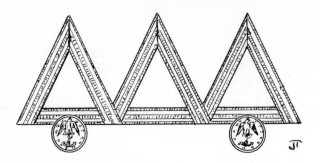

Lace of a captain's full-dress coat, above skirt buttons.

essary to be able to identify the most senior captains, and those lieutenants who had the more responsible assignments.

The full-dress coats of all captains were now lined with white, instead of blue of the previous order. Gold lace, not less than five-eighths nor more than three-quarters of an inch wide, was worn around the standing collar, down the edges of the long lapels, around the cuffs, and down the folds of the skirts, with two rows of lace on the pocket flaps. All buttonholes were to be trimmed with gold lace, half the width of that worn on other parts of the coat. Three triangles of lace were to be worn above the buttons at the top of the skirts of the coat, as shown in the sketch. All in all, a most elaborate full-dress coat! One could distinguish between the senior and junior captains only by their epaulets. Captains of more than five years' standing displayed two crossed silver anchors on the straps of their epaulets; those who had served less than five years had a single anchor. A "commodore" was directed to show a silver eagle above the anchors of his epaulets.

The coats of all junior officers were lined with blue cloth, and in general conformed to the 1813 order. A master commandant was now permitted to wear two plain gold epaulets. The lieutenants commandant, lieutenants of line battleships, and ordinary lieutenants wore the dress uniform of 1813, with lace around the standing collar and cuffs. They could be distinguished only by the location of the single epaulet. The first two groups of lieutenants wore the epaulet on the right shoulder; other lieutenants wore it on the left.

All officers, from "commodore" to lieutenant, wore gold-laced cocked hats in full dress. Now the lace was to show an inch and a quarter on each side of the fan, instead of the three-quarters of an inch of the previous order. With more lace on the coats and wider lace on cocked hats, business should have boomed for the uniform suppliers. All commis-

This portrait of Lieutenant A. B. Pinkham, the original of which is in the Nantucket Historical Society, shows that the style of uniforms can change, even though no new instructions are issued. Pinkham is wearing a full-dress coat, which conforms to the wording of the 1820 Uniform Regulations but entirely different in cut from those of the War of 1812 or the early 1820's. In this portrait, the buttons are no longer in straight rows, nor are the lapels buttoned across. Instead, the coat is cut with a swell, and the lapels are buttoned back as prescribed in 1830. This coat was worn before 1830, for the collar lace is as specified in 1820. In 1830, the collar would be decorated with live-oak leaf embroidery. This change in the style of the Navy's coats in the latter part of the 1820's evidently was the basis for the pattern of the full-dress coat prescribed in 1830.

Prior to 1830, sword belts were not described in uniform regulations, but portraits show them to be white, blue, or black. Pinkham's elaborately embroidered belt seems to have been an "adoption" but the oak-leaf motif was carried over into the 1830 regulations for cuff, collar, and pocket-flap decoration. Under the 1830 regulations, full-dress belts were of white webbing, with blue webbing for undress. However, many portraits of officers in the 1830 full-dress uniform show the embroidered belt.

(*Official Navy Photo.*)

sioned sea officers and the warranted sailing masters carried yellow-mounted cut-and-thrust swords. Midshipmen and pursers were instructed to carry dirks, and all officers in undress could carry dirks. Boatswains, gunners, carpenters, and sailmakers were directed not to carry side arms.

Another innovation of the 1820 order was the establishment of four types of buttons to identify classes of officers. A "No. 1" button was to be worn by all captains—an eagle with its head turned left, perched on the stock of an anchor, surrounded by thirteen stars. The "No. 2" button was to be worn by masters commandant, lieutenants commandant, lieutenants of line battleships, and mere lieutenants—an eagle looking to the right, perched on a branch and holding a shield with its left wing. For all non-combatants, including medical officers and pursers, a "No. 3" button was prescribed—the same as that worn by captains but without the circle of stars. Sailing masters, midshipmen, and all other warrant officers were instructed to wear "No. 4" buttons—similar to those of masters commandant, but with minor changes. Fortunately this rather odd button situation, which appears to have served no useful purpose, lasted only ten years. The 1830 uniform regulations directed that the "No. 1" button be worn by all officers. Now one design is worn by all officers of the United States Navy.

On June 10, 1821, just a month after the 1820 order was issued, the Secretary of the Navy issued a General Order modifying it. After July 4, 1820 all lieutenants commandant were to wear the dress of a master commandant, but with a single epaulet, and that on the right shoulder. Under this change, lieutenants were permitted to wear four buttons on the cuffs and at the pockets and to have lace down the lapels, on the pocket flaps, and down the skirts of the coat. The June 10 order also directed that all lieutenants who had served five years in grade by July 4 in any year, were to shift the epaulet from the left to the right shoulder.

It would seem that some simpler methods might have been developed to permit easier identification of naval rank. The simpler and more uniform means of showing rank and corps affiliation which developed during the Civil War certainly made it easier for the civilian population of the United States to determine an officer's rank and specialty.

UNIFORM REGULATION OF 1830

A Naval General Order approved by Secretary of the Navy John Branch on May 1, 1830, to be effective December 31, 1830, made some changes in the Navy's dress which are still reflected in the current uniform instructions. For the first time, distinctive devices were prescribed for civil or staff officers to distinguish them from the sea or line officers. A device is more readily recognized and understood than the amount or location of gold lace, or the number of buttons. All officers of the United States Navy today are identified with their corps by a system of devices, stemming from this 1830 order.

Another innovation in 1830 was the use of arrangements of live-oak leaves and acorns for decoration and for indicating rank. While the elaborate embroidery has disappeared from the present-day uniform of the United States Navy, the oak leaves and acorns still appear as indication of rank on the cap visors of senior officers. With exception of the Chaplain Corps, the devices of the staff corps all incorporate oak leaves and acorns. Customs and styles change, but in any service with a long tradition, certain things carry forward from year to year.

The full-dress coat of the 1830 order will be described in the words of the original order, since it is a complete change from earlier instructions and reflects the current fashion in civilian and military dress. The dress coat was to be of "dark blue cloth, double breasted, with long lapels; the width to be in proportion to the size of the coat, and cut with a swell, to be buttoned back with nine buttons on each lapel, and an equal number of blind button holes, worked with twist, as long as the width of the lapel will allow.—Standing collar to be lined with white . . ." The lapels were not to be buttoned across as they had been since 1802, but buttoned back on themselves. The two edges of the coat were to be fastened in the center of the chest with hooks and eyes. This coat, which represents a complete change in the Navy's dress, appears in many contemporary portraits, some of which are reproduced here. However, the coat could be buttoned across, and was so worn in inclement or cold weather.

The extent of the embroidery showing oak leaves and acorns determined an officer's rank—more for a captain and less as rank diminished. A captain's full-dress coat was trimmed with the leaves and acorn design on the standing collar, the cuffs, and the pocket flaps. Masters commandant had embroidery on collars and cuffs, while lieutenants had the decoration on the collar only. Passed midshipmen—that is, those who had passed the examination for promotion and were waiting for a vacancy in the rank of lieutenant—had a narrow band of oak-leaf embroidery on the top and front edges of the collars, and on either side a gold-embroidered foul anchor and star. Other midshipmen wore the same coat, but without the embroidered star. The anchor and star are still used as devices for midshipmen at the Naval Academy. Masters—the senior warrant officers, one day to be in line of promotion to commissioned rank—were not

This lithograph by Huddy and Duval is an excellent portrayal of the full dress of a captain according to the 1830 uniform regulations. The lapels are buttoned back as required by the order but have not been hooked closed in the center, so the white vest is visible. In full dress, either white pantaloons or breeches were prescribed, but, possibly in deference to cold weather, Captain Stewart posed in his undress blue trousers. Although the print is captioned "Commodore Charles Stewart," the epaulets do not indicate the star of an officer "entiled to wear a broad pendant" on the straps. Stewart had served in command of a squadron, and so would be known by the time-honored but still unauthorized title of "commodore." The cocked hat shows the newly introduced trim over the cockade, "six bullion loops, the inner ones twisted."

(*Courtesy of the Anne S. K. Brown Military Collection.*)

The Lieutenant, U. S. Navy, as depicted by Huddy and Duval in full dress is identified by the single epaulet on the right shoulder and by the absence of embroidery on the cuffs and pocket flaps. The coat is hooked together in the center, showing the prescribed button arrangement. The loop over the cockade is of flat lace, not the bullion loops of captains and masters commandant. The dress of the enlisted man is typical of the period: black, beribboned hat; short jacket with numerous small Navy buttons; white frock with blue collar and bib; full-bottomed white trousers; and pumps. These were the articles of clothing listed in purchase contracts and stocked in slop stores.

(Courtesy of the Anne S. K. Brown Military Collection.)

Huddy and Duval's "Passed Midshipman" is a rather relaxed full dress, for both the coat and vest are unfastened. This permits the white-web full-dress sword-belt to show. The border of oak leaves and acorns instead of the collar-covering embroidery of the three senior sea officers, allows room for a distinctive device. The gold foul anchor and star is today the insignia of distinguished midshipmen at the United States Naval Academy. The seaman shows the very full frock of the early years of the United States Navy.

(Courtesy of the Anne S. K. Brown Military Collection.)

permitted to wear the leaves and acorns on the collar, but had a button and slip of lace on either side of the full-dress collar. This was a carry-over from earlier regulations. All of these officers had double-breasted coats, with nine buttons on either breast. A captain retained the four buttons at the cuffs and pockets of the previous order, but the other officers now had three buttons on the cuffs and pockets.

To allow room for the distinctive devices introduced by the 1830 order, medical officers and pursers had the same narrow border of live-oak leaves and acorns around the full-dress collar as worn by midshipmen, with the device placed on either side. For medical officers the device was the "Staff of Esculapius," stemming from classical mythology. The symbol of Esculapius, the Roman god of medicine and healing, was a heavy staff with a serpent twined about it. For pursers the cornucopia,

Collar for surgeon's full dress.   Collar for purser's full dress.

The 1830 uniform regulations began the practice of indicating a staff officer's specialty by means of a distinctive corps device. Prior to 1830, attempts had been made to distinguish between sea officers, the line officers of today, and civil or non-ocmbatant officers by variations in the style or color of the uniforms. The introduction of staff corps devices in 1830 preceded the establishment of a common method of indicating rank by more than thirty years.

or horn of plenty, was selected as a device. It was quite appropriate for the officers responsible for paying and feeding the Navy, and providing small necessities, comforts, and clothing through "slop stores." Here again, the amount of embroidery indicates grade, for while surgeons and pursers had embroidery on both collars and cuffs, assistant surgeons had embroidery on the collar only. Medical officers and pursers wore the same arrangement of buttons as masters commandant: three at the pockets and on the cuffs.

At last, the Navy prescribed a uniform for chaplains! No, not a blue and gold uniform in the Navy tradition, but the somber garb of a clergyman: "Plain black coat, vest and pantaloons, to be worn over boots or shoes, or black breeches, silk stockings with shoes, coat to have three black covered buttons under the pocket flaps and on the cuffs." The only things which related a chaplain to the Navy were the three buttons on the

This portrait of Jonathan M. Foltz was painted in 1831 when he was a twenty-one-year-old Assistant Surgeon of the United States Navy. The standing collar shows the first device of the Medical Corps, the "club of Esculapius" in high relief. In 1871 Dr. Foltz became the Surgeon General of the Navy and Chief of the Bureau of Medicine and Surgery under President Grant.

(*Courtesy of the National Library of Medicine.*)

cuffs and at the pockets—which were not Navy buttons at that. A chaplain was not permitted to wear a cocked hat. Since the order is silent on what headpiece he could wear, it would appear that he could wear either the round hat or the cap authorized for undress.

Although both clerks and schoolmasters had been associated with the Navy for many years, it was not until 1830 that a uniform was prescribed for them. Their coat was "of plain blue cloth, single breasted, rolling collar, and made according to the prevailing fashion for the citizens of the time, with six Navy buttons on each breast, one on each hip and one at the bottom of the skirts." Here is another example of using buttons to indicate grade. Since a single-breasted coat was specified, it is rather difficult to visualize two rows of buttons! The practice of prescribing single-breasted coats for some non-combatant officers while sea officers and other non-combatants wore double-breasted coats was to continue for many years.

Boatswains, gunners, carpenters, and sailmakers were given a double-breasted coat very similar to that of commissioned officers. The collar was without ornamentation, and there were but eight buttons in each row. Such coats—similar to those of the senior officers, but with fewer buttons—continued to be one of the distinguishing marks of warrant officers.

Although knee breeches had not been specified for naval dress since the 1813 regulations, they reappeared in the 1830 order. In full dress, most officers—the exceptions being chaplains, forward warrant officers, schoolmasters, and clerks—had the option of wearing either white pantaloons or breeches with white silk stockings and buckled shoes. In undress, except in warm weather, blue pantaloons were worn.

Earlier orders had designated which officers could wear gold-laced cocked hats, but the style of the trim had not been specified. The 1830 order went into detail on the ornamentation of cocked hats, and used different styles of trim to indicate groups of officers. Captains' and masters commandants' hats were bound with one-and-a-half-inch gold lace, and had a tassel of five blue and five gold bullions at either end. Over the black silk cockade was additional decoration: six bullion loops, the two inner ones to be twisted together." The written description is somewhat misleading, as the sketches will show. It appears there were three loops from the top of the fan around the small Navy button below the cockade. Since this same description will be used to describe the cocked hats worn by senior officers for many years after 1830, it is advisable that it be completely understood, and a picture is the best means of clarifying the point. The cocked hats of other officers, except for chaplains, schoolmasters, clerks, and the forward warrant officers, were bound with one-and-a-half-inch lace, with tassels at either end; but the loop over the cockade was made of gold lace, not bullions. The Navy's cocked hats followed this general pattern until they were abolished after World War II. Those officers not entitled to cocked hats wore either round hats or the newly introduced blue cloth caps.

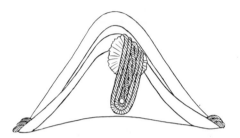 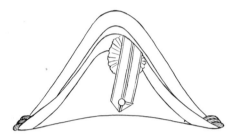

Cocked hat of captain and master commandant, 1830. Cocked hat of other officers, 1830.

(Sketch by Marvin H. Pakula.)

Caps were coming into style for both civilian and military use, so it is but natural that the Navy should have adopted this comfortable and serviceable headgear for undress use. Today, the cap is the only authorized head cover for male officers and chief petty officers, except the tropical helmet and the garrison and working caps which can be worn only with working dress. When the cap was first introduced, the overhang of the top, as shown in contemporary paintings of both civilians and military personnel, was quite wide. By the 1880's the overhang was practically nil, being just about the diameter of the band. Today's cap has a flare of approximately an inch and three-quarters, depending on the hat size.

In 1830, the caps of all officers except captains, masters commandant, and lieutenants, had blue bands. Those of the three senior officers had inch-and-a-half bands of gold lace. The caps of today also indicate classes of officers: the visors of flag officers are covered with embroidered oak leaves and acorns; captains and commanders have a border of similar embroidery on the outer edge of the visor; lieutenant commanders and all officers below that rank wear undecorated visors of black patent leather. The oak-leaf and acorn decorations on the bills of senior officers' caps today are similar to those of 1830.

The undress coat of 1830 carried forward the 1813 concept of a coat different from the one for full dress, with less embroidery. The undress coat of 1830 was described as of "dark blue cloth, lined with same, rolling collar, and made according to the prevailing fashion of citizens for the time." The first undress coat with its "rolling cape" had moved closer to the dress of civilians of the period. For senior sea officers, all lace and embroidery were omitted from the undress coat On the other hand, the undress coats of medical officers did have some decoration. The cuffs and collars were of black velvet, a throwback to the use, in 1797, of differently colored cloth to distinguish medical officers from their line associates. As a mark of identification, surgeons had a strip of half-inch lace around the velvet cuffs, while those of assistant medical officers were plain.

The need for a more convenient and comfortable coat for shipboard use was approved—the first of a long line of "service" coats. This short jacket had the same number of buttons as the more formal coat. Gray cloth or brown drilling trousers and black vests could be worn with the jacket. This was more suitable for work aboard ship, and certainly more comfortable than the high-collared dress coat, as well as less cumbersome than the undress frock coat.

Although straps of gold lace had been used for years to secure the epaulets to the coat at the shoulder seam, they were officially recognized by the 1830 regulations. The lace straps were to be three-quarters of an inch wide, and served a dual purpose: to hold the epaulet and to indicate an officer's status when he dispensed with the epaulets in undress. In 1830, this portion of the order concerned captains, masters commandant, and lieutenants, the only officers permitted to wear epaulets. Since there was no indication of rank on the straps, the only method of determining an officer's rank was to count his buttons. It was somewhat simpler to identify a lieutenant, for he had but one strap. However, from this first small beginning developed the system used during the Civil War, when an officer's rank and corps could be determined from his shoulder ornaments.

UNIFORM CHANGES 1830 TO 1841

The changes of uniform issued by the Navy Department from 1797 through 1820 had been few, covered only minor matters, and had little effect on the dress of the Navy. However, the 1830 uniform instructions included changes which showed a trend toward uniformity in dress for all officers of the Navy. A Naval General Order of January 20, 1832 changed the device of medical officers from the staff and serpent to a branch of live oak. Although the "Staff of Esculapius" had long been a recognized insignia of medicine, it evidently was not pleasing to the Medical Department. The 1832 change also removed the black velvet from the collars and cuffs of medical officers' undress coats, a small step toward

Captain Matthew Calbraith Perry in undress coat, circa 1838.

(Official Navy Photo.)

This full dress coat was worn by Surgeon Bailey Washington in the latter part of the 1830's. The collar shows the device of medical officers of January 20, 1832, which replaced the original staff and serpent of 1830. The coat is typical of the late thirties, for, instead of being "cut with a swell," the rows of buttons are nearly parallel, the style of the 1841 regulations. The back of the coat shows the arrangement of buttons for masters commandant and surgeons.

(Courtesy of the Smithsonian Institution.)

uniformity in the Navy's dress. Surgeons were differentiated from their assistants by a Navy button on either side of the rolling collar, while assistant surgeons had a strip of lace around the cuffs. This lace did not indicate rank, since in the 1830's medical officers did not have rank as we know it today. It was not until 1846 that they were assigned "relative" or "assimilated" rank with officers of the line.

An order of December 24, 1834, effective February 22, 1835, again modified the uniforms of officers of the Medical Department. It would appear that surgeons were not happy to have their assistants wear a strip of lace in undress, when they had none! Assistant surgeons retained the single strip, but surgeons were authorized to wear two half-inch strips on the cuffs in undress. Another move toward uniformity was permission for all medical officers to wear gold lace cap bands. The original 1830 regulation had limited this distinction to captains, masters commandant, and lieutenants, the three commissioned sea officers. Not to be outdone, midshipmen, who could succeed to command at sea, were authorized to display lace cap bands by an order of June 20, 1838. Once an exception is made to a uniform instruction, others follow!

UNIFORMS FOR ENGINEERS

The introduction of steam into the United States Navy brought about a change in its uniform not covered by an order from the Secretary. When the *Fulton,* the second ship by this name, was placed in commission in September 1837, it was deemed necessary to provide some form of dress which could serve to identify the engineers in charge of the boilers and machinery. The Secretary of the Navy, by a letter of November 21, 1837, authorized the commanding officer, Captain Matthew C. Perry, to prescribe a uniform for engineers. It may appear rather odd that the dress of engineers was not covered by a uniform change issued by the Navy Department. It is to be remembered that it was not until 1842 that Congress legalized the employment of this new class of officer. The uniform prescribed by Captain Perry was the undress of 1830: a double-breasted coat with a rolling collar. To set engineers apart from other officers, the collars and cuffs were to be of black velvet, like the undress uniform of medical officers prior to the 1832 change. Only the chief engineer was permitted to wear a cocked hat in full dress. The assistant engineers wore blue cloth caps on all occasions. To indicate the grade of engineers, the chief engineer displayed a gold-embroidered, five-pointed star on either side of the collar; the first assistant, a similarly placed pair

The lead article in the short-lived *Naval Magazine* of November, 1838 is entitled "The Boatswain's Mate," written by "A Brother Cruiser." The story is illustrated by this charming woodcut of "George Brown" in the uniform prescribed for muster by the then current "Regulation of the Government of the Navy." Not until 1841 were uniforms for enlisted men included in the Uniform Regulations. Such uniform instructions were not always strictly enforced, so the men vied with each other to add such decorative touches as are shown on the collar and bib of the white frock. The embroidery on the right sleeve is worthy of comment. The device is not that of a petty officer as prescribed in the 1841 regulations, a foul anchor and spread eagle, but the specialty mark of a boatswain's mate, of the 1866 uniform instructions! Many times, uniform regulations merely gave official sanction to the uniforms and devices previously worn.

Navy Engineer, circa 1841.

(Illustration taken from Bennett's Steam Navy of the United States.)

of silver stars; a second assistant, a silver star on the right side only; and a third assistant, a star on the left[4] Contemporary pictures show that at some time after 1837 the black velvet on the collars and cuffs was replaced with blue like that worn by other officers of the Navy.

UNIFORM REGULATIONS OF 1841

The "Regulations for the Uniform and Dress of the Navy of the United States" approved February 19, 1841 are of particular interest. In addition to many changes in the dress of officers, they contain the first instructions for the dress of enlisted men. Whereas this had been standardized to a large degree by the procurement of clothing under contract and by the use of patterns, enlisted men had not been covered before by the published uniform regulations.

In general, the 1841 uniform was much less elaborately decorated with embroidery than that of 1830, and the cut of the coat was drastically changed. Coats of this period are readily identifiable, for they were no longer "cut with a swell," buttoned back, or hooked together in the center. The coat was fuller and was worn buttoned across so that the rows of buttons were three inches apart from top to bottom. All the oak-leaf and acorn embroidery was removed from the full-dress coats of captains and commanders. (The rank of "master commandant" had been changed to "commander" by an Act of Congress on March 3, 1837.) Since the gold embroidery was omitted, rank was indicated only by buttons. While each officer had two rows of nine buttons on the breast, captains had four on the cuffs and under the pocket flaps; commanders but three in the same locations.

Evidently the Navy Department wished to spare lieutenants at least part of the cost of new dress uniforms. The order allowed them to wear the 1830 embroidery, oak and acorns, on the new standing collar. It appears that it would be rather difficult for a tailor to modify the 1830 coat, which fitted the figure rather snugly, to the looser coat of 1841 with its narrow lapels. Possibly the old collar could be attached to the new coat, thus salvaging the embroidery. The narrow border of embroidery was removed from the collars of passed midshipmen, but the anchor and star were retained. Midshipmen needed a new coat, now that they were permitted to wear a double-breasted one with a rolling collar—the undress coat of passed midshipmen—and with an anchor of buff cloth inserted in either side of the collar. Masters wore for dress the undress coat of the senior officers. On the collar were two loops of gold

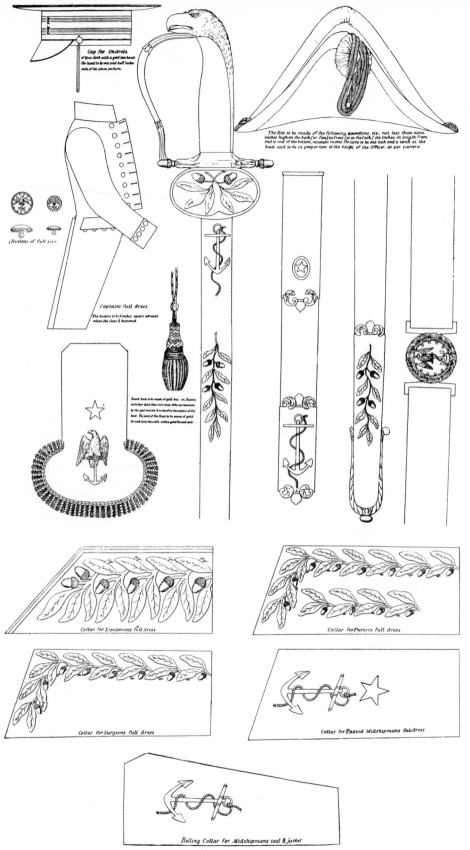

Illustrations from "Regulations for the Uniform and Dress of the Navy of the United States, 1841."

This miniature by L. Pellegrine of Captain Elin A. F. Lavallette shows the undress coat authorized by the 1841 regulations, "dark blue cloth, lined with the same, and with a rolling collar. Buttons to be the same in number and size, and arranged in the same manner as for the full dress coat." Except for the epaulets and gilt Navy buttons, it is the coat of civilians of the period.

(*Official Navy Photo.*)

lace, each four and a half inches long, with a button in each loop. Second masters wore the same coat, but with a single loop and button.

The undress coat for all officers entitled to wear the standing-collar full-dress coat was of dark blue, lined with the same, and with a rolling collar. The number and location of buttons was the same as in full dress. In effect, this was the same coat as in 1830, slightly modified in cut to conform to the civilian style of the day. Instead of the long frock coat for undress, midshipmen were instructed to wear short jackets while on duty, with the same number of small buttons as in full dress, and with the anchor, in buff, inserted in the collar. The 1841 order contained the first mention of cold or foul weather clothing. Officers could wear either pea jackets or overcoats, with the same arrangements of buttons as on other coats. The wearing of epaulets on this outer clothing was prohibited, but captains, commanders, and lieutenants were directed to display shoulder straps as an indication of rank and command.

Under the 1841 regulations, boatswains, gunners, carpenters, and sailmakers lost buttons. Instead of the two rows of eight buttons and the three under the pocket flaps of 1830, seven buttons were specified for the breasts of the double-breasted coat of 1841, and only two for the pockets. For many years, the Navy held rather consistently to the nine-button arrangement for the senior commissioned officers, and to the four-button pattern for the sleeves and pockets of captains, with three buttons for commanders, lieutenants, medical officers, and pursers. The number and arrangement of buttons for other officers seemed to be a matter of whim!

At the same time that the coats of captains and commanders had become plain, without lace or embroidery, those of medical officers had grown more elaborate. The border of leaves and acorns specified for full dress in 1830 was retained, but the device of 1832, the branch of live oak, was omitted. The band of embroidery was removed from the cuffs of surgeons. In compensation, a surgeon was directed to wear three strips of one-and-a-half-inch gold lace around the cuffs, the three buttons being between the two upper strips. Passed assistant surgeons had two strips of similar lace, and assistants, one. To the uninitiated, the well-laced surgeon might appear to be the most senior officer of the United States Navy. His cuffs showed lace, but those of a captain were plain. In most countries, a military man was judged by the amount of lace or embroidery; the more of it, the higher the rank. Although strips of lace had been used previously to indicate the grades of medical officers, this is the first time that all three grades were indicated by the number of stripes. A similar system for the rank identification of line officers would not be introduced until 1852.

Pursers retained the same embroidery as authorized in 1830, except that the device of the Purser Department, the cornucopia, was replaced by a strip of live-oak leaves and acorns of the same pattern as that around the full-dress collar. From 1841 on, the insignia of the officers who pay and feed the crews and who procure clothing and other supplies needed by the Navy, has been based on oak leaves and acorns. The device of the present-day Supply Corps is a sprig of three oak leaves and three acorns.

At long last, chaplains were permitted to wear a naval uniform: the undress coat of a lieutenant, with a black velvet collar and cuffs. Black velvet had been used to distingush medical officers in undress from 1830 to 1832, and was employed for engineers when they were placed in uniform in 1837. Chaplains had finally received recognition as commissioned officers, for the double-breasted coat had nine Navy buttons in each row, and there were three buttons on the cuffs and under the pocket flaps.

The legislation of 1835 which had made provision for professors of mathematics and secretaries to commanders of fleets or squadrons, is reflected in the 1841 uniform instruction. A secretary was directed to wear the double-breasted, rolling-collared, undress coat of a lieutenant, with two rows of nine buttons each, but with none on the cuffs: another exception to the general rule that commissioned officers display nine buttons and warrant officers a lesser number. Professors and clerks wore the same coats as secretaries, but with only seven buttons in a row. It would be some years before this matter of buttons was resolved.

The 1841 regulations expanded the system of showing some form of rank device on epaulets. Previously only a "commodore" had been assigned a device—a silver star. The new order directed all captains to wear a plain silver anchor and eagle on epaulets, and "commodores" a star above the anchor-eagle device. Although in 1841 the use of rank devices in any form was not extensive, the trend had been established. Stars have long been used to indicate top command, and since 1841 the silver spread eagle has been used to identify captains of the United States Navy. It is still employed as a pin-on device for the shoulders of Navy raincoats, for the collars of the khaki working shirts, and on the garrison cap.

Under the 1830 regulations, all officers entitled to wear epaulets displayed gold lace shoulder straps when epaulets were omitted. The 1841 regulation expanded the shoulder-strap system to incorporate some indication of rank. Now all captains were instructed to wear blue cloth straps, two and a half inches long and half an inch wide, with gold-embroidered edges. "Commodores" displayed the star in the center of the straps; for captains the straps were plain. Commanders and lieutenants wore gold lace straps, the same size as those of captains, but without devices. Since lieutenants were entitled to but one epaulet, they wore the strap on the right shoulder. From this small beginning was developed the Navy's system of shoulder straps, which came into full use during the Civil War and which lasted until late in the nineteenth century.

All officers except professors, clerks, and the forward warrant officers were permitted to wear cocked hats. The excepted officers wore blue cloth caps with blue bands. The use of bullion loops over the cockades introduced in 1830 was expanded. Captains and commanders retained the loop of six bullions, the center pair twisted; lieutenants, masters, and passed and other midshipmen now had a loop of four bullions, the center pair not twisted. The vignette shows the decoration of the hats of the junior officers. The civil officers entitled to wear cocked hats had a flat

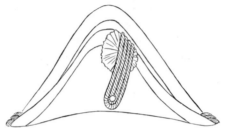

Cocked Hat, lieutenants, masters, and midshipmen, 1841.

(Sketch by Marvin H. Pakula.)

loop of lace, two inches wide, over the cockade. Under this system it was possible to identify the two senior officers, the rest of the seagoing officers, and finally, the commissioned civil officers. There was apparently one irregularity: secretaries, who were warranted, wore cocked hats.

In undress, the decoration of the blue cap, a gold lace band an inch and a half wide, indicated commissioned officers, including captains, commanders, lieutenants, all medical officers, chaplains, and pursers. All other officers had blue or black silk bands around the cap. However, the Navy introduced a cap device to identify midshipmen. Passed midshipmen wore an anchor with a star above it over the visor; other midshipmen, simply an anchor. These were the same devices as specified for midshipmen's coats.

Since the 1841 order was the first to include the dress of enlisted personnel, it is well to reproduce this section in its entirety.

> The outside clothing of petty officers, seamen, and ordinary seamen, landsmen and boys, for muster, shall consist of blue woolen frocks, with white linen or duck collars and cuffs, or blue cloth jacket and trousers, blue vests when vests are worn, black hat, black handkerchief and shoes, when weather is cold; when the weather is warm, it shall consist of white frock and

This lithograph of a painting by Lieutenant H. Walke is of interest for it shows the dress of both officers and men in 1847. Officers are in frock coats or jackets, and all seem to be wearing the visored blue cloth cap authorized in 1841. Instead of the very wide stiff overhang of the top of the cap pictured in the 1841 regulations, the caps indicate that the stiffening grommet had been removed in order to secure a more comfortable and casual headpiece. The men are in frocks, stiff hats, and trousers, the usual dress of seamen and petty officers.

(Courtesy of the Library of Congress.)

trousers, and black or white hats, as the commander may direct, having regard to the convenience and comfort of the crew, black handkerchiefs and shoes. The collars and breasts of the frocks to be lined or faced with blue cotton cloth, stitched with white thread or cotton.

This description covers in a general way the clothing of enlisted men since the creation of the United States Navy. It also summarizes the clothing carried in "slop stores," and purchased under contract. Since 1841, some description of enlisted clothing has appeared in all uniform instructions.

For the first time, a "mark of distinction" was prescribed for petty officers. The device was an "eagle and anchor . . . not more than three inches in length, and . . . of the same pattern as upon the Navy button (except stars) placed half way between the elbow and shoulder on the front of the sleeve. It shall be white when worn on a blue garment, and blue when worn on a white garment." Boatswains' mates, gunners' mates,

Petty officer's device, 1841.

(*Original Sketch by Marvin H. Pakula.*)

carpenters' mates, masters at arms, ship's stewards, and ship's cooks wore the device on the right sleeve. The other petty officers—quarter-masters, quarter-gunners, captains of forecastles, captains of tops, captains of afterguard, armorers, coopers, ship's corporals, and captains of the hold—wore the device on the left sleeve. Since distinctive rating badges, such as are now employed, were not used, it must have been difficult to determine whether a petty officer from another ship was a boatswain's mate or a cook, a quarter-master or a cooper! Specialty marks would not be prescribed until 1866, but now it was possible to distinguish between petty officers and other men. The duties of the petty officers of the period are described in Herman Melville's "White Jacket, or the World in a Man-of-War."

Eccentric hair styles appear to have caused concern, for the last paragraph of the 1841 order reads: "The hair of all persons belonging to the Navy, when in actual service is to be kept short. No part of the beard is to be worn long except the whiskers, which shall not descend more than one inch below the tip of the ear, and thence in a line towards the corners of the mouth." Melville's account of his cruise from the west coast of South America to the east coast of the United States devotes many pages to this matter of hair style. During the voyage around Cape Horn, the men had been permitted to grow heavy beards, of which they became inordinately proud. As the U.S.S. *Neversink* approached home port, the men were ordered to conform to regulations. Great was the anguish when the crew was forced to submit to the ship's barbers. A near mutiny occurred, but when the ship docked, the men were in conformance with the official orders.

The uniform order of 1841 made no mention of a uniform for engineers, having been issued before Congress legalized their employment. It is strange that no change in the 1841 uniform regulations was issued by the Department after the Act of Congress of 1842 which not only established the Engineer Corps, but also directed the Secretary to prescribe a uniform for this new class of officer.

UNIFORM CHANGES, 1841–1852

A Navy Department "Regulation, Changes and Modifications of Uniforms," issued on June 1, 1845, to be effective January 1, 1846, finally put lieutenants on even keel, by authorizing two plain gold epaulets. The system of employing distinctive devices on officers' shoulder ornaments was expanded. In addition to the epaulet devices previously ordered for "commodores" and captains, commanders were directed to wear a plain silver anchor. Changes were also made in the devices for shoulder straps. Captains other than those in command of squadrons now displayed a silver spread eagle. The Navy was moving inch by inch toward a system of rank devices.

The Navy's first cap devices had a short life, for the anchor and star of passed midshipmen, and the anchor of midshipmen, were removed from the front of the blue cap. All midshipmen were now permitted to wear a gold lace band an inch and a half wide, the same as authorized for captains, commanders, and lieutenants. Two concessions were made to warm climates. Lighter-weight frock (undress) coats of "dark blue summer-cloth" were authorized for summer or tropical use. A further concession was the permission to wear straw hats. The body of the hat was to be six inches high, and the brim three and a half inches wide. The wearing of straw hats in the United States Navy was indeed not

The order of May 27, 1847, directed medical officers to wear epaulets in dress, and shoulder straps in undress. As a distinguishing symbol, the shoulder ornaments were to be decorated with the letters *M.D.* in gold embroidery. The narrow shoulder straps of Assistant Surgeon Gerrard Alexander show only the initials of the Medical Corps. Passed assistants wore the same straps with a gold bar at either end.

(Official Navy Photo.)

new; it went back to the first cruises and actions in the Mediterranean. During the War of 1812, prisoners of war in England had made straw hats for sale. The ships of the Navy were serving more and more widely in tropical and semitropical waters as the interests of the United States expanded and merchant ships sailed the seven seas. This and the impending war with Mexico, undoubtedly had some bearing on the decision to provide more suitable clothing for hot weather.

The assignment in 1846 of relative rank to medical officers, and in 1847 to pursers, was the basis for the "Change and Modifications of Uniform" issued by Secretary of the Navy J. T. Mason on May 27, 1847. Now medical officers and pursers were permitted to wear epaulets similar to those of the sea officers with whom they had been given relative standing. However, the epaulets were of a different pattern, for the crescents were to be solid and bright, instead of embroidered. The bullions of the epaulets of surgeons and pursers of more than twelve years' standing were to be the same as those of commanders with whom they ranked, a half inch in diameter and three inches long. For surgeons and pursers of less than twelve years' service, the bullions were to be like those of lieutenants—three inches long, but only three-eighths of an inch in diameter. Passed assistant surgeons had the relative rank "next after lieutenants"—that is with masters. Assistant surgeons ranked "next after masters," or with second masters. As neither masters nor second masters wore epaulets, the Navy Department specified that the assistant surgeons wear the same type as their seniors, but with bullions a quarter of an inch in diameter. Within the crescents of the epaulets, all medical officers displayed the initials of the Medical Department, *M.D.* in Old English characters, worked in solid silver. Pursers wore the letters *P.D.* in Old English characters to indicate their respective department. "Surgeons of the Fleet" were identified by a rosette of burnished silver on the strap above the letters.

Since all officers entitled to wear epaulets wore shoulder straps to indicate their rank when epaulets were omitted, all medical officers and pursers were directed to wear straps of blue cloth with a gold-embroidered edge. The straps of surgeons and pursers had a quarter-inch border of embroidery, those for the passed assistant and assistant surgeons had borders an eighth of an inch wide. Medical officers displayed the letters *M.D.* in silver in the center of the straps. To indicate the classes of medical officers, devices were employed. "Surgeons of the Fleet" had a silver rosette at the strap ends. Surgeons of more than twelve years' service had a silver acorn at each end of the strap; surgeons who had served less than twelve years had no end devices. Passed assistant surgeons had a silver bar at each end of the strap; the bars were omitted for assistant surgeons. The senior pursers showed the *P.D.* in the center, with an oak leaf at either end. Pursers of less than twelve years' service wore the departmental letters, without end devices. Both the silver bars and oak leaves introduced by this uniform change have come down to the present day as rank insignia. Commanders are identified by silver oak leaves, lieutenant commanders by gold leaves, lieutenants by two silver bars, lieutenants (junior grade) by a single silver bar, and ensigns, by a gold bar.

Under the 1847 change, medical officers lost most of the lace and embroidery which had set them apart from the Line. The border of oak leaves and acorns which had been worn since 1830 was removed from the full-dress collar. As a device for the Medical Department, three embroidered sprigs of live oak were worn on either side of the standing full-dress collar. The strips of wide lace and the three buttons were removed from the cuffs. To distinguish surgeons, three embroidered sprigs of live oak, of the same pattern as on the collar but in smaller scale, were worn on the plain cuffs. Passed assistant and assistant surgeons had no embroidery on the cuffs.

The change in pursers' uniforms was less sweeping. They were permitted to retain the oak leaves and acorns around the dress collar, and the strip of embroidery on either side of the front edges of the collar. Perhaps pursers helped write this uniform change, for medical officers were put to the expense of modifying their coats and of purchasing epaulets and shoulder straps, and the only cost to the pursers was for the shoulder decorations.

The granting of relative rank was reflected in the cocked hats to be worn by surgeons and pursers. Those with more than twelve years in grade now wore the hat of a commander, with a loop of six bullions over the cockade. Those with less than twelve years wore the hats of lieutenants, with a loop of four bullions. Passed assistant and assistant surgeons retained the hats of the former order with a loop of gold lace instead of loops of bullions. The possession of rank could be determined from the uniform.

The use of rank devices was further extended by a "Regulation, Naval Uniform" of November 10, 1848. Commanders were directed to wear a gold-embroidered foul anchor, not to exceed one and an eighth inches long, in the center of the shoulder strap. It is to be remembered that the order of June 4, 1845 had directed commanders to show an anchor on the epaulets, but had left shoulder straps plain. The rank devices for shoulder straps of the senior line officers were: a "commodore," a silver star; other captains, a silver eagle; and commanders, an anchor.

The last change before new regulations were issued in 1852 concerned boatswains, gunners, carpenters, and sailmakers. Their coats, as
specified by the 1841 regulations, were devoid of any adornment except
the two rows of buttons on the breast. A "Regulation, Naval Uniform"
of April 5, 1849 permitted them to wear a large Navy button on either
side of the collar, with a blind buttonhole worked in black twist. As
a concession to their warrant rank, they were allowed to wear a band
of gold lace, one and a quarter inches wide, around the cap. Although
the lace was not so wide as that worn by commissioned officers, it was
more decorative than the blue or black bands worn by other warrant officers.

NOTES

[1] Lefferts, Charles M., *Uniforms of the American, British, French and German Armies
    in the War of the American Revolution, 1775–1783* (New York Historical
    Society, 19236), pp. 9–10.
[2] *Ibid.,* p. 10.
[3] Holcomb, Richmond P., *A Century with the Norfolk Naval Hospital 1830–1930*
    (Portsmouth, 1930), p. 162.
[4] Bennett, Frank M., *Steam Navy of the United States* (Pittsburgh, W. T. Nichol-
    son, 1896), pp. 713-717.

III

Uniforms, 1852–1862

The most important period in the development of the uniform of the United States Navy is that between 1852, when new uniform instructions were issued, and the end of the Civil War in 1865. It was during this time that the Navy established the policy of placing all officers in similar uniforms and initiated the system of rank indications in use today for officers of both line and staff. The use of distinctive devices to indicate an officer's specialty or corps was expanded to cover all groups of officers. Although there were to be many changes before the present uniformity in dress was fully developed, the pattern set between 1852 and 1865 has been continued.

In a comparatively small navy, with few ships and men, the original systems of showing rank and specialty by the arrangement, type, and amount of lace or embroidery, by the number and location of buttons, by the style or cut of the coat, by the design or ornamentation of shoulder ornaments, and by the decoration of the headgear, had been reasonably satisfactory. As the Navy expanded, when the United States emerged as a world power with interests in all corners of the globe, and when a major increase in men and ships was necessary to meet the threat of secession, it became necessary to develop a simple means of indicating not only an officer's rank, but his particular place in the naval organization. With the many changes brought about by advances in science, particularly the use of steam to propel men-of-war, more and more non-combatant officers with specialized training were required to support those who commanded at sea and manned the guns. A system of rank indication was not enough. A wider use of specialty devices was needed.

These needs were met by uniform instructions issued from 1852 to 1865.

The dress of officers and men of the United States Navy during the Civil War was based on the uniform order of March 8, 1852, modified many times to meet the requirements of a major war at sea. Since the changes were many and were covered by rather lengthy orders, it seems advisable to divide our discussion into two periods: from 1852 to 1862, when a major change was issued, and from 1862 through 1866.

UNIFORM INSTRUCTIONS OF 1852

The General Order approved by Secretary of the Navy Will A. Graham on March 8, 1852 was to become effective on July 4, 1852. This order was the first of those issued by the United States Navy to contain colored lithographs of the details of the uniforms and accessories. It also contained five plates showing full-length figures of officers in dress, undress, and service uniforms. Copies of this regulation are rather scarce. Many of the details shown were carried forward during the war. A black-and-white reproduction of this regulation is found in Appendix A. It is easier to visualize an item of military dress from a photograph than from a written description.

The 1852 instructions continued many of the features of the earlier orders on uniforms, and introduced many new features. For the first time, rank was indicated by means of strips of gold lace around an officer's sleeves. Such strips had been used under previous orders to indicate the grades of medical officers, but had never before been employed to show rank. Captains were directed to wear three strips of three-quarter-inch lace on their full-dress and undress coats; commanders, two strips; and lieutenants, one. Masters, who were fourth in the line of promotion, were identified by a row of three medium-sized buttons on the cuffs.

In full dress, in addition to the cuff decorations, sea officers had gold lace around the standing collars. A captain had a band of lace an inch and a half wide around the top and down the front edges, with a strip half an inch wide around the base of the collar. Commanders were similarly adorned, except that the lace on the upper edges of the collar was one and a quarter inches wide; lieutenants and masters had one-inch lace. Passed midshipmen had one-inch lace on the upper part of the collar, but none around the base; midshipmen, not passed, had a gold-embroidered anchor on either side of the collar instead of lace.

The 1852 order introduced gold-laced trousers for full dress, a practice which continued until dress uniforms were dropped during World

War II. Captains, commanders, and lieutenants wore lace on the pantaloons of the same width as around the collars; masters had gold cord,
three-eighths of an inch in diameter; and passed midshipmen, cord a
quarter of an inch in diameter.

The older practice of indicating the rank and specialty of civil or
staff officers was continued by the 1852 regulations. The dress uniforms
of medical officers remained as they had been since 1847: with the three
sprigs of live oak on the collars, and with similar embroidery on the cuffs
of surgeons. Passed assistant surgeons continued to have three medium
buttons around the cuffs; assistants had only the small buttons in the
cuff openings.

Again, pursers were required to make a minimum change in the full-
dress coat. The border of live-oak leaves and acorns first prescribed in
1830 as decoration for the top and front edges of the standing full dress
collar, was retained; only the strip of similar embroidery on either side
of the collar was done away with.

For the first time, engineers were assigned a uniform by official order
—a single-breasted, standing-collared full-dress coat, with a device for the
Engineer Corps. The insignia for engineers was a wheel in gold embroidery, with a silver anchor superimposed on it, and a branch of live
oak. This device is shown in Appendix A. The button system was employed to identify the classes of engineers. A chief engineer—a commissioned officer—had around the cuffs the three large Navy buttons previously used to indicate commissioned rank below that of captain; first
assistant engineers, three medium-sized buttons; second and third assistants,
none.

Chaplains continued to wear single-breasted coats of Navy blue, those
of the 1841 order, with black velvet collars and cuffs, and one row of
large Navy buttons. Professors, commodores' secretaries, and clerks wore
a blue single-breasted coat with a rolling collar, similar to the undress
coat of line officers, for both dress and undress. Identification was by
means of buttons on the breasts: a row of eight for professors and secretaries, and of seven for clerks. In all these instances, the coats were without
lace or embroidery and the cuffs without buttons.

The coats for boatswains, gunners, carpenters, and sailmakers were
double-breasted, with eight buttons in each row, a rolling collar with
a button and a slip of lace on either side, and three medium-sized buttons
around the cuffs. The coats were similar to those of 1841. Then, however, there had been but seven buttons in a row, and the cuffs had been
plain.

As had so often happened, the very general rule which had developed

Captain David Connor is pictured wearing the full-dress coat of the 1852 uniform regulations. His rank is indicated by the width of the lace around the top and down the front edges of the collar and by the epaulet devices. For a captain the insignia was a spread eagle perched on an anchor on the frog, with a star on the strap. A captain in command of a squadron, a "commodore," showed an additional star on the strap.

(*Official Navy Photo.*)

The undress frock coat of 1852 was of Navy blue cloth with a rolling collar and full skirts. The same sleeve lace was worn as in full dress. Commander William Francis displays the two three-quarter-inch lace strips of his rank. Either epaulets or shoulder straps were permitted in undress. These epaulets have the two crossed anchors of a commander on the frog.

(*Official Navy Photo.*)

over the years, that commissioned officers were to wear rows of nine buttons on their coats, and warrant officers a lesser number, and likewise that commissioned officers who had rank or assimilated rank were to wear double-breasted coats, was violated in the 1852 regulations. Chief engineers, who had been commissioned but as yet had not been given relative rank, wore a single row of nine buttons; but assistant engineers, who were appointed by warrant, also had nine buttons. Professors of mathematics, who had commissioned status but no relative rank, had but a single row of eight buttons. The forward warrant officers, who had continued to wear double-breasted coats since 1813, when they were first covered by an official uniform regulation, remained the exception to the general practice of allowing only officers with rank to wear double-breasted coats. However, by the end of the Civil War most officers were to be dressed in double-breasted coats, ending this form of distinction.

The undress coat was now described as "a frock-coat of Navy blue cloth, faced with the same, and lined with black serge . . ." The coat was double- or single-breasted, following the cut of the full-dress coat, and had the same number of buttons on the breast—with this exception: clerks, who had a row of seven buttons in full dress, had but six in undress! Sea officers wore the same sleeve stripes as in full dress, but of course without any collar decorations. In undress, a chaplain's coat was worn with blue collar and cuffs, the black velvet being reserved for full dress.

The methods of indicating rank on the shoulder ornaments were expanded and formalized. Captains' epaulets now bore the device formerly assigned to a "commodore"—the silver eagle and anchor, with a star on the strap. The commander of a squadron wore the same device as a captain, with a second star on the strap—the present two stars of a rear admiral. Captains had an eagle and anchor in the center of the shoulder straps. "Commodores" had the same center device, with a silver star at either end. The devices for commanders and lieutenants were the same on both epaulets and straps; two crossed foul anchors in silver for commanders, and a single foul anchor for lieutenants. The epaulets and shoulder straps for masters were unadorned.

The devices on the epaulets of medical officers and pursers, the only civil officers entitled previously to wear them, remained as under the 1847 order—the respective initials *M.D.* and *P.D.* The insignia on the shoulder straps was unchanged. Now that engineers were listed in the uniform regulations, epaulets and straps were specified for chief engineers, the only officers of the Engineer Corps who held commissioned rank. The epaulet had a plain, smooth gold crescent like that prescribed for medical officers and pursers, but the strap was of silver lace. All other officers had epaulet straps of gold lace. Since the device selected for chief engineers was the letter *E* in Old English characters, it was ordered to be of gold, to contrast with the silver strap. On the shoulder strap, however, the *E* was in silver, on a blue background.

A system of cap devices was adopted as an additional means of recognizing officers and of determining their rank or class. A captain's cap device was the silver eagle and anchor of his shoulder ornaments, encircled by a wreath of oak and olive branches in gold, worn above a gold lace band the width of that on his full-dress collar-one and a half inches. A commander displayed a similar wreath, with the crossed anchors of his epaulets, above a band one and a quarter inches wide; a lieutenant, and likewise a master, used the single silver foul anchor, above a band one inch wide. Passed and other midshipmen wore the device of a lieutenant without the gold lace band. Boatswains, gunners, carpenters, and sailmakers did not have either wreaths or lace bands, but displayed a gold-embroidered foul anchor.

Officers of the staff corps were readily identified by the insignia of their departments. Medical officers had a wreath of oak leaves with the initials *M.D.* in the center, and pursers the initials *P.D.* Engineers wore the same wreath as sea officers—oak and olive with a center insignia consisting of the wheel and anchor of the full-dress coat above a lace band one inch wide. It is interesting to note that medical officers and pursers, who had been permitted to wear a gold band around the cap before 1852, were now denied this privilege. Engineers, whose place on board ship had had not been formalized until 1842, were permitted the lace which had been an indication of rank. Since no officer likes to be deprived of what he considers his rights or prerogatives, we can expect a change to be forthcoming.

Professors, secretaries, and clerks were not identified as specific groups. They all wore an oak wreath, without other identification. The day had not come for each officer's specialty to be indicated by a device.

The instructions for the dress of enlisted personnel was basically the same as those in the 1841 order. The 1852 order stated "Thick blue cloth caps, without visors, may be worn by the crew at sea, except on holidays or at Muster." From this change has developed the so familiar blue hat of the United States Navy.

CHANGES IN UNIFORMS—1852 TO 1861

As might have been expected, the instructions of March 8, 1852 were soon changed. An order of September 24, 1852 authorized medical

Surgeons of over 12 years.

Pursers of over 12 years.

Surgeons of under 12 years.

Pursers of under 12 years.

Passed assistant Surgeons.

Assistant surgeons.

Central strap ornament 1¼ by ⁷⁄₁₀ inches. Acorn and leaf at the ends, ½ inch long.

Surgeons.

Pursers.

When the devices of surgeons and pursers were changed by the September 24, 1852, order, a new illustration was issued to amend the regulations of March 8, 1852. The shoulder straps are like those prescribed in 1847 and shown in the original 1852 order, except that the *M.D.* of the Medical Department was changed to a sprig of olive, and the *P.D.* of pursers to an oak sprig. The pursers' device, with the addition of another acorn at the stem, is the present insignia of the Supply Corps. The authority to wear gold-lace cap bands required a modification of the wreath. The original oak wreath was too tall to be worn above the band, so surgeons and pursers placed their new devices in the shallower olive and oak wreaths of the senior sea officers.

(Courtesy of the Naval Medical School.)

officers and pursers to wear gold lace bands around the undress cap. This necessitated changing the wreath of the cap device from the large one of oak leaves to that of oak and olive worn by the line officers. The devices of both groups of civil officers were changed. Medical officers replaced the initials *M.D.* with a sprig of olive, and for pursers, the *P.D.* was replaced with a sprig of oak. The same devices were employed on the shoulder straps, but no insignia was to be worn on the epaulets. The order also prescribed a uniform width-one and a half inches-for all officers' cap bands.

A "Regulation, Uniform for Engineers" of January 1, 1853 authorized second and third assistant engineers to wear cocked hats. The 1852 order had restricted cocked hats to chief and first assistant engineers. Although the wearing of shoulder straps had previously been limited to those officers entitled to wear epaulets, the order directed both first and second assistants to wear straps. Those of first assistants were to be of gold lace, four inches long and half an inch wide, bordered with gold bead cord one-eighth of an inch in diameter. The straps for second assistants were to be of blue cloth, but of the same size, with the same edging. It would appear that some indication of an engineer's rank and consequent authority was needed for proper performance of his duties aboard ship.

Once an order is modified, one can expect additional changes. A Regulation of February 17, 1853 ordered passed midshipmen to wear gold lace cap bands, and directed the old-line warrants, boatswains, gunners, carpenters, and sailmakers to wear ornamental bands. These were to be one and a quarter inches wide, made up of two strips of half-inch lace, with a quarter-inch strip of blue between. Gold lace separated by blue cloth is the distinctive sleeve lace of warrant officers today.

Chaplains, who had waited so long to be permitted to wear a Navy uniform, were again deprived of this privilege. A "Regulation, Uniform for Chaplains," dated March 3, 1853 directed them to wear in full dress a single-breasted black coat, with a single row of nine black cloth-covered buttons, and in undress a similar frock coat, with a turnover collar. Although the change is silent on headgear, it may be assumed that chaplains wore the blue cloth cap of the Navy with the wreath of oak leaves and acorns. The nine buttons on the coat still reflected their commissioned status, but, all in all, their dress showed little connection with the United States Navy. Chaplains would not be back in Navy blue until the Civil War.

The ever-present desire to wear as much lace as other officers effected the midshipmen. A regulation of May 6, 1853 permitted them to wear gold lace an inch and a half wide around the cap. Now all seagoing officers, from "commodores" to the most junior midshipmen, along with medical officers, pursers, and engineers, sported gold cap bands.

The Act of Congress of August 5, 1854 which confirmed the actions of the Secretary of the Navy in granting relative rank to medical officers in 1846 and to pursers in 1847, resulted in a change of uniform order which laid the foundation for the present practice of employing a single system for indicating the rank of both line and staff officers. Secretary of the Navy J. C. Dobbin on August 23, 1856 issued a General Order directing that "Surgeons and Pursers shall wear the Uniform of their relative rank with the exception of the lace on the pantaloons; but the epaulets, the shoulder straps, and the device upon the cap, of Surgeons and Pursers shall conform to existing regulations."

Although the order was limited to surgeons and pursers, and did not affect assistant surgeons, a major step was taken to establish a single system of rank indications. Surgeons and pursers of more than twelve years' service now wore the uniform of a commander, with one-and-a-quarter-inch lace around the top and down the edges of the full-dress collar, and two strips of three-quarter-inch lace on the cuffs of both dress and undress coats. Surgeons and pursers of less than twelve years' service had the one-inch lace of a lieutenant on the full-dress collar, and the single strip of lace on the sleeves. The order did begin the present use of a single system of sleeve lace for all officers of the Navy. It was deficient in that it did not provide for identification as to corps in full dress. True, one could determine that surgeons and pursers were staff officers, for they did not wear "railroad" trousers and the epaulets had plain, smooth crescents instead of the embroidered ones of the line, and were without devices. But no distinction was made between a surgeon and a purser. In undress the matter was simpler, for the devices of the two groups were shown on both caps and shoulder straps.

Only one change in the 1852 uniform regulations concerned the dress of enlisted personnel—that of March 26, 1859, directing that the blue woolen frock was no longer to have white duck cuffs and collar. For many years, the dress of enlisted men continued to be given scant coverage in official regulations.

In a Navy which was making the transition from sail to steam, it is understandable that engineers would press for full recognition as officers in all respects, including uniforms. Secretary Isaac Toucey on January 13, 1859 issued a General Order assigning relative rank to engineers.

Chief Engineers of more than twelve years will rank with Commanders.
Chief Engineers of less than twelve years with Lieutenants.

In 1857, Congress authorized the brevet rank of flag officer for captains in command of squadrons. Flag Officer Samuel F. DuPont is shown in the full-dress uniform of the 1852 uniform regulations for captains. The only indication of his rank of flag officer is a second star on each epaulet. One star is immediately above the eagle-anchor insignia on the frog, and the other is on the strap.

(*War Department General Staff Photo, National Archives.*)

First Assistant Engineers next after Lieutenants.
Second Assistant Engineers next after Masters.
Third Assistant Engineers with Midshipmen.

The action of the Secretary was confirmed in 1859, but the change in the status of engineers was not reflected in the uniform instructions until February 8, 1861. The regulations of that date directed that the coats of all engineers would henceforth be double-breasted—another move toward a standard uniform for all naval officers. Chief engineers were directed to wear the same number of strips of lace on the sleeves as did the line officers with whom they ranked: the three of a commander, or the two of a lieutenant. Assistant engineers retained the uniform as prescribed in 1852, just as did assistant surgeons when their seniors were directed to wear the uniforms of their relative rank.

Engineers' cap device, 1861.

(Courtesy of the Navy Library.)

The·device of the Engineer Corps—the wheel, anchor, and wreath—was removed from the standing full-dress collar, and replaced by an embroidered edging half an inch wide along the top of the collar and down the front edges. The wheel-and-anchor cap device was changed to a cross of four oak leaves, one and three-quarters of an inch in each dimension. The letter *E* was removed from the epaulets of chief engineers. This left them without a device, just as the change of September 24, 1852 had those of surgeons and pursers. No mention is made of a device for the shoulder straps, but it would appear that the cap device was employed in the same manner as for surgeons and pursers. The Navy Department Library contains a printed copy of the 1852 instruction, in which the various changes after March 8, 1852 have been inserted in longhand. The illustrations have been modified to reflect the various alterations. Pasted over the original 1852 illustration of the shoulder strap for chief engineers is a sketch which shows the cross of oak leaves used as a center device, with an acorn at either end for chief engineers ranking with commanders, and the notation that the acorns are omitted for chief engineers ranking with lieutenants. Since this sketch is in accord with the layouts of the shoulder straps for the senior medical officers and for pursers, it is to be inferred that the cross of oak leaves was worn on the straps, although this was not specifically noted in the 1861 change.

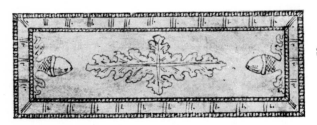

Shoulder strap, chief engineer, 1861.

(Courtesy of the Navy Library.)

An order of February 25, 1861, which directed the attention of all hands to the relative rank of officers of the Medical and Purser Departments, and of the Engineer Corps, as approved by Congress, contained a uniform instruction of particular interest. "Lieutenants while on duty as Executive Officers will wear on the cuffs a gold embroidered star, one and one quarter inches in diameter, to be placed one half of an inch above the strip of gold lace, and these will indicate the precedence to which they are by law entitled." While this star was not indicative of line officers as a group or corps, it is the first use of a star on the sleeve of officers of the United States Navy. Now the gold star has become the familiar insignia of the Line.

Until 1861 no provision had been made for assistant pursers, although the Medical Department and the Engineer Corps had long had assistants in various grades. Pursers previously had secured the necessary help by appointing clerks from among members of the crews, subject to the approval of the commanding officer. To meet the need of the growing Navy for more officers, Congress by an act of July 17, 1861 authorized that as many as 36 assistant paymasters could be commissioned. An Act of Congress of June 22, 1860 had changed the title of this group of officers from purser to paymaster. A Circular of September 6, 1861 prescribed for assistant paymasters the same uniform as for paymasters, but without lace on the cuffs. The epaulets were to be plain, with bullion a quarter inch in diameter. The blue cloth shoulder straps were to be four inches long and one and an eighth inches wide, bordered with gold embroidery three-sixteenth of an inch wide. The oak sprig of the Paymaster Department was omitted, although assistants to surgeons and engineers displayed the device of their corps on the shoulder straps.

The last alteration of the 1852 regulations prior to a major revision of July 1862 concerned the dress of masters' mates. The warranted masters' mates were to wear a single-breasted frock coat, with a row of nine buttons, a rolling collar without decoration, and plain cuffs. The blue cloth cap was to have a band made up of two strips of half-inch gold lace, separated by a half-inch blue band. This band was similar to that of the forward warrants, but was wider. The cap device was a plain silver anchor, worn without a wreath. Shipped or rated masters' mates—who were enlisted men—were directed to wear a blue jacket, double-breasted, with two rows of six medium Navy buttons. The silver anchor of their warranted counterparts was worn on the cap, but with the gold and blue band omitted. The Regulation was dated June 18, 1862.

IV

Uniforms, 1862–1866

The growth of the United States Navy during the period of the Civil War was tremendous—from a small force of 69 serviceable vessels prior to the outbreak of the war to a major fleet of 626, of all types, by 1865.[1] Congress appropriated funds for new construction, and any commercial craft which could possibly be converted to war use was acquired, all the way from large seagoing merchant steamers to small tugs. To man this rapidly growing fleet, an Act of Congress of July 24, 1861 authorized the commissioning of temporary officers and the enlisting of seamen. The number of seamen increased from approximately 7,600, just prior to the war, to 51,500.[2] The Bureau of the Census' Historical Statistics of the United States (Washington: G.P.O., 1960) shows the strength of the Navy and Marine Corps late in 1861 and in 1865 as follows:

	1861	1865
Navy		
Officers	1,114	6,759
Enlisted	26,767	51,537
Marine Corps		
Officers	48	87
Enlisted	2,338	3,773

As has been the custom in recent wars, temporary officers were not required to own all the articles of dress specified by the uniform instructions. On September 6, 1861, Acting Secretary G. V. Fox issued a Circular reading:

116

Sir:

   The Department does not require Officers appointed on "Temporary
Service" to supply themselves with full dress Uniforms. It only obliges them
to obtain Undress Uniforms and side arms.

This was the first step toward the abolition of the full-dress uniform
and decorative accessories for all officers, regular or temporary, during
the war. Matters of ceremony and social occasions, when the dress uniform
was worn in times of peace, took second place to the business of blockading the coast of the South and tracking down commerce raiders.

   The legislation of July 16, 1862 which created the additional ranks
of rear admiral, commodore, lieutenant commander, and ensign necessitated a change in the uniform instructions in order that these new
grades might be identified. On July 31, 1862 President Lincoln's able
Secretary of the Navy, Gideon Welles, issued a General Order which
not only established the indications of rank of officers of the Navy, but
modified the uniform to suit wartime conditions. The full-dress coat, with
its tails and standing collar and its elaborate trimmings of lace, was
abolished. The undress frock coat was to serve for all purposes: full dress,
undress, and service dress. Since the full effects of war at sea were not as
yet felt, some of the former grandeur of the uniform was retained. A
full dress was specified, the frock coat to be worn with epaulets, cocked
hat, sword, and sword knot, but without the laced trousers of the
1852 order. In undress, the frock coat was to be worn with or without
epaulets or sword, but the cocked hat was to be replaced by the cap.
The uniform most frequently seen in contemporary photographs is the
service dress: a frock coat with shoulder straps, a cap, with or without
a sword, but without a sword knot. There was little time for the more
formal affairs of Navy life.

   With the introduction of new ranks, it was necessary to modify
the sleeve lace prescribed by the original 1852 order and its frequent
modifications. Now there were eight grades of commissioned sea officers
to identify instead of the original three. The insignia of a rear admiral
was three strips of three-quarter-inch lace, with a strip of quarter-inch
lace between the first and second and the second and third strips, and an
additional quarter-inch strip above the upper wide lace. Since all bands of
lace were placed one-quarter of an inch apart, those worn by a rear admiral
measured ten inches from top to bottom! A commodore had the same
lace as an admiral, except for the upper quarter-inch strip. A captain
retained the three strips of three-quarter-inch lace prescribed in 1852, the
strips being half an inch apart. For a commander, two strips of three-

Rear Admiral Andrew H. Foote, 1862.

(*Army Signal Corps Photo, National Archives*) (*Brady Collection.*)

quarter-inch lace, with a quarter-inch strip between them, were specified. A lieutenant commander inherited the two strips of wide lace formerly worn by a commander; a lieutenant displayed the single strip of ¾″ lace previously prescribed for this grade, but with a strip of quarter-inch lace above it; a master had a single strip of three-quarter-inch lace, and an ensign a strip a quarter of an inch wide. None of these arrangements has lasted until today, although an ensign is still identified by a single strip of lace—which is now half an inch wide—on the sleeves. Since rank was also indicated on the epaulets, it was necessary to modify the former instructions. A rear admiral wore the devices formerly prescribed for a flag officer—the eagle and anchor on the frog, with two silver stars on the epaulet strap. The former device of a captain—the eagle, anchor, and single star—was displayed by a commodore. The rank devices ordered for the other commissioned officers bear a very close resemblance to the pin-on devices now worn by officers of the Navy and also of the Army and Air Force. A captain's device was a spread eagle perched on a foul anchor, The following officers all had the foul anchor in the center, with varying end devices: commanders, silver oak leaves; lieutenant commanders, gold oak leaves; lieutenants, two gold bars; masters, a single gold bar; and ensigns, simply the anchor in the center with no end devices. The gold bars for lieutenants and masters (later lieutenants, junior grade) were changed to silver in 1877, but it was not until 1922 that ensigns were directed to wear a single gold bar as an indication of rank. Under the 1862 uniform change, the anchor became a device for officers of the Line, rather than part of the insignia of rank as it had been previously.

The anchor was similarly used on the shoulder straps as a device of the Line. The eagle was omitted from the straps of rear admirals and commodores, but the anchor was retained. A rear admiral's straps had the anchor in the center, with a star at either end. The straps of a commodore showed the anchor at one end and a star at the other. All other sea officers wore the same arrangement of devices as on the epaulets, with the anchor in the center.

The 1862 order was silent on the type of cocked hat to be worn, but by inference rear admirals through commanders retained the decoration prescribed for the senior officers in 1852—a loop of six bullions, the center pair twisted. Other commissioned officers had the loop of four bullions. The blue cloth cap with the band of gold lace was worn by all the commissioned line officers. However, the cap devices were modified. That for a rear admiral now became a silver star, one inch in diameter, worn in the center of the wreath of oak and olive branches. Commodores, captains, commanders, and lieutenant commanders retained the cap device formerly prescribed for captains—a silver eagle and anchor in the wreath. Lieutenants, masters, and ensigns had the insignia of lieutenants and masters of the former order—a horizontal foul anchor in the wreath. The device for midshipmen was modified to a plain silver anchor placed vertically within the wreath. The cap devices of warrant officers were unchanged, except that shipped or rated master's mates lost the plain silver anchor, and wore caps without any device.

While the uniforms and insignia of seagoing officers were described in detail in the General Order of July 31, 1862, only two short statements refer to the dress of civil or staff officers. These are: "Coats of all other officers to be the same as those now prescribed for Undress of their respective grades, except the cuffs will be closed and without the small buttons, and with the same arrangement of lace as that worn by 'line officers' of the same relative rank." The other statement referred to all officers of the Navy: "No other changes than those herein specified are to be made in the uniform at present prescribed." It is evident that the uniform regulations of 1852 were still in force, and that the order of July 31, 1862 was merely another change, albeit a major one.

The instruction that all staff officers were to wear "the same arrangement of lace as worn by 'line officers' of the same relative rank" did modify the dress of certain civil officers. Surgeons, paymasters, and chief engineers of more than twelve years' standing now had two strips of three-quarter-inch lace with a quarter-inch strip between them on the sleeves, instead of the two strips of $\frac{3}{4}''$ lace worn formerly. Those of less than twelve years' standing, who ranked with lieutenants, had one strip of $\frac{3}{4}''$ lace, with a strip of quarter-inch lace above it. Certain staff officers, who had not been authorized to wear sleeve lace previously, now were permitted to display the lace of their line counterparts. Passed assistant surgeons and first assistant engineers, who ranked "next after lieutenants," wore the lace of a master, a single three-quarter-inch strip. Assistant surgeons and second assistant engineers, who ranked "after masters," now ranked with ensigns and had one strip of quarter-inch lace.

The sweeping change of 1862 was a major step toward uniformity in that a single system of showing rank by means of sleeve lace had been adopted for all officers who had rank or relative rank. Corps affiliation was indicated by a series of devices on epaulets and shoulder straps, with the foul anchor becoming the insignia of a line officer. With the exception of chaplains and professors of mathematics, all commissioned officers wore identical double-breasted coats. A step was taken toward a standard cap device for line officers, for now they were grouped into three classes instead of being identified by a different insignia for each grade. Rear admirals, the most senior officers, showed a star in the wreath; commodores through lieutenant commanders, an eagle and an anchor; and lieutenants through ensigns, an anchor. Staff officers showed their corps device in the center of the wreath, and those without corps affiliation wore the wreath alone. It was to be many years before one device would be used to indicate a commissioned officer of the United States Navy; however, the change was under way.

A most important change in the Navy's system of identifying insignia occurred when an order of May 23, 1863 directed all officers of the Line to wear a gold-embroidered five-pointed star, placed a quarter of an inch above the upper strip of sleeve lace. Since that date, the star has been the symbol of the line officer. This same order replaced the combinations of three-quarter- and one-quarter-inch lace with a system of varying numbers of strips of quarter-inch lace for both line and staff officers with rank or relative rank. No copy of this change can be located in the archives of either the Navy Department or any other branch of the Government. It was found in a catalog of Tomes, Son and Melvain, New York manufacturers and suppliers of military accessories and insignia. This firm published a reproduction of the Navy's uniform regulations of March 8, 1852, complete with the same colored lithographs used by the Navy. A copy of this publication in the personal collection of Colonel Frederick P. Todd, Director of the Museum at the United States Military Academy, West Point, has a copy of an "Appendix No. 3" pasted inside the front cover. The appendix reprinted a Navy uniform instruction which directed that all line officers display a gold-embroidered five-pointed star above the gold sleeve lace. The text of the appendix is reproduced below.

CHANGE OF UNIFORM IN SLEEVE ORNAMENTS

as issued from Navy Department, Washington. May 23, 1863

Lace ¼ inch. Spaces ¼ inch between each row, except otherwise specified.

Rear Admiral, 8 rows of Lace, 1st row 2 inches from edge of cuff, with ½ inch space between 1st and 2d row, 4th and 5th row, and 7th and 8th row, with 1 inch gold embroidered star placed ¼ inch above last row in center of sleeve.

Commodore, 7 rows of Lace, ½ inch space between 3d and 4th rows, and 4th and 5th row. Star as Admiral.

Captain, 6 rows of Lace, ½ inch space between 3d and 4th rows. Star as Admiral.

Commander, 5 rows of Lace, ½ space between 1st and 2d row, and 4th and 5th row. Star as Admiral.

Official records show that D. G. H. E. Baumgarten was commissioned an assistant surgeon of the Navy in 1862, so it becomes rather easy to date this photograph. When he was commissioned in 1862, assistant surgeons had the relative rank of "next after masters," or actually with passed midshipmen. In consequence, the cuffs would be without buttons or lace. Secretary Welles's relative-rank order of March, 1863, gave assistant surgeons the relative rank of masters, so the cuffs would be decorated with the three buttons of a master, as shown in the photograph. The uniform change of May, 1863, directed masters and all officers of the same relative rank to wear two stripes of one-quarter-inch lace around the closed cuffs. It is evident that Dr. Baumgarten is wearing the prescribed uniform of an assistant surgeon of the period between March and May, 1863. The device of the shoulder straps and the gold lace cap band are in accord with the modified 1852 uniform order, and were not changed until November, 1863, when the shoulder straps were modified and the lace bands abolished.

(Official Navy Photo.)

Rear Admiral Joseph Smith is seen in the uniform of his rank as prescribed by the Navy's uniform instruction for the period from May, 1863 to 1869. Admiral Smith, a line officer, became chief of the Bureau of Yards and Docks in 1846, four years after the bureau system had been established, and served as chief until 1869—a tenure of office of twenty-three years. His tour of duty as chief of the bureau covered the period of transition from sail to steam, and from wooden ships to ironclads. His principal assistant was William P. S. Sanger, who, in 1867, was the first civil engineer to become a commissioned officer of the United States Navy.

(Courtesy of the Bureau of Yards and Docks.)

Lt. Commander, 4 rows of Lace, ½ inch space between 3d and 4th row. Star as Admiral.

Lieutenant, 3 rows of Lace. Star as Admiral.

Master, 2 rows of Lace. Star as Admiral.

Ensign, 1 row of Lace. Star as Admiral.

Staff Officers of assimilated rank, to be the same with the exception of the Star.

While the instruction of May 23, 1863 cannot be located in any Navy uniform order prior to that of January 28, 1864, there is evidence that the change in sleeve lace and the use of the star as a device for the Line was effective before that date. The Rare Book Section of the Navy Department Library has a copy of the official uniform regulations of 1852 in which various changes have been inserted in longhand. This copy also contains what appear to be printers' proofs of the illustrations contained in the uniform order issued in January 1864. Several of the proofs are dated March 1863, and give the name of the printer as J. F. Gedney of Washington. Those proofs showing the arrangement of quarter-inch lace indicate that all spacing was to be a quarter of an inch. Long-hand corrections have been made to show the special half-inch spacing specified in the appendix to the Tomes, Son and Melvain catalog, and there credited to a Navy Department change of May 23, 1863. There are also proofs illustrating the shoulder straps as they appeared in the 1864 order, except that those of paymasters and naval constructors are missing. All proofs are marked:

Adopted July 15, 1863
G. Welles
Secretary of the Navy

The words above and below the signature are in one handwriting, and the signature appears to be that of the Secretary himself.

There is no reason to doubt that Tomes, Son and Melvain were in possession of an official, written order when they issued "Appendix No. 3." Their business would naturally have required that they keep abreast of all changes in the military dress of the United States. It would appear then, that orders were issued in written form during 1863 adding the star to the sleeves of line officers, and modifying the sleeve lace and shoulder straps. When it was decided to cover the many changes by a new instruction, the printer would normally submit proofs of any illustrations. The corrections noted for the spacing between strips of lace indicate that the artist had not understood the written instructions.

That changes in the uniform regulations of 1863 had been issued

This photograph of Dr. Michael Brady is of particular interest, for he is wearing the insignia of two uniform instructions. Passed Assistant Surgeon Brady has the three strips of one-quarter-inch lace of his relative rank (lieutenant) as prescribed in May, 1863, and which remained in use until 1869. The cap device is the wreath and oak leaf of the uniform change of November, 1863. The shoulder strap is decorated with a sprig of olive in the center, and without end devices. This is the shoulder strap of an assistant surgeon, his former rank, under the 1852 regulations. The proper shoulder straps for the period after November, 1863 had no center corps device, but the two gold-embroidered bars of a lieutenant at either end. With the frequent changes in insignia of rank and corps from 1862 to 1864, it is understandable that many officers were unable to procure the proper insignia as soon as the change became effective.

(Official Navy Photo.)

is further borne out by an article in the U. S. Army and Navy Journal of November 21, 1863. This semiofficial publication, published in New York, includes an article headed "Changes in the Navy Uniform," and credits Tomes, Son and Melvain of 6 Maiden Lane, New York with the information. Reference is made here to a Navy Department order of November 11, 1863. It is to be remembered that the Secretary of the Navy issued a General Order on March 13, 1863 modifying the relative rank of surgeons, paymasters, and engineers, and granting relative rank to chaplains, professors of mathematics, naval constructors, secretaries, and clerks. In addition, chiefs of the various staff bureaus were assigned the relative rank of commodore. The text of the change as reported in the U. S. Army and Navy Journal is exactly the same as that later shown in the 1864 uniform regulations, and the description of the insignia to be shown on the shoulder straps conforms exactly to that shown in the printer's proofs approved by Secretary Welles on July 15, 1863.

There is further confirmation that some modification of the uniform instructions had been made official in 1863, for a Circular dated December 21, 1863 and sent to the commanders of fleets and squadrons, reads as follows:

NAVY DEPARTMENT

Washington, 21st December, 1863

SIRS   The Department regrets to perceive that the new designations for uniforms, such as shoulder straps, cap ornaments, and the cap itself, are so varied by the manufacturers, that the prescribed uniform can hardly be recognized.

You will require all officers within the limits of your command to conform, without unnecessary delay, to the precise style and dimensions of the plates issued by the Department, and you will inform it of any neglect to comply with this order.

Very Respectfully,
GIDEON WELLES
Secretary of the Navy.

It appears not only that printed changes were issued, but also that the plates showing the details of the accessories to the uniform were released prior to the printed order of 1864. None of these has as yet been located.

For convenience, the two major changes in the insignia during 1863—the one of May 23 affecting the sleeve lace and star, and the November 11 order establishing the devices of staff corps—have been shown on pages 326-329, Appendix C, 1864-1866. The most readily available and complete description of the uniform and devices is contained in the uniform regulations issued January 28, 1864. It will be well to discuss the changes introduced in the November 11 order at this time, for it represents the biggest single step toward a uniform system of devices.

The order recognized the increased ranks granted certain staff officers, and the assignment of rank to others who previously had had no relative rank. The same symbols of rank established for the Line in the General Order of July 31, 1862 were employed to indicate staff officers of the same relative rank. In lieu of the anchor, the center device of the Line, staff officers showed the device pertinent to their corps. Chiefs of the staff bureaus, who now held the relative rank of commodore, wore the single silver star of their rank, superimposed on a gold corps device in the center of the shoulder strap. Staff officers of the relative rank of captain displayed the eagle of rank, perched on a gold corps device. Officers of lesser rank were directed to wear a silver corps device in the center of the strap, with a rank device at either end: silver oak leaves for a commander; gold oak leaves for a lieutenant commander; two gold bars for a lieutenant; a single gold bar for a master. Since ensigns were not authorized to wear end devices on the shoulder straps, staff officers with the relative rank of ensign showed only the corps device in silver in the center. The exception to this system was that medical officers, who had not been assigned a corps device for shoulder straps, displayed only the standard rank devices on their straps.

The change of November 11, 1863 concerned staff officers primarily, but two sections, on caps and cap ornaments, affected all officers of the Navy. The style of the cap was modified slightly: the overhang of the top was reduced to a width of only a quarter of an inch more than the band. Gold bands were removed, and the cap device was now to be worn on the blue band, instead of above the gold lace band as in the 1852 order. Except for rear admirals, all line officers were to wear the same device, a silver foul anchor, in the center of the wreath of oak and olive leaves. An admiral was identified by two silver stars, each five-eighths of an inch in diameter. This was another step toward a uniform cap device, although in 1863 it referred only to the Line. Staff officers were identified by the devices of their corps in the center of the wreath.

The corps devices for the Staff for both caps and shoulder straps were:

Medical Corps—a spread oak leaf for the cap, but no device for the shoulder straps.
Paymasters Corps—an oak sprig, of three leaves and two acorns.
Engineer Corps—a cross of four oak leaves.

Professors of Mathematics—the letter *P*, Old English, in silver, on a gold circle.

Naval Constructors—a sprig of two live-oak leaves and two acorns.

Chaplains—a cross, set obliquely.

Secretaries—the letter *S*, Old English.

All center insignia of the cap ornament were in silver, except that of professors, which was gold and silver as noted above.

Midshipmen, boatswains, gunners, carpenters, sailmakers, clerks, and master's mates receiving $40 a month all wore the wreath, without any center device.

The practice of showing rank insignia on the collar is not of recent origin, for a Circular issued on December 24, 1863 directed that all officers wear an indication of their rank on the points of the overcoat collar. This practice is in use today: rank is shown on the points of khaki, blue flannel, and tropical khaki shirts. The rank devices shown on the shoulder straps were employed, with the exception that the two bars of a lieutenant and the single bar of a master were to be in silver, not gold. Ensigns, who were without rank devices, were instructed to wear a small gold cord on the front edge of the collar. When the overcoat was worn, the corps could be determined only by the cap device.

UNIFORM REGULATIONS OF 1864

The uniform instruction of 1852 had been so drastically amended during its twelve-year existence that a new instruction for the dress of the Navy was needed. In the "Regulations for the Uniform of the Navy of the United States" approved by Gideon Welles on January 28, 1864 certain new features were incorporated; and although a full-dress uniform was prescribed, it was not to be worn during the war. The cocked hats, epaulets, and sword knots were to remain in storage until the war's end—in fact, until new instructions were issued in 1866.

No complete copy of the 1864 regulations has been located in Navy Department files or archives—the descriptive text is not accompanied by the referenced illustrations. Some, but not all, of the illustrations are in the National Archives. Fortunately for students of the dress of the United States Navy, the order, with the illustrations, was reproduced in the *Illustrated Catalog of Arms and Military Goods* published by Schuyler, Harley and Graham, 19 Maiden Lane, New York, in 1864. This catalog has been reproduced and is now available for purchase.[3] It includes the then current uniform regulations for the Army, Navy, Marine Corps, made a major move toward the present use of one uniform for all officers, Line or Staff, with a single system of rank designation by sleeve stripes and insignia, and a series of devices to indicate corps. After World War I the transition to the present system was completed. Never again would the Navy make it so difficult for the uninitiated to determine rank or specialty.

UNIFORM CHANGES, 1864 TO 1866

The first Uniform Circular amending the January 28, 1864 regulations was issued on January 14, 1865. The change made provision for the rank of vice admiral, authorized by an Act of Congress on December 21, 1864. The uniform prescribed for Admiral Farragut was the same as that for rear admirals under the 1864 order, except for the necessary indication of higher rank. The cap device was three silver stars, placed to form an equilateral triangle, with the point down, on a gold-embroidered foul anchor. The shoulder straps displayed the same three stars: one at either end and one in the center superimposed on the anchor, the device of the Line. A two-inch strip of lace was placed an inch from the bottom of the sleeve, with two strips of one-inch lace, spaced at half-inch intervals, and the gold star of the Line above it. This was a change from the strips of quarter-inch lace established in 1863, and the first use of the two-inch lace now worn by flag officers. The three stars in the form of an equilateral triangle were worn on the ends of the overcoat collar.

Uniform Circular No. 1 also modified the sleeve lace worn by rear admirals to conform to the style established for the Vice Admiral—a two-inch band of lace, with a single one-inch strip of lace above it. This arrangement of sleeve lace is the basis for the sleeve stripes of flag officers today: a two-inch strip with a half-inch strip above it for a rear admiral; two half-inch strips above the wide lace for a vice admiral; three half-inch strips above the wide strip for an admiral; and four above the wide one for a fleet admiral.

The January 1865 change also made provision for a sack coat to be worn as "service dress" for certain occasions, both afloat and ashore. The Navy had for many years permitted the wearing of a jacket as "service dress" under limited conditions. The sack coat was merely another instance where the Navy's dress followed current civilian styles. The single-breasted, five-button sack coat could be worn either with sleeve lace and shoulder straps or without them, but for line officers it invariably

Rear Admiral David Dixon Porter, 1865.

(Army Signal Corps Photo, National Archives.)

Although the sack coat was not officially authorized until January 14, 1865, it had been adopted unofficially prior to that date and shows in many photographs taken in 1864. The coat could be worn with sleeve ornaments and shoulder straps, or with rank and corps insignia on the collar. In the latter case, only the star was retained on the sleeves by line officers and the shoulder straps were omitted by all officers.

(*Official Navy Photo.*)

retained the star on each sleeve. When lace and straps were lacking, indications of rank were shown on the collar in the same manner as on the overcoat: that is, by means of the end device of the shoulder strap. For those officers whose straps had no end devices—chiefs of staff bureaus, captains, and ensigns—the center rank device was shown, but without any corps device underneath.

Uniform Circular No 2 dated July 31, 1865 was directed solely to midshipmen. The gold wreath cap device was abolished and replaced by a plain gold anchor in a vertical position. This was in effect the cap device specified for midshipmen in the uniform instructions of 1841, which had been replaced by the change of 1845. Circular No. 2 also directed midshipmen to wear a jacket that had a standing collar, with a gold-embroidered plain anchor on either side. This again was a return to earlier uniforms. Today, midshipmen at the Naval Academy display the gold anchor on the collar. Over the years, devices have come and gone, only to be reemployed at some later date.

The last revision of the 1864 order was Uniform Change No. 3 dated January 18, 1866. The detailed description of the undress cap was accompanied by a pattern, for the avowed purpose of the order was "to establish a uniformity of make which will be followed in the future." Although the order states that the dimensions and form of the cap are to be unaltered, a careful reading both of the section on the cap in the 1864 order and of Change No. 3 indicates a definite change. Now officers were to wear a gilt chin strap, with a small Navy button at either end—the current practice. In a section entitled "Miscellaneous Provisions," ensigns were directed to wear a small gold cord on the edges of the collar of the sack coat. This was the same provision for indicating rank as employed on the overcoat.

The war years had convinced those responsible for specifying the dress of the Navy that uniforms should be uniform! The small and apparently reluctant steps taken prior to the Civil War toward providing a common coat for all officers, and a system of readily identifiable rank and corps devices, could not meet the needs of a large wartime navy. Those nice distinctions enjoyed by officers of a small peacetime navy—elaborate embroidery and gold lace in proportion to rank—had no place in a major sea war. The changes in the dress of the United States Navy from 1861 through 1865 laid a solid foundation for the current regulations and the system of indicating rank and corps now employed. Many of the changes made in those four years are still reflected in the dress of the Navy.

While major changes were made, and to a large degree uniformity was achieved, there were still some differences between the dress of the Line and that of the Staff. When the Navy went back to a peacetime footing after the Civil War, some of the earlier differentiations between those officers who could command at sea and those whose mission was to support the men who manned the guns, again showed up in the Navy's dress. It was not until the United States was involved in a global war that true uniformity in dress came about. A study of the Navy's dress in 1861 through 1865, the period of major change, should be supplemented by a review of the developments and changes leading up to the present uniform.

NOTES

[1] Knox, Dudley W., *A History of the United States Navy.*, *rev. ed.* (New York Putnam, 1948) , p. 317.

[2] *Ibid.*, p. 317.

[3] Reproduced by Norman Flayderman, Greenwich, Conn., 1961.

Benjamin F. Isherwood, who had been serving as Chief Engineer in the Bureau of Construction, Equipment, and Repairs, was made Chief of the Bureau of Steam Engineering when it was established by Congress in 1862. His insignia is that of a chief engineer with more than twelve years service, and the two stripes of three-quarter-inch lace indicate his relative rank of commander. The shoulder straps show the cross of four oak leaves, the Engineers insignia since 1861, and an acorn at either end of the strap indicating a senior chief engineer. The three officers standing behind Isherwood are either 1st or 2nd assistant engineers, for there are no devices on their shoulder straps, and 3rd assistants did not wear straps. The engineer in the center is a second assistant engineer for the cuffs are plain. A first assistant would have had a row of three buttons on the top of the cuff. The grade of the other two officers can not be determined for their cuffs are not visable. However, one of them is a first assistant engineer, for Isherwood's cap and one other have gold lace bands, worn only by chief and first assistant engineers.

(Courtesy of the National Archives.)

The pivot gun crew of the U.S.S. *Miami* is at drill during the period in 1864 when the gunboat was part of the force blockading the Confederate ram *Albemarle* in Roanoke Sound. The details of the blue uniform are particularly clear in this photograph. Of interest are the side arms—the brass hilted cutlass and the holstered Navy Colts. A white-crossbelted Marine has been pressed into service as a member of the gun crew.

(Courtesy of the National Archives.)

This photograph of Divine services on the deck of a monitor is interesting for it shows a chaplain in uniform with sleeve lace and shoulder straps, the indication of relative rank granted by Secretary Welles's order of 1863.

(Courtesy of the National Archives.)

The photographer must have spent considerable time aboard the *Hunchback,* for this landing piece and the walking beam of the steam engine are to be seen in a number of pictures. The swords are evidently props for neither officer is wearing a sword belt, and no slings are attached to the scabbards. The man on the left has no lace on the sleeves and no shoulder straps, and since he is wearing a straw hat, it is difficult to determine his grade. However, he appears to be a "Master's Mate, receiving $25 per month." The officer on the right shows the star of the Line on the sleeve, without sleeve lace. This was the indication of a "Master's Mate, receiving $40 per month." If the two warrant officers had posed for the photograph wearing blue caps, positive identification could be made. Senior master's mates wore a wreath, without a center insignia, as a cap device, and juniors had no cap ornament.

(*Courtesy of the National Archives.*)

The uniform regulations described the articles of clothing to be worn by officers, but the manner in which the uniform was worn depended on the skipper. From the dress of the two officers, it is evident the *Hunchback* was not a "spit and polish" ship. If the officer on the left buttoned his coat to the neck, the checked shirt would not show, and perhaps he could pass inspection! His sleeve ornaments, the single strip of one-quarter-inch lace, and the star indicate he is a line officer of the rank of ensign. The shoulder strap device detail can not be seen; it was a horizontal foul anchor in the center, with no end-rank devices. The officer on the right is of the Staff, for there is no star above the two stripes of a master. His corps can not be determined, for the shoulder straps can not be read, and there were no cap devices for straw hats.

(*Courtesy of the Library of Congress.*)

This stripling is typical of the boys of the Civil War Navy who were swept into the service by the excitement, speaches, and martial music. On the bulkhead behind him are cutlasses, ready to be taken up when someone shouted "Repel boarders!"

(*Courtesy of the Library of Congress.*)

Most of the men of the U.S.S. *Mendota* are wearing a white cover over the blue cap, and show the name of the ship on the cap band. The stripes of white tape on the upper arms are watch marks; on the right for the starboard watch, on the left for the port watch. The officer, on the right, behind the capstan, is without shoulder straps and displays only the wreath on his cap. This, and the star of the Line on his sleeve, indicate he is a master's mate. The officers on the pilot house deck are wearing a variety of head gear; uniform caps, white straw hats, and a plantation owner's large, floppy, straw hat. All coats are of the sack variety, worn with the narrow sleeve lace of the 1863 order. The unbuttoned and partially buttoned sack coats, the white and blue trousers, the checked and white shirts, all add to the informal feeling.

(Courtesy of the National Archives.)

B-599

This picture indicates the general laxity in the enforcement of the uniform instructions during the Civil War. Stiff flat-topped white straw hats were prescribed for wear in warm climates, but the hat of the officer on the left certainly does not conform to regulations. The officer holding the newspaper has the five strips of gold lace of the 1863 change around the cuffs and the star of the Line, but the spacing of the lace is non-regulation. The spaces between the lace are all a quarter of an inch. The regulations specified that the first and second, and fourth and fifth stripes were to be a half-inch apart. Order after order was issued by the Navy Department. Squadron commanders directed compliance with the uniform regulations, but with little effect.

(Courtesy of the National Archives.)

The men and their uniforms are typical of the crews of the ships of the United States Navy during the Civil War. Their reaction to being photographed may be considered normal for any group of service men. The Marine sergeant in the foreground has taken time from the checker game to look at the camera, but his Navy opponent appears to be planning his next move. The two men seated on the deck at the right continue to mend their clothes through the whole procedure. Although the Marine appears to be strumming his banjo, it is only a pose, for the day of snapshots and fast film was many years in the future. If his hand had moved, there would have been a blur. It is to be noted that all the petty officers are wearing the rating badge of their class, without any specialty distinctions. Boatswain's, gunner's, carpenter's, and sailmaker's mates and ship's cooks wore the device on the right sleeve. All other petty officers wore the badge on the left arm.

(Courtesy of the National Archives.)

This is evidently a photograph of the engineering force of a small naval vessel taken in 1863. Three of the officers are wearing caps which show the device of the Engineer Corps, the cross of four oak leaves, in the standard cap wreath. The officer seated in the center has the 1863 sleeve lace of a master, so he is a first assistant engineer. The narrow shoulder straps are without any form of device or insignia, typical of the period from 1861 to November, 1863, for 1st and 2nd assistant engineers. The officer, second from the right, is a second assistant engineer, with the relative rank of ensign, as indicated by the single strip of one-quarter-inch lace. The two officers on the left, and the one on the extreme right are third assistant engineers, who wore neither sleeve lace nor shoulder straps.

(*Courtesy of the National Archives.*)

This is a typical petty officer of the Civil War, tough and whiskered. We can determine that he is a petty officer by the eagle-anchor device with a star above it. There is no way to determine his specialty. Since his badge is on the left arm, we know he is not a boatswain's, gunner's, carpenter's, or sailmaker's mate, nor a ship's cook, who wore the device on the right sleeve. It is probable that he was a quartermaster, standing deck watch.

(Courtesy of the Library of Congress.)

B-6193

This photograph of drill with a landing piece is of particular interest for it shows the short, blue, officer's jacket in detail. The uniform instructions in effect during the Civil War authorized single- or double-breasted blue jackets, with the same number of buttons as worn on the frock coat. As can be seen, the jacket is similar to the frock coat, but cut off at the waist and more closely fitted to the body. Shoulder straps and sleeve lace were to be worn on the jacket in the same manner as on the frock coat. Lacking sleeve lace, the officer is a warrant. The ranks of boatswain, gunner, carpenter, and sailmaker can be ruled out, for the forward warrant officers in 1864 wore narrow gold lace shoulder straps, and were the only warrant officers to have shoulder ornaments. The officer can be identified as a "master's mate, receiving $40 per month" by the star on the sleeve and the wreath on the cap.

(Courtesy of the National Archives.)

This is one of the very few pictures which shows Navy personnel in cold weather gear. Some seamen are shown in short blue jackets, and others in the pea coat. The Marine drummer is bundled up in the caped overcoat of the Corps.

(Courtesy of the Library of Congress.)

This picture could be titled The Casually Dressed Navy, for it is certainly typical of the Navy in the Civil War. The officers on the boat deck appear in every conceivable costume from checked shirts to frock coats, and from blue caps to farmers' straws. Of special interest are the blue jackets, for this garment does not stand out in many contemporary photographs. The officers, third and fourth from the left and third from the right, are in the short jackets first authorized in 1830. The officers, fourth, fifth, and sixth from the right, are shown in the frock coat, the coat most frequently seen in Civil War photographs. Examples of the sack coat, which was introduced during the war, are shown on the extreme right and left. The assortment of head gear is worth noting. The range runs from the regulation blue cap to a civilian felt hat, and includes regulation and non-regulation straw hats.

(*Courtesy of the National Archives.*)

This is a rather typical assortment, not only of enlisted uniforms, but also of enlisted men of the Civil War period. Some men are in the customary blues, others are wearing red flannel undershirts. The men wearing sack coats are shipped or rated master's mates who wore no insignia on sleeves or shoulders, and a plain blue cap without a device. The sack coats are almost as long as the frock coat of the officer standing on top of the turret.

(Courtesy of the National Archives.)

This view of the gun deck of Admiral Farragut's flagship, the U.S.S. *Hartford*, off Mobile Bay in July, 1864, shows two officers in jackets. The officer in the straw hat appears to have the three stripes of a lieutenant on the cuffs. It is not possible to determine the rank of the capped officer from this photograph.

(*Navy Department Photo, National Archives.*)

Farragut's sleeve shows the eight strips of one-quarter-inch wide lace prescribed for a rear admiral in 1863, with the star of the Line above the upper stripe. The shoulder straps have a silver foul anchor in the center, with a silver star at either end. The cap device of a rear admiral was the wreath of oak and olive branches, with two silver stars in the center. The two officers in the center, whose rank and corps can not be determined, are wearing frock coats, and the officer on the extreme right is wearing a jacket.

(*Audio-Visual Collection, National Archives.*)

This photograph of Captain John A. Winslow and his staff on the deck of the U.S.S. *Keargsarge* is of interest, for it indicates that officers did not always conform to the latest uniform regulations. All officers, except Captain Winslow, third from left, have the one-quarter-inch sleeve lace as prescribed by the uniform instructions of January, 1864. In contrast, Winslow's sleeves display the three three-quarter-inch-wide strips of lace of a captain as directed by the July 31, 1862 revision of the 1852 uniform regulations. A change of May 23, 1863 had directed that all sleeve ornaments be made up of combinations of one-quarter-inch lace, and that all line officers show a gold star on the sleeve above the upper stripe. To conform to the current regulations, Winslow's sleeves should have shown six strips of narrow lace, with a quarter inch spacing between the strips except that the third and fourth strips were to be a half inch apart, and with a star above the upper strip. Captain Winslow is also wearing a cap of the earlier instructions. A change of November 1863 had removed the gold lace band of previous instructions, and directed that the cap device be worn on the plain blue cap band, immediately above the visor.

Winslow is not the only officer in this group out of uniform. The master, third from the right, has a cap device according to the General Order of July 31, 1863, not the one of the regulations of January, 1864. His silver anchor is placed in the gold wreath horizontally, instead of vertically as worn by the line officers on either side of him. The location of the star on his sleeves is not in accordance with instructions. It should have been a quarter of an inch above the upper lace, not the several inches as shown. The introduction of the gold star as a sleeve device for line officers made it easy to differentiate between Line and Staff. However, to determine a staff officer's specialty, it was necessary to study the shoulder strap device or the insignia in the cap wreath. The cross of four oak leaves worn as a cap device by all engineers is rather easy to spot. The officer on the extreme left is a chief engineer with the relative rank of lieutenant commander. Other engineers appear in this group, but their rank is not easily determined for the sleeve lace cannot be seen. There are three engineers in the second row; first, third, and fourth from the right. Since the engineer third from the right does not have shoulder straps, it is safe to assume that he is a third assistant engineer. The staff officer with the relative rank of lieutenant commander on Winslow's right is a paymaster, with the sprig of live oak of the Pay Department within the cap wreath. The officer on the extreme right is a surgeon, with the relative rank of lieutenant commander, for the center device of the cap ornament is the silver spread oak leaf of the Medical Department. The officers whose caps displays the wreath without a center device are warrant officers.

(*U. S. Signal Corps Photo, Brady Collection, National Archives.*)

Rear Admiral Dahlgren is shown with his staff on the deck of his flagship off Charleston, South Carolina. With the exception of the ensign leaning on the gun, and the staff officer extreme right, all officers are wearing the frock coat, the most commonly worn service coat. The ensign is shown in the short double-breasted jacket with two rows of nine small buttons, authorized as service dress except at general muster and occasions of special ceremony. The staff officer with the relative rank of captain on the right is wearing the single-breasted sack coat, authorized officially in January, 1865, but worn unofficially prior to that date.

There are three staff officers with the relative rank of captain in the photograph—first and third from the right and third from the left. The corps of these officers can not be identified for the cap devices are not visible and the insignia on the shoulder straps can not be identified. Since the relative rank of captain was reserved for the most senior officers of the staff corps, and fleet surgeons, paymasters, and engineers, it is reasonable to assume that the three officers are the fleet surgeon, the fleet engineer, and the fleet paymaster assigned to Admiral Dahlgren's squadron.

(Gift Picture Collection, National Archives.)

Enlisted men of the United States Navy appear in many photographs of the Civil War period. It is unusual to find one which includes a seaman wearing a jacket. The old timer, second from the left, is in a short double-breasted jacket with rows of small buttons. This had been a standard article of clothing from the time the first crews were signed on the new frigates in 1797. The style of the jacket had changed but little over the years. The one shown is basically the same as that worn by the boatswain's mate of 1836. The seaman's jacket was included in uniform regulations from 1841, the first to include the dress of enlisted men, until the pea jacket was introduced in 1886.

(*Courtesy of the Library of Congress.*)

V

Navy Department, 1865—1962:

Legislation, Administration, Management

In order to follow the developments in the dress of the United States Navy from the Civil War to the present it is necessary to review the changes in administration, legislation, and the various orders of the Navy Department which influenced naval attire.

Although at the end of the Civil War the United States had the strongest navy in the world, this supremacy was to be of short duration.[1] During 1865, most of the vessels that had been purchased and converted to military use were sold, along with some of the ships which had been built of poor materials during the war. Many of the vessels still on the stocks were allowed to rot without ever being completed. The ironclads were laid up in ordinary, their guns stored, and vast stocks of materials were sold. The number of ships in service decreased rapidly; by 1870 only 81 were in commission, and 125 were in ordinary or under construction.[2] This was a far cry from the fleet of more than 600 men-of-war in service during the latter part of the Civil War. Many of the better ships in service in 1870 were those built, and well built, prior to the war.

The reduction of the ships in service, the rapid release of officers and men who had served during the war, the lack of adequate appropriations to support a Navy, lack of public or Congressional support for a strong seagoing force, all had an effect on the Navy Department and the position of the United States as a strong sea power. The decline of American naval strength after the war and the beginnings of a "New Navy" in 1881 are discussed in detail in *The Rise of American Naval Power, 1776–1918* by Harold and Margaret Sprout.

155

Admiral Farragut, undress, 1866.

(*Courtesy of the Library of Congress.*)

The shot of the wardroom officers of the *Congress* in 1871 is interesting because it shows both the uniforms and a ship of the doldrum period of the United States Navy. It is evident that sail was the order of the day, with steam to be used only in an emergency. In black and white it is difficult to determine the classes of staff corps officers represented. Line officers are easily identified by the star on the sleeves. The staff officer seated second from the left is either a surgeon or paymaster, for there is either light blue or white cloth between the strips of sleeve lace. The officers extreme left, third from left, and standing extreme right are probably engineers, for the red corps cloth would photograph black. It is to be noted that all officers below the rank of master (a stripe and a half) are wearing shoulder loops instead of straps. The ship's Marine officer is seated on the right.

(Courtesy, U. S. Naval Medical School.)

RELATIVE RANK

An Act of Congress of July 25, 1866 "To define the Number and regulate the Appointment of Officers in the Navy, and for other Purposes," provided for an admiral, a vice admiral, and an increase in the number of line officers between the rank of ensign and rear admiral. The number of staff officers was held to that authorized in earlier legislation. In addition, the Secretary of the Navy was authorized to appoint a board to consider the qualifications of volunteer officers for appointment in the regular Navy. Under this proviso, five lieutenant commanders, twenty lieutenants, fifty masters, and seventy-five ensigns could be selected and appointed. As the peacetime strength of the Line increased, the number of staff officers remained basically at prewar levels. The end result was a much higher percentage of line in proportion to staff. Farragut was immediately appointed to the newly created rank of admiral, and Porter succeeded Farragut as vice admiral.

The July 25, 1866 act also provided that naval constructors and first assistant engineers be appointed by the President and confirmed by the Senate—as commissioned officers. They were to have naval rank and pay as "officers of the Navy," but no actual ranks were established, presumably because their relative ranks had been covered by Secretary Welles' order of 1863.

An Act of Congress of March 2, 1867 gave civil engineers commissioned status. Since the first employment of civil engineers in the early years of the nineteenth century, they had been appointed by the Secretary of the Navy, and had served in a civilian capacity. Their position was somewhat different from that of other staff officers. Surgeons, paymasters, chaplains, engineers, and professors served on board ship; civil engineers performed functions in the shore establishment. The 1867 legislation placed civil engineers on a par with other staff officers. William P. S. Sanger, who had served in the Bureau of Yards and Docks since its inception in 1842, and as "Civil Engineer of the Navy" under the Board of Navy Commissioners since 1836, was the first of this group to be given a commission. Six other civil engineers were commissioned on March 28, 1867, making a Civil Engineer Corps of seven officers! This was the small beginning of a corps whose officers in World War II numbered about 10,000.

When General Grant assumed the Presidency in 1869, he appointed Adolph P. Borie Secretary of the Navy. There appears to have been a definite agreement that Vice Admiral Porter was to be in fact the guiding hand of the Navy.[3] An order issued by Secretary Borie on March 12, 1869, directed that "all matters relating to the navy coming under the cognizance of the different bureaus be submitted to Vice-Admiral Porter before being transmitted to the Secretary of the Navy."[4] This order certainly was not in conformity with the basic legislation that had created the Bureau system in 1842, by whose wording the bureau chiefs were to be the advisers to the Secretary and to have direct access to him.

On the basis of a decision by the Attorney General of the United States, General Order No. 120 was issued on April 1, 1869. With the major expansion of the fleet during the war, and the almost total employment of steam-powered vessels, the numbers of staff officers particularly in the Engineer Corps, had multiplied. Secretary Welles in 1863 had recognized the importance of staff corps to support the Line. He had increased the relative rank of the three older corps—Medical, Paymaster, and Engineer—and had granted relative rank to chaplains, constructors, and professors. This recognition of the Staff could not be entirely palatable to the old-line Navy.

General Order No. 120 read as follows:

The Attorney General having advised the Department that Congress alone can fix the relavtive rank of line and staff officers in the Navy, and that only those officers whose relative rank has thus been legally established being below mentioned, the order of March 3, 1863, and the Naval Regulations, Article II, paragraphs six to twenty-eight (both inclusive), are hereby revoked and annulled.

Surgeons of the fleet, paymasters of the fleet, and fleet engineers; and surgeons, paymasters, and chief engineers of more than twelve years, rank with commanders.

Surgeons, paymasters, and chief engineers of less than twelve years, and the secretary of the Admiral and the secretary of the Vice-Admiral, rank with lieutenants.

Passed assistant surgeons and first assistant engineers next after lieutenants.

Assistant surgeons, assistant paymasters, and second assistant engineers rank next after masters.

Third assistant engineers rank with midshipmen.

A. E. BORIE
Secretary of the Navy

The order of March 3, 1863 is of course, Secretary Welles' action modifying the relative rank structure of the Navy.

Although staff officers did not lose pay when their relative rank was reduced, or—as with chaplains, constructors, and professors—when relative rank was taken from them, they did lose prestige. The reason for making no change in salaries was that there was no direct correlation between the pay of a lieutenant, and that of a surgeon who had the relative rank of lieutenant. Pay schedules for the various grades of officers in each staff corps were entirely distinct from the pay schedule for line officers.

This reversal of a procedure which had been established by Secretary Welles in 1863, and not questioned by Congress since that date, brought about congressional action. Legislation of March 3, 1871 granted relative rank to all classes of staff officers covered by the 1863 order, with the exception of professors of mathematics. Secretary of the Navy George M. Robeson, who had assumed office when Borie resigned on June 25, 1869, issued a Naval Regulation Circular on December 1, 1871, setting forth the relative rank "between line officers and medical, pay, engineer and other officers not of the line," as follows:

Medical Directors
Pay Directors
Chief Engineers—first 10   } Relative rank of captain
Naval Constructors—first 2
Chaplains—first 4

Medical Inspectors
Pay Inspectors
Chief Engineers—next 15   } Relative rank of commander
Naval Constructors—next 3
Chief Engineers—next 45

Surgeons
Paymasters
Chief Engineers—next 45   } Relative rank of lieutenant commander
Naval Constructors—remainder
Chaplains—next 7

Passed Assistant Surgeons
Passed Assistant Paymasters   } Relative rank of lieutenant or master
First Assistant Engineers
Assistant Naval Constructors

Assistant Surgeons
Assistant Paymasters   } Relative rank of master or ensign
Second Assistant Engineers

Secretary to the Admiral   } Relative rank of lieutenant
Secretary to the Vice Admiral

Among Staff officers who might rank with line officers in either of two grades, those with the longest service ranked with the more senior grade. It is to be noted that the act permitted relative rank for only eighteen chaplains. Since the total number of chaplains allowed was twenty four, six were of necessity without rank. Third assistant engineers continued to rank with midshipmen, as under Secretary Welles' order.

The act of March 3, 1871 had also authorized the President "to determine and fix the relative rank of civil engineers." No action was taken by the Department on this authority until 1881.

Legislation of May 31, 1872 granted relative rank to professors of mathematics, the one group omitted from the 1871 act. Three professors were to rank with captains, four with commanders, and five with either lieutenant commanders or lieutenants. It is to be remembered that earlier legislation had limited the number of professors to twelve. Now, with only minor exceptions, the relative rank of staff officers had been restored to that granted by Secretary Welles in 1863. The only commissioned staff officers without relative rank were civil engineers.

General Order 263, issued by Secretary William H. Hunt on February 24, 1881, finally assigned relative rank to civil engineers. The text of the order was as follows:

> The President of the United States has this day, under the provisions of Section 1,478 of the Revised Statutes, conferred relative rank on Civil Engineers of the Navy, and fixed the same as follows:
> One with the relative rank of Captain. Two with the relative rank of Commander. Three with the relative rank of Lieutenant Commander. Four with the relative rank of Lieutenant.
> Civil Engineers will take precedence in their Corps and with other officers with whom they hold relative rank, in accordance with the law regulating precedence of officers of the Navy.

It is evident from a letter of June 17, 1881 from the Attorney General to the Secretary of the Navy, that civil engineers had pressed their claim for recognition as officers of the United States Navy and for the prerogatives that went with relative rank. A properly executed commission, although it can be framed and hung on a wall, is of little value in indicating an officer's place in the Navy family. A uniform and the accompanying prerogatives are the preferred tokens of military status. The Attorney General's decision of June 17, 1881 is based on a letter of April 12, 1881 from "B. F. Chandler and other civil engineers in the Navy" which in effect had asked whether civil engineers were officers in the Navy or "civil officers connected with the Navy." The decision was that civil engineers were officers of the Navy and entitled to all the rights and

The U.S.S. *Atlanta* was one of the ships of the new Navy of the 1880's. Congress laid the foundation for a modern Navy in 1883 by providing funds for the construction of four, small, steel cruisers, the *Chicago*, the *Boston*, the *Atlanta*, and the *Dolphin*. Sail had not been forgotten, but now it was used as an auxiliary to steam, not as the primary motive power.

(*Official Navy Photo.*)

benefits of officers. It is evident from the correspondence that civil engineers had raised a question as to their status in 1878. Then the ruling had been adverse. Why the Navy Department had delayed so long in putting into effect the authority granted in 1871 to arrange relative rank for civil engineers cannot now be determined. This small group of officers, whose function was to build, maintain, and in some degree operate the shore establishment of the Navy, did not serve on ships at sea. The fact that the Chief of the Bureau of Yards and Docks was a line officer may have had some bearing on the delay in granting relative rank. All other staff bureaus were headed by officers of the same professional background as their subordinates and could present their cases directly to the Secretary. Not until 1898 was the Chief of the Bureau of Yards and Docks, and thus of Civil Engineers, himself a civil engineer.

The question of rank and relative rank was finally resolved at the end of the nineteenth century. The Personnel Act of March 3, 1899 included a proviso "That all sections of the revised statutes which, in defining rank or positions in the Navy, contain the words 'the relative rank of' are hereby amended to read 'the rank of,' but officers whose rank is so defined shall not be entitled, in virtue of their rank to command in the line or in other staff corps." While this legislation could not be palatable to all line officers, it was a step which had been inevitable from the day in 1846 when surgeons were assigned relative rank.

Another section of the 1899 act stated that nothing in the legislation was to "be construed as changing the titles of officers in the staff corps." As a result, a medical director with the rank of captain, continued to be addressed as "Medical Director." A civil engineer with the rank of lieutenant would be called "Assistant Civil Engineer," and all chaplains would have that title and no other regardless of their rank. The title of rank was considered applicable only to the line. Secretary Daniels, in a change in Naval Regulations dated September 12, 1918, directed that thereafter ". . . every officer in the Navy shall be designated and addressed by the title of his rank without any discrimination whatever. In written communication the name of the corps to which a staff officer belongs shall be stated immediately after his name." This is current Navy practice; an officer of the Civil Engineer Corps of the rank of captain is addressed as "Captain" and in written correspondence is designated as "Captain John Doe, Civil Engineer Corps [or CEC], United States Navy [or USN]." Tradition changes slowly; thus one may still hear an older officer address a captain of the Supply Corps as "Pay," or an officer of the Medical Corps, whatever his rank, as "Surgeon." Of course the most widespread use of the earlier form is in addressing any officer of the Chaplain Corps simply as "Chaplain."

NAVY MANAGEMENT

It is of interest to follow the changes in the Navy's system of management since the creation of the eight bureaus in 1862. This same system, modified from time to time to meet changing conditions in military thinking, technology, and business procedures, is still in effect. There was no major change in the management setup of the Navy Department for about twenty years after the Civil War. This was a period of retrogression and stagnation, with little public or congressional interest in naval affairs. The period is excellently covered by Paullin, Knox and the Sprouts.[5]

The task of trying to coordinate the work of eight bureaus, especially those of Construction and Repair, Steam Engineering, and Equipment and Recruiting, was a task beyond the capacity of a single individual, the Secretary of the Navy. To correlate the work of the bureaus, Secretary of the Navy Richard W. Thompson in March 1877 organized a board composed of chiefs of bureaus. The idea of creating some panel to assist the Secretary was not new, for it had been considered during Secretary Welles' administration, 1861–1869. Although between 1869 and 1881 there was much agitation for the creation of a permanent board, nothing concrete developed.[6]

When the building of a new Navy got under way in 1881, the partition of shipbuilding responsibilities among three bureaus became a major problem. Secretary William E. Chandler, in his annual report of 1883, recommended combining the Bureaus of Construction and Repair and of Steam Engineering into a new Bureau of Construction, Engineering, and Repair. This would have restored the setup of 1842, except that the equipment functions would be left with the Bureau of Equipment and Recruiting. Such a shift would not solve the problem entirely, for equipment was definitely tied into shipbuilding and repair, and recruiting was a personnel matter. Nothing came of the many proposals to centralize responsibility for the ship program until the twentieth century. In 1889, since legislation could not be secured to resolve the situation, Secretary of the Navy Benjamin F. Tracy organized a Construction Board made up of the chiefs of the Bureaus of Construction and Repair, Steam Engineering, Equipment and Recruiting, Ordnance, and Yards and Docks. The latter bureau had no direct responsibility for ship construction and repairs, but performed functions at the shore facilities which made these operations possible.

In a further effort to improve the administration and to centralize responsibility, Tracy made modifications within the basic bureau framework as established by Congress, by transferring functions from one bureau to another. As originally established in 1862, the Bureau of Navigation was intended to be the scientific division. In 1865 Secretary Welles had transferred the Office of Detail, which he had established within the Secretary's office to handle officer personnel, to the Bureau of Navigation. This had resulted in split responsibility for personnel: the men in Equipment and Recruiting, and officers in Navigation. An order of June 25, 1889 moved recruiting to Navigation, and such equipment functions as the procurement of chronometers, compasses and similar items, from Navigation to Equipment and Recruiting. The latter bureau was renamed the Bureau of Equipment.[7] Under later secretaries, the remaining functions of the Bureau of Equipment were absorbed by other bureaus, and by an act of June 30, 1914 the Bureau of Equipment was abolished.

The next management change was a minor one. The act of June 22, 1860 had directed that pursers were to be known as paymasters, and an act of March 3, 1871 had established the Pay Corps of the Navy. The name of the parent bureau had remained Provisions and Clothing, its title under the Bureau Act of 1842. Congress in July 1892 changed the name to Supplies and Accounts, the current designation. The new designation was considered more descriptive of the functions to be performed by this group of officers, who had gradually been assigned greater responsibilities for the purchase of supplies and materials, their custody and storage, and for financial matters. Not until 1919 were officers of the Bureau of Supplies and Accounts called Supply Officers, and their corps the Supply Corps.

In a further effort to improve the management of the Navy Department, Secretary of the Navy John D. Long in March 1900 established the General Board. This group of senior line officers—headed by Admiral George Dewey, the most distinguished naval officer of the period—provided valuable assistance to the Secretary. An attempt in 1904 to give the Board legal status and administrative responsibility failed, and left it a purely advisory body.[8]

The next step taken to improve the administrative system and to coordinate the work of the bureaus was the creation of the Naval Aide system in 1909. Secretary of the Navy George von L. Meyer established four general divisions in the Department: Operations of the Fleet, Personnel, Material, and Inspections. Each division was headed by a senior line officer, designated an Aide. The Secretary believed that the system had merit, but was unable to secure congressional authority for it. It was abandoned when Josephus Daniels became Secretary of the Navy in 1913.[9]

The possibility that the United States might become involved in the war raging in Europe finally convinced Congress that the Bureau system of management required some form of coordinating authority for

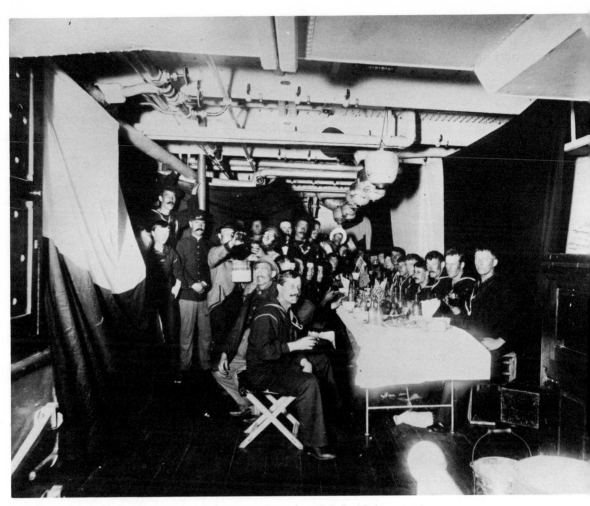

A gala occasion in the seamen's mess, U.S.S. *Maine*, 1896.

(*Detroit Photographic Company Collection, Library of Congress.*)

assistance to the Secretary. An Act of Congress of March 3, 1915 created the office of the Chief of Naval Operations. The bill read: "There shall be a Chief of Naval Operations who shall be an officer on the active list of the Navy, appointed by the President, not below the grade of Captain for four years, who shall under the direction of the Secretary of the Navy be charged with the operations of the fleet, and with the preparation and readiness of plans for its use in war."[10] Congress in August 1916 authorized the grade of admiral for the Chief of Naval Operations and provided that "all orders issued by the Chief of Naval Operations in performing the duties assigned him shall be performed under the authority of the Secretary of the Navy, and his orders shall be considered as emanating from the Secretary and shall have the full force and effect as such."

The first expansion of the Bureau system since 1862 took place in 1921, when on July 12 the Bureau of Aeronautics was created by Congress. The airplane, first employed in a major war during 1914–1918, had become a major part of the arsenal of military powers, and could no longer be handled under management systems established prior to World War I. The United States Navy's first interest in what was to become an all-important military weapon began in 1898 when two naval officers were detailed to serve on the "Joint Army-Navy Board to examine the Langley Flying Machine." Although the Langley machine was wrecked, the successful flight of the Wright Brothers in 1903 kept interest alive. In September 1910 Captain W. I. Chambers, an assistant Aide for Material, was detailed to handle the growing correspondence in connection with aviation. The office was transferred to the Division of Operations in the Secretary's office in January 1914. When the office of the Chief of Naval Operations was established in 1915, the cognizance of aviation matters was transferred to this new division of the Navy Department, where it remained until the Bureau of Aeronautics was established in 1921.[11]

The beginnings of naval aviation were small. To demonstrate the possible value of the airplane to the Navy, Eugene Ely, a civilian pilot employed by Glenn Curtiss, a pioneer aircraft builder, landed a Curtiss pusher on a specially built platform aboard the U.S.S. *Pennsylvania* in December 1911. Lieutenant T. G. Ellyson, who was ordered to the Curtiss Aviation Camp for flight training in December 1910, was the first of a long line of officers of the United States Navy to wear Navy wings.

As further tests and a growing world-wide interest in aviation indicated that airplanes would be of definite value to the military, the Navy purchased three planes in 1911. The technical responsibilities for aviation

This picture of the Navy's first seaplane was taken in 1911. The builder, Glenn Curtiss, in cap, white shirt, and black tie, is at the left of the controls. The first naval aviator, Lieutenant T. G. Ellyson, in rubber boots, is standing next to Captain W. I. Chambers, the officer then in charge of aviation matters in the Navy Department, Lieutenant John H. Towers, who later became Chief of the Bureau of Aeronautics, is standing on Captain Chambers' left. The others shown are Curtiss personnel.

(*Official Navy Photo.*)

were distributed within the Bureau system. Although the aeronautical engineers were still in the future, the Navy did have skilled engineers in many fields. The specialists in ship design and construction of the Bureau of Construction and Repair became experts in the design of aircraft, and their counterparts in the Bureau of Engineering assumed responsibility for power units. In this early stage of the design and construction of the airplane, the Navy had the necessary skills, and made many innovations to adapt the plane to Navy use.

Originally officers received flight training at the facilities of the plane builders. The need for more Navy control became evident as the future air arm of the Navy developed. A temporary Aviation Camp was established at Annapolis, Maryland in September 1911, and in January 1913 the entire naval aviation unit was transferred to Guantanamo Bay, Cuba, for exercises with the Fleet. To provide more permanent facilities, the unit was moved to the old abandoned Navy yard at Pensacola, Florida, in January 1914. Pensacola is now the primary station for aviation training. The first use of a naval seaplane in combat occurred during the landing of American troops at Veracruz, Mexico, in the spring of 1914. On a reconnaissance flight over enemy positions, a Curtiss hydroplane was hit by enemy rifle fire.

After the Mexican affair, training was continued at Pensacola for officers and men of both Navy and Marine Corps, so that when the United States entered World War I in April 1917, there were forty-eight officers and men in training and a total of fifty-four aircraft. By the end of the war, naval aviation had expanded to 42,051 officers and men and 2,127 aircraft. The shore establishment for aviation grew from the single facility at Pensacola to twenty-five air stations overseas, thirteen in the United States, two in Canada, and one in the Azores. Aviation had come of age and had demonstrated beyond question that it was an essential part of the Navy.[12]

During the period of expansion, the technical phases of naval aviation had been handled within the framework of the existing Bureau system, with naval constructors and engineers playing major roles. The continuing advances in aeronautical technology and science now indicated that change was required to administer the many and diverse phases of aviation. The result was the creation in 1921 of the Bureau of Aeronautics.

The authority of the Chief of Naval Operations had been somewhat vaguely defined in the 1915 legislation creating the office. President Roosevelt in a memorandum of March 2, 1934, stated that the Chief of Naval

Operations was charged with the coordination of the bureaus and offices, but that orders to these bureaus and offices should come directly from the Secretary of the Navy.[13]

The next modification of the Bureau system was long overdue—the placing of the responsibility for ship construction and repair in one bureau.The legislation of 1862 had divided this responsibility among three separate bureaus. Since the Civil War, the Bureau of Ordnance had also become involved. The introduction of armor and the development of modern armament, which became in many cases an integral part of the vessel, spread the responsibility further. In spite of many plans and recommendations, the matter was not rectified. Again it was the buildup for possible involvement in a global war that triggered the action to consolidate authority. By legislation of June 20, 1940, the Bureaus of Construction and Repair and of Engineering were merged into the Bureau of Ships. Guns and armor remained with the Bureau of Ordnance. To insure that neither the naval constructors nor the engineers would dominate the new bureau, the law provided that "the Chief of the Bureau of Ships shall be appointed . . . from among the officers of the active list of the Navy who are specially qualified and experienced in naval engineering or naval architecture. . . . An officer on the active list of the Navy who is especially qualified in naval engineering or naval architecture shall be detailed as Assistant Chief of the Bureau of Ships. . . . Provided that if the Chief of the Bureau of Ships be specially qualified in naval engineering the Assistant Chief of the Bureau of Ships be specially qualified in naval architecture, and vice versa." The first chief of the new bureau was an engineer, Rear Admiral S. M. Robinson, who had been head of the Bureau of Engineering, and his assistant was Rear Admiral A. H. Van Keuren, the former Chief of Construction and Repair. With this merger, the Corps of Naval Constructors went out of existence, and the naval constructors themselves became line officers for engineering duty, as had the engineers after they were amalgamated into the Line in 1899.[14]

By an Executive Order of March 12, 1942, President Roosevelt combined the officers of Chief of Naval Operations and Commander in Chief, U. S. Fleet in one person. The relationship of the Chief of Naval Operations and the various bureaus was resolved by a section of the order stating that the Chief of Naval Operations "shall be charged with the preparation, readiness, and logistic support of the operating forces comprising the several fleets, seagoing forces and set frontier forces of the United States Navy, and with the coordination and direction of effort to this end of the bureaus and offices of the Navy Department except such offices

The Navy's first air station, Pensacola, Florida, 1914.

(*Official Navy Photograph.*)

Assembling planes, United States Naval Air Station, Brest, France, 1918.

(Courtesy of the National Archives.)

(other than bureaus) as the Secretary of the Navy may specifically exempt."[15]

Legislation of May 13, 1942 renamed the Bureau of Navigation as the Bureau of Naval Personnel—a title certainly more descriptive of the duties it performed. When it was first established in 1861, Navigation had been a proper name for the bureau, but as the years passed, the bureau lost its scientific responsibilities and took over administration of personnel —officers in 1865, and enlisted men in 1889. In 1941 the Bureau of Navigation was responsible not only for administering officers and men, but also for their training, including that at the Naval Academy, and also for all welfare activities and for the administration of the Chaplain Corps

The most recent change in the Navy administrative and management pattern has been the consolidation of the Bureaus of Ordnance and Aeronautics into a Bureau of Naval Weapons by an Act of Congress of August 18, 1959. A press release of August 19, 1959 stated in part:

One of the objectives of the merger is to provide an effective organization for the development and procurement of Naval weapons and weapons systems. This will bring a unified approach to the development of weapons rather than two parallel approaches, which particularly in the missile field, have been common under the current two related systems.

Secretary of the Navy Franke commented further on the merger:

The problems occasioned by technical advance in supersonic aircraft, guided missiles, electronics and similar fields and matters of cognizance concluded that the Bureaus of Ordnance and Aeronautics should be combined to form a new Bureau of Weapons. The long-continued history of outstanding accomplishment of the Bureau of Ordnance, since its inception in 1842, and the equally dynamic accomplishments of the Bureau of Aeronautics in 38 years were recognized but the consolidation of these two distinguished organizations is essential and will produce a significant improvement in the total weapon system effort in the Department.

The organization of the Navy Department today is basically as it was in World War II. Certain offices and boards report to the Secretary of the Navy; the bureaus, the Marine Corps, and in time of war the Coast Guard, report to the Chief of Naval Operations—Commander in Chief, U. S. Fleet. After years of trial and error, transfer of functions from one bureau to another, creation and abolishment of bureaus, and variation in the staff organization, the present management system meets the needs of today's Navy. The pattern is flexible enough so that changed conditions can be handled, and, if necessary, Congress can modify the arrangements to cope with any major situation outside the latitude of current legislative authority.

OTHER CONGRESSIONAL ACTIONS

During the period from 1865 to date, there have been numerous Acts of Congress with a bearing on the dress of the United States Navy. The most important of these will be reviewed briefly so that one may follow the many changes in uniform regulations which finally authorized a common uniform for all officers, with recognizable methods of indicating rank and corps.

Congress in an act of March 3, 1883 granting appropriations for the naval service, modified the titles of two grades of officers. The grade of master was "changed to that of lieutenant, the masters now on the list to constitute a junior grade of, and be commissioned as lieutenants, having the same rank and pay as now provided by law for masters; and the title of the grade of midshipman is changed to that of ensign, the midshipmen now on the list to constitute a junior grade of and be commissioned as ensigns, having the same rank and pay as now provided by law for midshipmen." As a result of this legislation, the historic title of "sailing master," changed to "master" in 1837, disappeared from the United States Navy. Now officers with a rank between those of lieutenant and ensign are known as "lieutenant (junior grade)" and rank with first lieutenants of the Army and Air Force. The change in the designation of midshipmen is a little more difficult to understand. Originally there was but one class of midshipmen; later, provision was made for those midshipmen who had passed an examination for promotion and were waiting for a vacancy in the grade of lieutenant. This group was known as "passed midshipmen." The title of "ensign (junior grade)" does not appear in the uniform regulations of 1883. Instead there were provisions for "naval cadets" or "cadet engineers" who had completed the four year courses at the Naval Academy. Today, of course, midshipmen upon graduation and upon entering the service are immediately commissioned ensigns in the Navy, or Second Lieutenants in the Marine Corps.

U. S. Navy Regulations Circular No. 41 of January 8, 1885, grouped the enlisted men of the Navy into classes, and established the ratings of first-, second-, and third-class petty officers, thus superseding the former all-inclusive rating of "petty officer." The table below indicates how the various ratings were grouped:

Gun Crew, U.S.S. *Hist*, Battle of Santiago, July, 1898.

(*Official Navy Photo.*)

	SEAMEN CLASS	SPECIAL CLASS	ARTIFICER CLASS
PETTY OFFICERS 1ST CLASS	Chief Boatswain's Mates Chief Quartermasters Chief Gunner's Mates	Masters-at-Arms Equipment Yeomen Apothecaries Paymaster's Yeomen Ship's Writers School Masters Band Masters Engineer's Yeomen	Machinists
PETTY OFFICERS 2ND CLASS	Boatswain's Mates Quartermasters Gunner's Mates Coxswains to Commander-in-Chief	Ship's Corporals Ship's Cooks Chief Musicians	Boilermakers Armorers Carpenter's Mates Blacksmiths Sailmaker's Mates Water Tenders
PETTY OFFICERS 3RD CLASS	Captains of Forecastle Captains of Main Top Captains of Fore Top Captains of Mizzen Top Captains of Afterguard Coxswains Quarter-Gunners Seamen Gunners	Captains of Hold	Printers Painters Oilers
SEAMEN 1ST CLASS	Seamen Seamen-Apprentices, 1st Class	Lamplighters Jacks-of-the-Dust Buglers Musicans, 1st Class Tailors Barbers	Firemen, 1st Class Carpenters Calkers
SEAMEN 2ND CLASS	Ordinary Seamen Seamen-Apprentices 2nd Class	Baymen Muscians	Firemen, 2nd Class
SEAMEN 3RD CLASS	Landsmen Apprentices, 1st, 2nd and 3rd Class Boys		Coal Heavers

The separation of petty officers into three classes was a definite improvement upon the original system. In the uniform regulations to be approved on July 1, 1885, the ratings of first-, second-, and third-class petty officers would be indicated by chevrons in a manner similar to that employed at present.

The Navy had provided enlisted assistants to medical officers ever since the first frigate went to sea in the eighteenth century. It was not until 1898 that a definite branch of the service was established for the training of men who were employed in the sick bays aboard ship or in the hospitals ashore. Originally a boy or a seaman who was not able to perform arduous duties of handling sail or similar work was assigned to care for the sick and wounded under a surgeon's supervision. Later, ratings were established for "surgeon's stewards," "apothocaries," and "baymen" to identify men employed in the medical departments. The need for a better organization and for training personnel in these specialized duties was evident. An act of June 17, 1898 established the Hospital Corps to provide trained assistance to medical officers, and male nurses to care for the sick and wounded. The new corps became part of the Medical Department, under the Bureau of Medicine and Surgery. The act made provision for "twenty-five pharmicists with the rank, pay, and privileges of Warrant Officers, to be appointed by the Secretary of the Navy and removable at his discretion, and as many hospital stewards, hospital apprentices, first class, and hospital apprentices as in the judgment of the Secretary of the Navy were necessary and that it [the corps] should be attached permanently to the Medical Department of the Navy." This was a major forward step in the medical care of naval personnel.

In recognition of Rear Admiral George Dewey's service in the Spanish-American War, Congress by an act of March 2, 1899 established the rank of Admiral of the Navy especially for that officer, the rank to cease upon his death. The title of admiral created for Farragut in 1865, and taken over by Porter after Farragut's death in 1870, lapsed upon Porter's death in 1891. Until the rank of admiral was authorized in 1916 for the Chief of Naval Operations, the title had been authorized only for the purpose of honoring particular officers of the Navy.

On March 3, 1899 "An act to reorganize and increase the efficiency of the personnel of the Navy and Marine Corps of the United States" became law. One of its provisions, under which staff officers were given rank in place of relative rank, has already been discussed. Another section of the act provided that officers of the Engineer Corps were to be amalgamated into the Line. The day of sail had passed, and in modern men-of-war every officer was required to have some knowledge of engineering. Younger engineering officers were permitted to qualify for general line duties, but the older and more senior engineers were to be restricted to shore billets and duties in their special field. The Engineer Corps, established in 1842 after some years of unauthorized existence, was abolished. Engineers, who for years had struggled for equality with the Line, had finally attained it. The device of the corps, the cross of four oak leaves, disappeared from the uniforms of officers of the United States Navy, to be replaced by the star.[16] An Engineer Corps was never reestablished, but the need for engineering specialists remained. An act of August 29, 1916 made provision for "Officers for Engineering Duty Only." Officers not below the rank of lieutenant could apply for engineering duty and be so assigned with the approval of the Secretary of the Navy. They could serve at sea, as the younger engineers had done under the 1889 legislation, but after reaching the rank of commander their duties would be on shore. The only exception to this rule was that E.D.O. commanders could serve as fleet or squadron engineers.[17]

Section 12 of the Naval Personnel Act of 1899 directed that warrant boatswains, gunners, carpenters, and sailmakers—the original forward warrants of the Navy—after ten years' service from the date of their original warrants were to be commissioned "chief warrant" officers. As a result, the Navy now had two classes of warrants instead of one. This change would be reflected in the major revision of the 1896 uniform instruction which was to be issued on May 8, 1899.

Congress on May 13, 1908 established the female Nurse Corps as a part of the Medical Department of the Navy. The head of the corps was to be a Superintendent of Nurses, appointed by the Secretary of the Navy. Under the superintendent there were to be as many chief nurses, nurses, and reserve nurses as might be required, all to be appointed by the Surgeon General of the Navy, with approval of the Secretary. The nurses were required to be graduates of a nursing school and to have passed both physical and professional examinations. Members of this newest staff corps were to serve at naval hospitals, on board hospital ships, and at dispensaries, and to perform such other duty as might be approved by the Secretary of the Navy The status of nurses remained vague, without actual or relative ranks, just as had that of staff officers until 1846, when surgeons received relative rank. On July 3, 1942 Congress granted Navy nurses relative rank, but not commissioned status. For male officers, the often disputed business of absolute, assimilated, or relative rank had been settled in 1899. The work of the Nurse Corps in World War II, when its personnel grew from 800 to more than 11,000, most of whom were reserves, finally brought recognition to its members.[18] An act of February 28, 1944 gave nurses actual rank for the duration of the war and for six months thereafter, or to such earlier time as the Congress or the President might designate. Legislation of April 16, 1947 made the Nurse Corps a regular staff corps of the Navy and gave its members commissioned status and rank.

The Navy originally had made no provision for dentists; but legislation of August 22, 1912 authorized the appointment of not more than thirty assistant dental surgeons, to be part of the Navy's Medical Department and to receive the same pay and allowances and to take rank in the same manner as the Medical Corps. From this beginning grew the excellent Dental Corps of the United States Navy, which numbered about 7,000 officers, mostly reserves, in World War II.[19] A portion of the act establishing the Dental Corps also made provision for a Medical Reserve Corps, to provide for additional doctors in the event of a national emergency. The Medical Reserve Corps was to be an integral part of the Navy's Medical Department, under the Bureau of Medicine and Surgery. It provided a large proportion of the doctors needed in World War I and in World War II, 85 per cent of approximately 14,000 doctors on duty were reserves.[20] In 1913 a Dental Reserve Corps was established. From these first steps toward creating a backup for the regular Navy grew the present-day Naval Reserve, which provided most of the officers and men required for the world-wide conflict of 1941-1945.

NAVAL MILITIA AND NAVAL RESERVE

The cost of maintaining regular navies was high. Late in the nineteenth century, to provide a means of augmenting the regular establishment in time of war, the major maritime powers established the policy of training civilian volunteers. The first such action in the United States was the establishment of the Medical and Dental Reserves. To expand the program, the United States first supported the state naval militias, and later created a Naval Reserve Force. The creation of non-regular components to serve with the Navy in time of war had its effect on the uniform.

The Constitution of the United States gave Congress the powers to "raise and support armies," to "provide and maintain a navy," and also to "call forth the militia to execute the laws of the Union, suppress insurrections and repel invasion," The militia units were to be under state control, and followed the pattern established during the Revolution. Subsequent legislation clarified the position of the militia, and in the early twentieth century placed the organized land militia under control of the War Department. No action had been taken to create a naval branch of the militia in time of war. The possible need for a sea branch of the states' militias was not disregarded: during the formative years of the Federal Government, the matter received serious consideration from time to time. It was assumed that in any crisis, officers and men could be drawn for the Navy from the merchant marine, since the seaborne carrying trade would be greatly curtailed during any war, and there would thus be a vast reservoir of trained seamen. This policy was effective during the War of 1812, when American vessels were for the most part denied the sea by the British fleet.

During the Civil War, land militia units were brought into Federal service, but there was no similar provision to supplement the small professional Navy. Congress on July 24, 1861 authorized the appointment of officers in an acting capacity and made provision for the recruitment of seamen. These men were volunteers, and had no previous commitment to serve in an emergency as did the land militia. After the war, this volunteer force was released, except for a limited number of officers who were permitted to transfer to the regular Navy.

In the 1880's, legislation was introduced in Congress to create a naval militia, the counterpart of the land forces of the states. Although Congress took no action to establish such a force, various states did add naval branches to their militia organizations. The first such unit was established in Massachusetts in 1888; by 1894 there were twenty-five branches of the militias.

The first action by Congress to support this non-regular auxiliary to the Navy took the form of a clause in the Naval Appropriations Act of March 2, 1891, which made $25,000 available for arms and equipment for the naval militias, under such regulations as the Secretary of the Navy should deem necessary. By an act of August 3, 1894 the Navy was authorized to loan such vessels which were "not suitable nor required for general use, charts, shipkeepers, not to exceed 6, of the regular Navy . . ." to the states upon application by their governors. A Joint Resolution of Congress on May 26, 1898 created a United States Auxiliary Naval Force during the war with Spain. One section provided that officers and men of the state naval militias, with the consent of the governors of the states, could be mustered into the new Auxiliary Naval Force for active service with the United States Navy. Those members of the naval militias who did not transfer to the Auxiliary Naval Force manned old-style vessels, many of them monitors of Civil War vintage, for coast and harbor protection within the boundaries of their respective states. After the war, members of the auxiliary force were released from Federal service under the terms of the congressional resolution.

The events of 1898 clearly pointed to the desirability of having some form of naval reserve force under Federal control. Those in charge of the state naval militia units were reluctant to lose control of them. Legislation of January 21, 1903 revised the law concerning the land militias and provided that one portion of the militia would in effect be a "ready reserve, known as the 'National Guard,'" while the balance of the militiamen would make up a "reserve militia." The National Guard was to receive financial assistance from the Federal Government, and to be organized, armed, and disciplined in accordance with the regulations covering the regular Army. The Guard could be called into Federal service for a nine months' period by order of the President. This was the first real reorganization of the land militia since its creation in 1789. The way was thus paved for the establishment of Navy control of the naval militias of the states, which took place a few years later.

An Act of Congress of February 16, 1914, "to promote the efficiency of the Naval Militia and for other purposes," gave the Navy Department the same relation to and responsibilities for the state naval militias as the War Department had for the state units of the National Guard. In the event of an emergency, the naval militias were to be called into Federal service before any volunteer force.

The Naval Reserve as such was created by the Naval Appropriations Act of March 3, 1915. The sections concerning the Reserve state in part, "There is hereby established a United States Naval Reserve which shall consist of citizens of the United States who have been or may be entitled to be honorably discharged from the Navy." The Reserve was to consist of two classes: those men who enlisted in the Naval Reserve within four months after discharge, and those who enlisted more than four months after discharge. This would shortly be known as the "Fleet Reserve," for its members were required to have served honorably in the Navy.

The Naval Reserve was expanded by an Act of Congress of August 29; 1916, part of the preparedness program on the eve of the entrance of the United States into World War I. The expanded reserve force was to be divided into six classes:

Class I: The Fleet Naval Reserve, to be made up of former naval personnel under the conditions of the 1915 legislation.

Class II: The Naval Reserve, made up of members of the seagoing profession who had served at least two years aboard a vessel on the high seas or large lakes.

Class III: Naval Auxiliary Reserve, to consist of persons who had served or were serving in the merchant marine of the United States.

Class IV: Naval Coast Defense Reserve, drawn from those who were cap-

able of performing special and useful service in the Navy in time
of war.

Class V: Volunteer Naval Reserve, to be made up of those persons who
could qualify for other classes of the Naval Reserve, and who
were willing to serve without pay or gratuity in time of peace.

Class VI: Naval Reserve Flying Corps, to be drawn from officers and
student flyers who transferred from the Naval Flying Corps,
and enlisted men with training in flying.

The act also provided for a Naval Flying Corps of 150 officers and
350 men, as a branch of the Regular Navy, and established a National
Naval Volunteer Force to tie the members of the naval militia into Federal service. No member of the naval militia was entitled to retirement
pay until he was found qualified and had been enrolled in the National
Naval Volunteers. In effect, naval militiamen served two masters: the
state and the Federal governments. The obligation to the Federal Government was paramount, for under it a member could be called into
active service with the Navy without the consent of the governor of
his state. The 1916 act also provided that if members of the various
naval militias were not enrolled in the Naval Volunteers, they could be
drafted into this branch. The transfer to Federal service relieved persons
from any obligation to the naval militia.

The authority of the state naval militia was further reduced, and
the Naval Reserve strengthened, by legislation of July 1, 1918 em-
powering the President to transfer personnel of the National Naval Volunteers to appropriate classes of the Naval Reserve Force. Subsequent
legislation of June 4 and 20, 1920 and February 28, 1925 modified the
Naval Reserve and naval militia setups. The classes of the Reserve were
reduced to three—the Fleet Reserve, the Merchant Marine Reserve, and
the Volunteer Reserve. To be eligible for Federal assistance, 95 per cent
of the officers and men of a naval militia unit had to be enrolled in the Naval
Reserve. An act of July 1, 1938 divided the reserve into four classes:

Fleet Reserve
Organized Reserve
Merchant Marine Reserve
Volunteer Reserve

With the establishment of the Naval Reserve Force, interest in the naval
militia waned, and in most states the organizations were disbanded, or
were perpetuated in name only, training being accomplished by the
Naval Reserve program.

The legislation of March 3, 1915, which created the Naval Reserve, permitted "citizens of the United States" to enroll, with no restriction as to sex. It was under this broad authority that women were enlisted in the Navy and served as "Yeomanettes" in World War I. Acts subsequent to that of 1915 limited membership to "male Citizens." On July 30, 1942 the Reserve Act of July 1938 was amended to permit women to be enrolled, both as officers and in an enlisted status, in order to release officers and men for duties at sea and overseas. The women of the Navy—the Waves—provided many needed services during the war. In recognition of this, on June 12, 1948, Congress authorized regular commissioned and enlisted status for women in the Navy.

To review the changes affecting the dress of the Navy, it will be necessary to return to 1916. An act of August 29, 1916 provided that "hereafter no further appointments shall be made to the Corps of Professors of Mathematics, and that the corps shall cease to exist upon the death, resignation, or dismissal of the officers now carried in that corps on the active and retired lists of the Navy." With the retirement of its last officer from active duty on July 1, 1936, the Corps of Professors of Mathematics in effect passed out of existence, and with it the device of an oak leaf and an acorn. Although naval officers are still assigned to duties in connection with education in the Navy, they now wear the device of their particular corps.

No story of the United States Navy, its officers and men, and the uniforms and insignia they wore, would be complete without some mention of the Seabees, the special construction forces of World War II. Before World War II the construction program of the Navy was carried out under contract with civilian construction firms, supervised by the Bureau of Yards and Docks, with officers of the Civil Engineer Corps directly in charge. Before the war, many projects were under way at possessions in the Pacific and the Caribbean. After November 1940, when fifty destroyers were traded to Great Britain for base rights in the British islands of the West Indies, the Navy's program to expand shore facilities for the Navy grew rapidly. It soon became necessary to provide the civil engineers at the sites of the work with draftsmen, surveryors, inspectors, clerks, and accountants in such numbers that it was not considered possible to recruit civilians for these positions. To meet the demand, the Bureau of Navigation authorized the formation of "Headquarters Construction Companies," to consist of experienced men secured through Naval Reserve recruitment.

After the attack on Pearl Harbor on December 7, 1941 it was impossible to continue the use of contractors and their civilian employees for construction work in combat areas. If a civilian attempted to defend himself when attacked by enemy forces, he would be considered a guerrilla under military law, and be subject to execution. Construction had to proceed, and to provide the men necessary to push the program forward, Construction Battalions were organized by recruiting men who had the necessary skills and experience. The question of command arose, since in general the naval regulations vested military command in the Line. Early orders concerning relative rank had plainly said, "This order confers no authority to exercise military command." However, a surgeon always had control and supervision over personnel attached to the Medical Department, as did a paymaster in the Pay Department, or an engineer in the engineer force. It was essential that officers of the Civil Engineer Corps have complete jurisdiction over the personnel of their units, not only the skilled construction workers, but also the supply, medical, or other officers, Line or Staff, detailed to a battalion. A letter from the Secretary of the Navy on March 19, 1942 directed that appropriate orders were to be issued "to all officers attached to a construction unit so that there would be no doubt on their part that they are to be under the authority of the officer assigned to duty as commander thereof." In effect, Civil Engineers were in command of an expanded department.

The Seabees (Construction Battalion = C.B. = Seabee) worked and, when necessary, fought to build the bases which provided the stepping

In January, 1943, all enlisted personnel attached to United States Navy construction battalions were directed to wear a shoulder patch with the letters C.B. as a means of unit identification.. On October 14, 1944, the patch was changed to the Fighting Bee. The new symbol was appropriate for men who could fight and build.

(*Courtesy of the Bureau of Yards and Docks.*)

stones for the long, slow advance across the Pacific. They supported the amphibious landings in Africa, in Europe, and at the locations where United

States troops went ashore. The exploits of the construction men of the Navy and their peculiar *esprit de corps* are familiar to all. From the original handful of men recruited for the first Headquarters Construction Companies in 1941, the Seabees and their civil engineer officers increased to nearly 260,000. The officer strength grew from 159 in June 1939 to over 10,000 by VJ-Day in August 1945. This gives some indication of the volume of work handled by the Navy's construction personnel.[21]

The most recent addition to the staff corps of the United States Navy is the Medical Service Corps, established in 1947. In accordance with an act of April 18, 1946, commissioned and other warrant officers had been given temporary appointments to ranks up to and including that of commander. Congress by legislation of August 4, 1947 established the Medical Service Corps, under the Medical Department of the Navy. The corps is composed of commissioned officers, from the rank of ensign to that of captain, who are specialists in medical supply, optometry, pharmacy, administration, and related areas in medical and hospital fields. Members of the Hospital Corps eligible for rank above that of chief medical service warrant officer are transferred to the Medical Service Corps.

It is interesting to note that the most recent additions to the staff corps have been those connected with the Bureau of Medicine and Surgery: Hospital Corps, 1898; Nurse Corps, 1908; Dental Corps, 1912; and Medical Service Corps, 1947. In the same span of time some staff corps have been abolished: the Engineer Corps in 1899; that of the Professors of Mathematics in 1916; and the Corps of Naval Constructors in 1940, when the Bureau of Ships was established. It may be assumed that as technology changes and new skills are needed by the Navy, the list of staff corps will be modified further.

While changes in officer classifications and corps reflect a changing Navy, a better indication of the specialties required to operate the complex machinery and equipment of an atomic-age establishment is shown by the specialty marks used today. From the first list of eight badges, which represented thirteen ratings, the list has grown to ninety-seven general ratings, emergency ratings, and distinguishing marks for enlisted men, as shown in the illustrations of the current uniform regulations. The construction men are identified both by "general service" ratings and by some marks which apply only to Seabees.

NOTES

[1] Knox Dudley W., *A History of the United States Navy*, rev. ed. (New York, Putnam, 1948), p. 317.

2 Paullin, Charles Oscar, "A Half Century of Naval Administration in America, 1861–1911," *U.S. Naval Institute Proceedings*, Vol. 39, No. 2 (June 1913), p. 739.

3 *Ibid.*, pp. 748–749; Soley, J. R., *Admiral Porter*, pp. 458–460.

4 Paullin, *op cit.*, p. 749.

5 Paullin, Charles Oscar, "A Half Century of Naval Administration in America, 1861–1911," *U.S. Naval Institute Proceedings*, Vol. 38 (Dec. 1912) Vol. 39, March, June, Sept., Dec. 1913; Vol. 40 (Jan., March, May, July 1914); Knox, *op cit.*; Sprout, Harold and Margaret, *The Rise of American Naval Power*, 1776–1918 (Princeton, Princeton University Press, 1939).

6 Paullin, *op cit.*, Vol. 39, No. 2 (June 1913), p. 756.

7 Paullin, *op cit.*, Vol. 39, No. 2 (Sept. 1913), p.1266.

8 Furer, Julius Augustus, *Administration of the Navy in World War II* (Washington, Navy Department, 1959 [G.P.O. 1960]), pp. 107–108.

9 *Ibid.*, pp. 109–109.

10 *Ibid.*, pp. 109–110.

11 *United States Naval Aviation*, 1898–1956 (Bureau of Aeronautics, 1956); Furer, *op cit.*, pp. 352–359.

12 Furer, *op cit.*, pp. 357–358.

13 *Ibid.*, p. 112.

14 *Ibid.*, pp. 217–222; Madden, Robert B., "The Bureau of Ships and Its E. D. Officers," *Journal of the American Society of Naval Engineers*, February 1954.

15 Furer, *op cit.*, pp. 125–134.

16 Robert, William P., *History of the Construction Corps of the United States Navy* (Washington, G. P. O., 1937); "Designated Engineering Duty Only," *Journal of the American Society of Naval Engineers*, Vol. 63, No. 4 (Nov. 1951).

17 Public Law No. 241, 64th Congress, approved August 29, 1916.

18 Furer, *op cit.*, p. 485.

19 *Ibid.*, p. 484.

20 *Ibid.*, p. 483.

21 Moreell, Ben, *Naval Institute Proceedings*, Vol. 88, No. 3 (March 1962), pp. 84–107; Furer, *op cit.*, pp. 421–424.

VI

Uniforms, 1866–1962

When the new uniform regulations of December 1, 1866 were issued, so far as the dress of the United States Navy was concerned there could be no doubt that the war was over. Gold lace and bullion again appeared on officers' uniforms. The full-dress body coat, with standing collar, tails, and epaulets, and the cocked hat once again became part of the well-dressed naval officer's wardrobe. However, not all the lessons learned during the grim period from 1861 to 1865 were forgotten. The war had forced the Navy to adopt a standard uniform for officers and to use easily identifiable indications of rank and corps. Many more years passed before the dress of the Navy became truly "uniform," but the major steps had been taken, and the clock would never be completely turned back. A system of rank indication, common to both Line and Staff, had developed for both sleeves and shoulder ornaments. The gold, five-pointed star had become the principal insignia of line officers, with the foul anchor as a supplementary device for shoulder and collar ornaments. Devices had been established for the various staff corps. These would be modified from time to time. But today each staff corps has its own distinctive insignia, and many of these can be traced to the developments of the Civil War period. The changes which took place in the four war years have a direct bearing on the dress of the United States Navy of the present.

Complete uniformity, however, was not attained until the United States was involved in another major war. In the meantime, there were attempts to restore the distinctions between Line and Staff which must be reviewed.

UNIFORM REGULATIONS OF 1866

The Regulations for the Uniform of the United States Navy approved by Secretary of the Navy Gideon Welles on December 1, 1866 continued to use the frock coat—the all-purpose coat of 1862—for full, service, and undress. The double-breasted body coat, a direct descendant of the dress coat originally prescribed by the infant Navy Department in 1802, was restored; but its wear was limited to "occasions of special ceremony." The wartime need for a service coat more comfortable and convenient than the long frock coat continued to be recognized. For more casual dress, single-breasted sack coats or short jackets were worn. In warm weather, white linen or grass cloth jackets could be used. For more formal occasions, a frock coat of light-weight wool, with medium buttons, was authorized. From these concessions to working conditions and warm weather, the present working and tropical uniforms have developed.

The special full-dress coat of 1866 was described in practically the same language as in the 1852 regulations. The standing collar was to be trimmed with different widths of gold lace, similar to those of the earlier order, but modified to cover the new ranks authorized during the war. For the Admiral, the lace was to be one inch wide; for the Vice Admiral and for rear admirals and commodores, three-quarters of an inch; for captains, commanders, and lieutenant commanders, half an inch; and for lieutenants, masters, and ensigns, a quarter of an inch. Midshipmen, third assistant engineers, and forward warrant officers were not permitted to wear the special full-dress coat. All staff officers wore the body coat with the same collar lace and sleeve stripes as the officers with whom they had relative rank—without, of course, the star on the sleeves. Epaulets, cocked hats, swords, and sword knots were worn, and trousers were either plain blue or white. Not for some years were the gold-laced trousers of 1852 reinstated.

The frock coat, with its two rows of nine large Navy buttons on each breast, was identical for all commissioned officers, boatswains, gunners, carpenters, and sailmakers. The identification by means of buttons had not entirely disappeared. Midshipmen and third assistant engineers—both warrant officers—wore the frock coat of the more senior officers, but with rows of medium-sized buttons. A feature of earlier instructions, the single-breasted coat for certain classes of officers, was continued. Clerks and mates were directed to wear single-breasted frock coats, with a row of nine medium-sized buttons.

The frock coat, with epaulets and either cocked hat or cap, was worn as full dress for "general duty and official visits on shore." For both undress and service dress, the coat was worn with shoulder straps and cap.

The sleeve lace for all commissioned officers, Line and Staff, was basically the same as that prescribed in the 1864 regulations, with modifications necessary to indicate the new ranks of admiral and vice admiral. The Admiral's sleeve decorations were two strips of two-inch lace with a one-inch strip between them, all spaced half an inch apart. The Vice Admiral displayed a two-inch strip with two one-inch strips above it, all spaced three-quarters of an inch apart. Rear admirals had a band of two-inch lace with a half-inch strip three-quarters of an inch above it. Commodores had only the two-inch band. All other officers wore the quarter-inch lace of the 1864 regulations, with the same spacings as before. All line officers except the Admiral wore the gold-embroidered star, one inch in diameter, above the upper sleeve stripe. The special star for the Admiral was two inches in diameter, with a steam frigate in silver in the center. Since Farragut was Admiral, it is understandable that the frigate was the *Hartford,* his flagship at Mobile Bay.

The same arrangement of sleeve lace was worn on the single- or double-breasted blue service jacket. The white jacket was worn without any indication of rank, both sleeve lace and shoulder ornaments being omitted. The sack coat was worn without sleeve lace, but retained the star on the sleeves for line officers, and on the collar were the same arrangements of rank and corps devices as in 1865, the foul anchor being used as the corps device of the Line. This method of showing rank and corps on coat collars continued, with only minor modifications, until 1919, when the single-breasted service coat, as seen in photographs of naval officers in World War I, was abolished. The display of rank and corps insignia on shirt collars is currently prescribed for khaki and tropical dress.

The devices for the newly reinstated epaulets and shoulder straps were as prescribed for shoulder straps in the 1864 uniform instruction. For the Admiral and Vice Admiral, who were not covered in the 1864 order, these were, respectively, four silver stars with a gold foul anchor under each of the two outer ones, and three stars with the gold anchor under the center one. The same decorations appeared on the collar of the sack coat.

The cocked hats prescribed in 1866 were similar to those of 1852, but with the height of the "fan" reduced from the earlier "eight to six and a half inches" to anywhere from six to five and a half inches. The "cock" was reduced proportionately. The "loop of six bullions, the center two twisted," was reserved for flag officers. All other officers entitled to wear cocked hats had the loop of four bullions of the 1852 order. In

This 1870 photograph of Commander Stephen B. Luce shows the prescribed arrangement of rank and corps devices on the collar of the sack coat. When the sack coat was replaced by the single-breasted, fly-front service coat in 1877, the same general arrangement was followed.

(*Official Navy Photo.*)

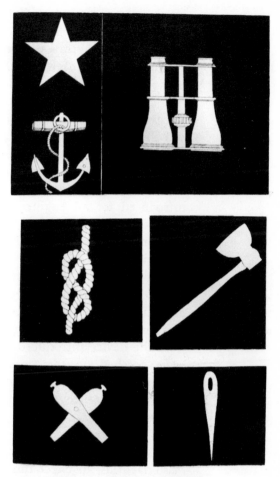

Prior to 1866, all petty officers wore the same device, with no indication of their specialties. The petty officers' badge, upper left, was a modified form of that introduced in 1841. In 1866, it was worn by all Line petty officers on the right sleeve, halfway between elbow and shoulder. Staff petty officers wore the device, without the star, on the left sleeve. Although only eight specialty marks were prescribed and shown, by varying the location on which they were worn, twelve ratings could be identified.

(Courtesy of the Navy Department Library.)

another step toward uniformity all commissioned officers other than naval constructors, chaplains, and professors of mathematics, were ordered to wear identical cap devices. The common device showed a silver-embroidered spread eagle, standing on a gold-embroidered foul anchor set in an inclined position. Midshipmen, after graduation from the Naval Academy, were permitted to wear the cap device of commissioned line officers. The commissioned officers excepted from the order wore the oak-and-olive wreath of previous orders, with the corps device in the center: a sprig of live oak for constructors, an inclined silver cross for chaplains, a gold disk with a silver P for professors, and the same with a silver S for secretaries. The cap device for warranted third assistant engineers was that introduced for all engineers in 1861—a cross of four oak leaves in the center of a gold wreath. Midshipmen at the Academy displayed a plain gold anchor placed vertically. Other warrant officers wore the wreath as a cap device.

For the first time a system of rating badges for enlisted men was included in a uniform regulation. Prior to the 1866 order, a sleeve mark had been used only to indicate petty officers as a group, with no indication as to their ratings. Under this new instruction petty officers wore the device introduced in 1841—a vertical foul anchor with a spread eagle perched on the stock—placed on the sleeve between the elbow and shoulder. Line petty officers were to wear the device with a star above it on the right sleeve; other petty officers—and first class firemen—on the left, without the star.

The rating marks used to show a man's specialty were very few as compared with the wide range of such marks in today's Navy. The master-at-arms, in effect the chief of police aboard ship, showed on both sleeves a vertical foul anchor, with a star above it in the same position as the star on the sleeves of line officers. A coxswain to the commanders-in-chief wore two crossed anchors on either side of the collar of the frock or jacket. A coxswain to any other commanding officer wore a single anchor on either side of the collar. All quartermasters employed a double marine glass as their mark. The chief or signal quatermaster had the device on both sleeves. Other quartermasters had the device on the right or left sleeve according to the watch assigned—on the right sleeve for the starboard watch and on the left for the port watch. Boatswain's mates used the same device as coxswains to commanding officers—the vertical foul anchor—placed, however, on the sleeve instead of on the collar. The chief boatswain's mate wore the device on both sleeves, and other boatswains had the anchor on the sleeve according to their watch. The device of gunner's mates was readily identifiable—two crossed cannons, muzzles down. Gunner's mates had the mark on both sleeves; the quarter-gunners used the location of the mark to indicate their watch. Captains of forecastle wore the crossed anchors of coxswains to the commanders-in-chief on the right or left sleeve, depending on the watch to which they were assigned. Captains of tops employed an open figure-eight knot as their mark, placed to indicate their watch. The latter two ratings were relics of the age of sail.

Carpenter's and sailmaker's mates, as staff petty officers, wore the eagle anchor device on the left arm, between elbow and shoulder, and their rating badges on both sleeves, between cuff and elbow. The mark of carpenter's mates was a tool of their trade, a broad axe; that of sailmaker's mates, likewise an instrument needed for their work, a fid.

The only enlisted men who were not petty officers and who wore a sleeve mark were ships' writers, identified by the letter *W*; ships' schoolmasters, by the letter *S* and Naval apprentices, by the letter *A*. Writers and schoolmasters wore the mark on the lower left sleeve, indicating staff status, and apprentices wore the mark according to their watch.

All petty officers' devices and rating badges were blue on white clothing and white on blue.

The illustrations of the 1866 regulations show the rating badges for eight petty officers; thus with the three marks for other enlisted men, the total number of identifying marks employed in 1866, comes to eleven. The uniform regulations of 1959 picture sixty-four general ratings and twenty-one distinguishing marks for enlisted men. Improvement in technology and the advances of science have increased the specialties needed to operate the vessels of the fleet and the Navy's air arm.

Now that the Navy had developed a standard sleeve lace for officers, a similar method of identifying classes of enlisted men was instituted. Petty officers, seamen, and first-class firemen had three rows of white tape stitched around the collars of their blue frocks, with a white, five-pointed star in each corner. Ordinary seamen and second-class firemen had two rows of tape, and landsmen, coal-heavers, and boys a single strip of tape. A corresponding number of strips was worn around the cuffs.

According to another innovation in the dress of enlisted men, masters-at-arms, yeomen, surgeon's stewards, and paymaster's stewards—all petty officers—were instructed to "wear blue jackets with rolling collars, double-breasted; two rows of medium size navy buttons on the breast, six in each row. Slashed sleeves or cuffs, with three small navy buttons. Plain blue caps with visor. They will be allowed to wear white cotton or linen shirts (in place of duck frocks with turn-over collars,) and uniform vests, with six small navy buttons." The petty officer's badge was worn on the sleeves; in addition, the jacket of a master-at-arms showed the anchor and star above the cuffs of both sleeves. This was the first step toward specifying a coat and cap for chief petty officers different from the frock or jacket worn by other petty officers and men.

CHANGES TO THE 1866 UNIFORM REGULATIONS

On March 11, 1869, General Order No. 90, issued by Secretary of the Navy A. E. Borie just two days after he took office, foreshadowed things to come for members of the staff corps. One section of the order concerned the uniforms to be worn by staff officers. Medical officers were directed to wear cobalt blue cloth around the sleeves, between the gold lace rank stripes. Paymasters were assigned white cloth as a corps indication, and engineers, red. It is to be noted that only the three groups of staff officers who had possessed relative rank before Secretary Welles' order of 1863 were included in the order. There was no mention of chaplains, naval constructors, or professors of mathematics. It would appear that the decision to reduce the rank of surgeons, paymasters, and engineers, and to take relative rank from chaplains, naval constructors, and professors had been made at the time General Order No. 90 was issued on March 11. An order on relative rank was not issued until April 1, twenty days later.

The decision to indicate the specialties of civil or staff officers by colored cloth between the strips of sleeve lace served a useful purpose. Now that all officers with actual or relative rank wore caps with the same device, the specialties could be determined only by noting the corps devices on the epaulets or shoulder straps. One could differentiate between officers of the Line and Staff, for only line officers wore a star above the sleeve lace. But the specialties of staff officers could not be so readily identified. This practice of differentiation of specialties by colored cloth had been introduced into the British Navy in 1863: navigators had white; medical officers, scarlet; accountants, white; and engineers, purple.[1]

Not all of the March 11, 1869 order was devoted to staff officers. Important changes were made in Navy dress, some of which are still reflected in the present current practice. Instead of using multiple stripes of quarter-inch lace to indicate ranks from captain to ensign, a new system was introduced—the various combinations of half-inch and quarter-inch lace employed today. Those prescribed in 1869 differ from the present practice in that captains were identified by three strips of half-inch lace. Commanders showed two strips of half-inch lace, with a quarter-inch strip between them; lieutenant commanders, two strips of half-inch

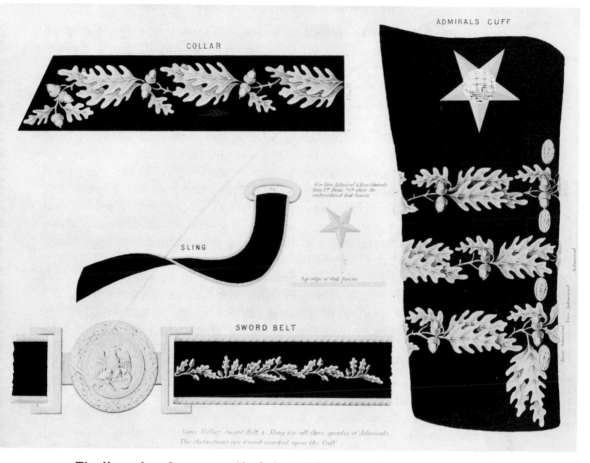

COLLAR

ADMIRALS CUFF

SLING

SWORD BELT

The live-oak and acorn motif of the 1830's was used as decoration for the cuffs and collars of the special full-dress coats of the admiral, vice admiral, and rear admiral in 1869. The decoration of the collar was the same for all three grades. The number of rows of cuff embroidery indicated rank—three for the admiral, two for the vice admiral, and a single row for rear admirals. Of special interest is the *"Hartford"* star, worn only by Admiral Farragut.

lace; lieutenants, a strip of half-inch lace, with another a quarter of an inch wide above it; masters, a single half-inch strip; and ensigns, a quarter-inch strip.

In undress, flag officers wore the same arrangements of sleeve lace as they do today—the Admiral, a two-inch strip with three strips of half-inch lace above it; the Vice Admiral, a two-inch strip with two half-inch strips; rear admirals, a wide strip, with a half-inch strip above it; and commodores, a single wide strip. However, in special full dress—that is, the body coat—a more elaborate means of showing rank was authorized for flag officers other than commodores. Embroidery in the live-oak leaf and acorn pattern of 1830 was used as sleeve decoration. The Admiral had three bands around the sleeves, with the special *Hartford* star above them; the Vice Admiral had two bands, and rear admirals, a single band, both with the gold star of the Line above the upper stripe.

Order No. 90 introduced a new cap device to be worn by all commissioned officers, "a silver shield with two crossed anchors in gold." However, the illustration of the cap device shows that a small silver spread eagle was perched on the top of the shield. In general, the 1869 cap device bears a very close resemblance to that worn at present. The Navy was taking a step backward in directing staff officers to wear a distinctive corps color between the strips of sleeve lace. A common cap device, on the other hand, was a step forward.

Another uniform change, General Order No. 126, issued on May 27, 1869 by Secretary Borie, modified the sleeve lace of captains and commanders. Captains were directed to wear four strips of half-inch lace, and commanders three. Since 1869, a captain has been a "four-striper" and a commander a "three-striper." The pattern of sleeve lace was inching toward that worn in the present day.

UNIFORM INSTRUCTIONS OF 1869

New uniform regulations were approved by Secretary of the Navy George M. Robeson on July 14, 1869. Since Robeson took office under an interim appointment on June 25 1869, the day of Borie's resignation, it is evident that the instructions were practically ready for release before the new Secretary took office. The new instructions incorporated the changes of General Orders Nos. 90 and 126, with a single addition. The sleeve lace of the Admiral in undress was changed to two strips of two-inch lace, with a strip of one-inch lace between them. The *Hartford* star—Farragut's personal insignia—was retained for both full and undress.

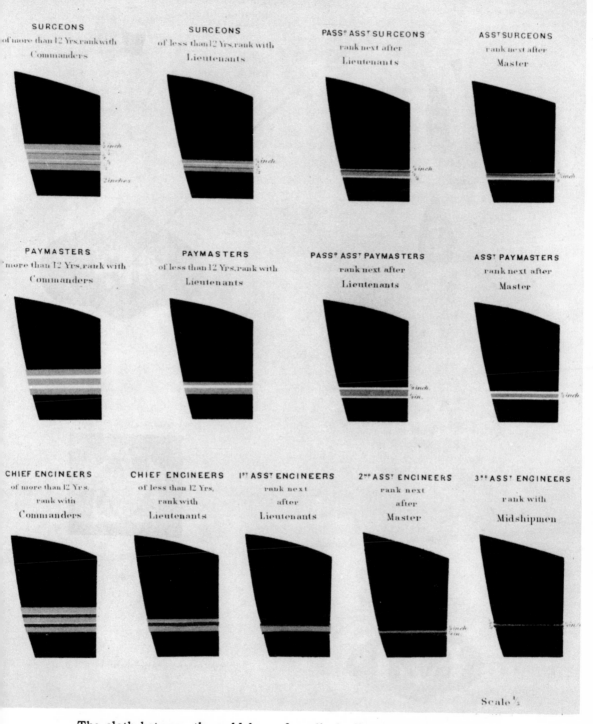

SLEEVES
FOR STAFF OFFICERS

SURGEONS
of more than 12 Yrs. rank with
Commanders

SURGEONS
of less than 12 Yrs. rank with
Lieutenants

PASS⁰ ASS⁰ SURGEONS
rank next after
Lieutenants

ASS⁰ SURGEONS
rank next after
Master

PAYMASTERS
more than 12 Yrs. rank with
Commanders

PAYMASTERS
of less than 12 Yrs. rank with
Lieutenants

PASS⁰ ASS⁰ PAYMASTERS
rank next after
Lieutenants

ASS⁰ PAYMASTERS
rank next after
Master

CHIEF ENGINEERS
of more than 12 Yrs.
rank with
Commanders

CHIEF ENGINEERS
of less than 12 Yrs,
rank with
Lieutenants

1ˢᵗ ASS⁰ ENGINEERS
rank next
after
Lieutenants

2ⁿᵈ ASS⁰ ENGINEERS
rank next
after
Master

3ʳᵈ ASS⁰ ENGINEERS
rank with
Midshipmen

Scale ⅓

The cloth between the gold lace of medical officers was cobalt blue; for paymasters, white; and for engineers, red. Unfortunately, red photographs black, so the red of the Engineer Corps is not visible, but the pattern is evident from the illustrations of the sleeves of surgeons and paymasters.

(Courtesy of the Naval Medical School.)

MIDSHIPMAN
(after graduation)

Gold Embroidered with Silver Anchor.

ENSIGN.

Shoulder Loops
Length to be not less than 5½ not more than 6 inches.

To be made to Ship & Unship the same as a Marine Officers knot.

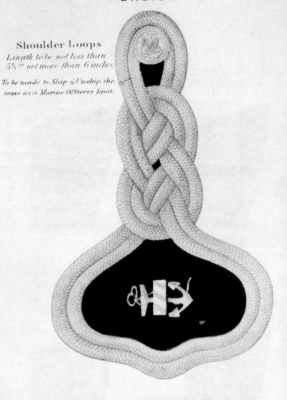

MASTER.

Shoulder Loops
Length to be not less than 5½ not more than 6 inches.

To be made to Ship & Unship the same as a Marine Officers knot.

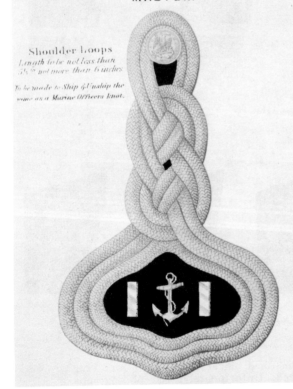

Cap Ornament
for all
Commissioned Officers.

Anchors embroidered in Gold only as much as shown no embroidery under the Shield. Extreme length of Anchor and Ring 1½ inch.
Shield and Eagle of Solid Silver (moveable)
Shield ⅝ths high and ½th wide

¼in Gold Cap Cord.

The cap device introduced in 1869 is like that of 1962 except that the spread eagle then was much smaller. The shoulder loops of 1869 were an innovation which had a comparatively short life. All officers above the rank of master wore epaulets in full dress and shoulder straps in undress. By 1883, all officers were permitted to wear epaulets and straps, except midshipmen at the Naval Academy The gold cap cord was replaced by a flat gold lace chin strap in 1883.

The order of April 1, 1869, modifying relative rank, is reflected in the text of the regulations and also in the illustrations. Surgeons, paymasters, and chief engineers were directed to wear the three half-inch stripes of a commander; surgeons, paymasters, and chief engineers of less than twelve years' service, the half-inch strip with a quarter-inch lace above it, worn by a lieutenant. Passed assistant surgeons, paymasters, and first assistant engineers wore the lace of a master; assistant surgeons, paymasters, and second assistant engineers, who now ranked "next after masters," wore the single quarter-inch lace of an ensign. Third assistant engineers, who ranked with midshipmen, had a gold cord, an eighth of an inch in diameter, around the sleeves—the same as worn by midshipmen after graduation. The distinctive corps colors—cobalt blue for medical officers, white for the Pay Corps, and red for engineers—were worn between the strips. When a staff officer ranked with a single-striped officer, the colored cloth showed a quarter of an inch on either side of the gold lace. This method of indicating the officers of the staff corps was continued until after World War I, when the cloth was removed and the staff corps devices were placed on the sleeve in the same position as the star of the Line.

The reduction in relative rank was also reflected in the description and illustrations of the shoulder ornaments. The highest relative rank granted any staff officer was that of commander; accordingly, the rank device was the silver oak leaf worn on either side of the corps device. For medical officers, the center of the shoulder strap and the middle of the frog of the epaulet were devoid of any insignia, since the Medical Corps had not as yet been assigned a device. Under the new regulations, no officer below the rank or assimilated rank of lieutenant was permitted to wear a cocked hat, epaulets, or shoulder straps. As shoulder ornaments, these junior officers wore gold-embroidered shoulder loops in full dress, undress, and service dress. The shoulder loops are shown in the page reproduced from the 1869 regulations. Staff officers holding relative rank with masters, ensigns, and midshipmen after graduation, wore similar loops, without any indication of their corps.

The only staff rank mentioned in the 1869 regulations besides those of surgeons, paymasters, and engineers, was that of secretaries to commanders of fleets and squadrons, who ranked with lieutenants. The secretaries' device remained the letter S in silver, and was worn on the shoulder straps and epaulets. However, no distinctive colored sleeve cloth was specified for this small group of non-combatant officers.

Further instructions for the cap device, which had been established for all commissioned officers by General Order No. 90 appeared in the 1869 uniform regulations. Warrant officers were directed to wear two gold anchors, crossed, on the front of the cap. This device has remained in use. Mates were to wear a plain vertical anchor, and clerks a foul anchor, in gold.

The 1869 uniform regulation made no specific mention of uniforms for three groups of commissioned officers—chaplains, naval constructors, and professors. They had been deprived of their relative rank by the order of April 1, 1869, but were permitted to wear certain articles of the Navy's dress. All commissioned officers were permitted to wear the frock and sack coats, and the jacket, with the uniform cap and new device. Since they were without relative rank, none of these staff officers could wear sleeve lace, shoulder ornaments, or cocked hats. They were identified as officers of the Navy by the Navy buttons on their coats and by their caps. The General Regulations that established the conditions under which various uniforms were to be worn contains the following statement, which had been included in earlier instructions: "Chaplains, when performing divine service, may wear either the vestments of the church to which they belong or the uniform prescribed in the regulations." From this, it is evident that the commissioned officers without relative rank could wear the dress of the Navy, except for the special full dress, without any indications of rank or grade.

The instructions for the dress of enlisted personnel remained basically those of the 1866 order, but modified the method of indicating the various classes of men. The tape on the blue collars of the blue and white frocks was eliminated, although the white star was retained. In place of the tape, the collars were to be "neatly stitched with white thread—two rows, one-eighth of an inch apart, the first row close to the edge." The tape around the cuffs was retained as a means of classification. One strip of tape indicated landsmen, coal-heavers, and boys; two strips, ordinary seamen and second-class firemen; three, seamen; and four, those petty officers who were not permitted to wear the blue double-breasted jacket.

Two new rating badges for enlisted men were introduced. Machinists wore as a distinguishing mark, a paddle-wheel, with a star above it, on both sleeves of the double-breasted jacket. Why a paddle-wheel was adopted instead of the screw propellor is difficult to imagine, since the Navy's steam-propelled vessels now employed the screw in all except the older craft. A rating of seaman gunner was established, and this group of jacketed petty officers wore the mark of gunners' mates—the two crossed cannon of 1866 with a star above—on both sleeves of the rolling-collared jacket. With these exceptions, the rating marks remained as they had been established in 1866.

One item in the 1869 regulations is noteworthy—the first working uniform prescribed by the Navy. For enlisted personnel this consisted of a pair of overalls and a jumper of white cotton duck. In the past, enlisted men had worn their oldest blues or whites for work which might soil the uniform. The use of steam for propulsion and machinery aboard ship made it mandatory that the men have for dirty work, clothing which could be washed aboard ship frequently and thus be kept reasonably presentable. Years later the Navy was to realize that a working uniform was needed by officers as well as men.

CHANGES TO 1869 UNIFORM REGULATIONS

When Congress on March 3, 1871 revised the relative rank of medical officers, paymasters, and engineers, and granted relative rank to chaplains and naval constructors, it was not necessary to issue a uniform change to cover the three groups of staff officers who had held relative rank prior to 1863. The 1869 regulation had described the devices and insignia to be worn by officers of the Medical, Paymaster, and Engineer corps, and had stated that staff officers were to wear the same lace and rank devices as the officers with whom they had relative rank. The same was not true for naval constructors and chaplains, both of whom had been omitted from the 1869 regulations. On March 21, 1872 a Circular directed that the uniforms for naval constructors and their assistants be the same as for the officers of the Line with whom they had relative rank, with the same exceptions that applied to other staff officers. The star of the Line was to be omitted from the sleeves, and in lieu thereof, dark violet cloth was to be worn between the bands of gold sleeve lace. A sprig of two live-oak leaves and an acorn, the device of 1866, was to be worn on epaulets and shoulder straps. The Navy made no provision for the uniforms of chaplains, even though relative rank had been restored in 1871.

The legislation of May 31, 1872 restoring relative rank to professors of mathematics was promptly followed by a uniform change. A Uniform Circular of June 12, 1872 provided professors with the same uniforms as those worn by the Line, and with insignia in accordance with their relative rank. The sleeve cloth was to be olive green, and the corps device— the sprig of a single oak leaf and an acorn—of silver, as specified in 1866.

A circular of February 7, 1873 introduced an officers' white cap for warm-weather use. Either a white cap or the blue cap with a white cover could be worn. A change of July 31, 1873 modified the sleeve lace of the special full-dress coat of flag officers. Only the Admiral and Vice Admiral were allowed to wear the elaborate oak-and-acorn motif, and rear admirals had to be content with gold lace strips in both full and undress—a band of two-inch lace with a half-inch strip above it, as is worn by a rear admiral today. The July 1873 order also introduced a coat for evening social occasions, tailored in the same manner as civilian full dress for evening. The tail coat was cut to the waist in front, and had five Navy buttons on each side. The same sleeve lace was worn on the evening dress coat as on the full-dress uniform coat, and epaulets could be worn or not at the officer's option. The present uniform regulations provide a similar evening dress coat, patterned on the current civilian style, with three buttons on each side, and with sleeve lace and corps devices on the sleeves. Now the shoulders are without ornaments, for epaulets have not been part of the uniform instructions since those of 1941. Their use was abandoned during World War II, and they have not been reinstated.

A revision of the uniform instructions dated August 12, 1874 brought the uniform of principal petty officers closer to that of officers. Earlier instructions had directed certain petty officers to wear double-breasted jackets, white shirts, and visored caps instead of the frocks of other enlisted men. Now masters-at-arms, machinists, yeomen, apothecaries, boilermakers, coppersmiths, ships' writers, and nurses were to wear a single-breasted sack coat like the one authorized for service dress for officers, with five medium-sized buttons. Today, all chief petty officers wear a blue service coat of the same cut as officers.

It will be recalled that when the special full-dress body coat was reinstated in 1866, along with the cocked hat and epaulets, the gold-laced trousers of 1852 were not worn. A Uniform Circular of November 7, 1874 directed that all officers wear gold-laced trousers with both the special full-dress and the full-dress frock coat. The lace was to be of the same width as that worn on the collars of the special full-dress coat. This order is perfectly clear in regard to the width of the trouser lace for all except flag officers. The 1869 order had not prescribed lace for the collar of the body coat for the Admiral, Vice Admiral, and rear admirals, but instead directed that the collar be decorated with oak-leaf and acorn embroidery. It can only be assumed, in the absence of more specific instructions, that the lace for admirals was to be the width of the collar embroidery, an inch and a half. All officers from commodores through commanders wore one-inch trouser lace; all with the rank of lieutenant commander through ensign, half-inch lace. Staff officers wore a strip the same width as the line officers with whom they had relative rank. This same order modified the sleeve lace of lieutenant commanders and lieutenants, and officers of the same relative ranks. The first of these were directed to wear two strips of half-inch lace, with a quarter-inch strip between them; lieutenants, two strips of half-inch lace. The spacing between strips was to be a quarter of an inch. This sleeve lace arrangement is now used to denote lieutenant commanders and lieutenants.

General Order No. 202 of January 20, 1876 modified the dress of enlisted men. The use of white tape on frock collars and cuffs had been introduced in 1866 to identify the various classes of enlisted personnel; the 1869 regulations had eliminated the white tape from the collars, leaving the sleeve tapes as before. The new order directed that the frocks of all enlisted men have three rows of tape three-sixteenths of an inch wide on the collars, retaining the white star at the corners. This was decorative only; the number of rows of tape on the cuffs indicated a man's class.

UNIFORM REGULATIONS OF 1876

It had been the practice of the Navy Department to issue uniform instructions as separate publications—instructions, orders, changes—and then later to incorporate them into the next edition of the official Navy Regulations. In those approved on August 7, 1876, Section VIII—"Uniform" merely specified when and how the uniform was to be worn. The details were contained in "Appendix No. 3, Uniform Regulations of the United States Navy." It would appear that in 1876 the uniform instructions were not issued as a separate publication, as they had been prior to and have been since that date. As a result, students of naval dress often overlook this particular instruction.

Fundamentally, this was a revision of the 1869 order, incorporating the changes issued since 1869. One change was in the collar decoration of the special full-dress coat of rear admirals. The oak-leaf and acorn embroidery was changed to a one-inch strip of gold lace—the same width as worn by officers of the rank of commodore through commander under the 1869 order. The major change in the dress of enlisted personnel related to the sack coat authorized for eight ratings of petty officer in 1874. Now the sack coat could be worn only by masters-at-arms, machinists, and apothecaries. The question of which petty officers were permitted to wear sack coats was to be simplified some years later when the rating of chief petty officer was authorized.

CHANGES TO THE UNIFORM REGULATIONS OF 1876

In an order of January 16, 1877, the sack coat introduced in 1865 was replaced by a new service coat. The 1865 service coat had been tailored like the civilian sack coat in 1865; the new service coat was modeled on the tight-fitting military tunic in vogue in the 1870's. It will be recalled that the Navy's first undress coats had been the same as those for full dress, without lace or embroidery, and that in 1830 the undress coat was described as "made according to the prevailing fashion of citizens of the time." The frock coat of 1852 was similar to that worn by civilians, and as civilian fashions changed, the Navy had followed them for the style of the service coat. The sack coat of 1865 is an example. However, in 1877 the new coat was military rather than civilian in cut.

The new service coat was to be worn after July 1, 1878 by all commissioned officers and midshipmen who had graduated from the Naval Academy, and by cadet midshipmen and cadet engineers. It was described as single-breasted, with a fly front and a standing collar, and fitting close to the body. This is the coat worn in World War I and not abolished until afterward, when the double-breasted, roll-collared coat now worn was introduced. The style of the 1877 coat is still reflected in the Navy's white service coat—a snug-fitting one with a standing collar. The service coat had lustrous black braid on the standing collar, on the front edge, around the bottom, and up the back seams. Rank was indicated by strips of black braid instead of by gold lace as on other blue coats, and the star of the Line was omitted. Rank was also indicated by placing the rank insignia used on the epaulets and shoulder straps, embroidered in high relief, on either side of the standing collar. Instead of the gold devices of the shoulder ornaments, lieutenants wore two silver bars, masters a single silver bar. Eventually, silver would be used for the grade ornaments of both these two groups of officers. Since there was no indication of corps on either the collar or the cuffs of the service coat, it was impossible to differentiate between Line and Staff. This must have been confusing in that earlier orders had ordered devices to be worn on the collars of overcoats and sack coats with both rank and corps indicated—a satisfactory system. The senior officers of the Navy of 1877 had served in the Civil War and should have remembered how the matter was handled then.

The Navy took another step toward uniformity in dress in July 1878, when paymasters' clerks were authorized to wear the new service coat, and in October, when the forward warrant officers were directed to do likewise. Line warrants—boatswains and gunners—were directed to wear a gold-embroidered star on either sleeve, and a similar silver star on either side of the collar. The staff warrant officers—carpenters, sailmakers, and paymasters' stewards—omitted the star from the sleeves and displayed embroidered diamonds on the collar. On June 11, 1880 mates were ordered to discard the former sack coat for the new single-breasted service coat, with stars on the cuffs and collar.

A Uniform Circular of June 10, 1881 prescribed a rating badge more representative of the steam Navy for petty officers of the engineering force —a screw propeller superimposed on a foul anchor. The rating of machinist was abolished, and its mark, a paddle-wheel, disappeared.

A change of June 21, 1881 modified the dress of ensigns and staff officers of the same relative rank. Shoulder knots were to be worn only in full dress, and shoulder straps were prescribed for undress. The straps were to be worn with the corps device in the center, and without end devices. It would not be until the twentieth century that ensigns were identified by a single gold bar. Now ensigns were permitted to wear cocked hats with a loop of two bullions. This was to be the final change in the arrangement over the cockades of cocked hats. On August 10, 1881 the sleeve lace was brought into line with the practice of today. Masters had a strip of half-inch lace, with a quarter-inch strip above it—the indication at present of a lieutenant, junior grade—and ensigns were permitted to wear a single strip half an inch wide instead of the quarter-inch strip first authorized in 1862.

A uniform was authorized for the Civil Engineers of the Navy in 1881, fourteen years after they had been given commissioned status, and six months from the day they had finally been given relative rank. A Uniform Circular of August 24, 1881 described the distinctive marks and devices as follows:

> The sleeve lace will be light blue velvet.
> Shoulder-straps: border embroidered gold, body light blue cloth, and the letters C.E. (Old English) embroidered in silver in the center.
> The same letters will be similarly embroidered on the frogs of epaulets.

Prescribing light blue cloth for the background of the shoulder straps was a departure from the pattern that had developed since the introduction of shoulder straps before the Civil War. In all previous orders, the background of the straps had been Navy blue. In directing that the device of the Civil Engineer Corps be the letters C.E., the Navy reverted to a pattern first established in 1847, when the letters M.D. and P.D. were used to indicate officers of the Medical and Purser Departments respectively. Gradually, from 1847 on, more and more officers of the staff corps were directed to wear corps devices incorporating oak leaves and acorns. In 1881, all staff corps devices except those of the Medical Corps, which had no device, and of civil engineers, were of the leaf-and-acorn motif.

Although the illustration depicts the dress of officers of the Civil Engineer Corps in 1881, the uniforms are typical of all officers of the period. The civil engineer with the rank of commander, on the left, is in full dress. His corps is identified by the light blue cloth between the gold sleeve lace and by the insignia of the corps on the epaulets. The vignette in the center shows the silver corps device in the center, with the silver oak leaves of a commander on either side. The same frock coat was worn in undress with shoulder straps replacing the epaulets, plain trousers, and a cap. The shoulder strap of a civil engineer of the relative rank of captain is shown upper left. The light blue background was changed to dark blue in 1883.

The right hand figure could be any officer of the United States Navy of the rank or relative rank of lieutenant. The two strips of black braid and the two silver bars on the collar indicate rank; there is no corps device. The uniform instruction of 1883 directed that the corps device be placed on the collar behind the rank insignia, as shown in the upper right detail.

A new uniform regulation, approved November 1, 1883 by Secretary of the Navy William E. Chandler, covered the dress of officers only. The instructions followed those of the modified 1876 order, with some innovations. A white service coat was introduced, of the same pattern as the 1877 blue coat but with white braid trimming and sleeve stripes. No rank devices were worn on the collar. "Whites" were to be worn with either a white cap or a white tropical helmet. Another modification concerned the blue service coat. When this was introduced in 1877, no provision had been made to indicate the wearer's corps. The same system of collar devices as that employed in 1865, when the sack coat was introduced, was to be employed: in general, the rank device was to be placed on either side of the collar, with a corps device behind it. The exception to this pattern was that the Admiral wore the four silver stars of his rank, with a gold foul anchor under each of the outer stars.

After so many years of being distinguished by the absence of a corps device, medical officers were directed to wear a "spread oak leaf embroidered in dead gold, with an acorn embroidered in silver on it" as a corps device. This is the present-day insignia of the Medical Corps, and the basis for all other devices worn by officers of the Bureau of Medicine and Surgery. The distinctive colored cloth to be worn between the strips of gold sleeve lace was changed, from the cobalt blue assigned medical officers in 1869 to dark maroon.

A new cap device was ordered for all commissioned officers and midshipmen who had graduated from the Academy: "a silver shield, emblazoned paleways, of thirteen pieces, with a chief strewn with stars surmounted by a silver spread eagle, the whole being placed upon two crossed foul anchors embroidered in gold." The basic difference between the 1883 cap device and that of 1962 is that whereas originally the eagle was facing left (sinister), since 1941 it has faced to the right (dexter).

The cap device for warrant officers, mates, and pay clerks consisted of two crossed foul anchors, such as are worn by warrant officers at present. Another change concerned warrant officers; those with twenty or more years of service had the frock coat collar devices in silver, and those of less than twenty years had the same devices embroidered in gold. Boatswains wore two crossed foul anchors; gunners a flaming spherical shell; carpenters a chevron, point down (a carpenter's square); mates a binocular glass; and pay clerks, the oak-leaf and acorn device of the Paymaster's Corps.

The decoration of the cocked hat was finally changed. The loops of bullions over the cockades were replaced by a loop of flat gold lace, the same width as worn on the standing collar of the special full-dress body coat. Flag officers' cocked hats were bound on the outer rims of the fans with gold lace, and the trim for those of all other officers was black silk. From this time on up until the hats were abolished after World War II, the decorations of cocked hats were unchanged.

UNIFORM REGULATIONS OF 1886

A new uniform regulation, illustrated in color, was approved by Secretary of the Navy W. C. Whitney on July 1, 1885. Issued by the Government Printing Office in 1886, it is commonly known as the Regulation of that year. The portion on officers' dress is practically identical with that issued in 1883. The section on enlisted men's dress was completely illustrated for the first time, so that it is very simple to follow the printed uniform descriptions. These illustrations show all the various uniforms, the sleeve marks, caps, hats, foul weather clothing, and working dress.

In line with the Regulation Circular of January 1885, which had divided petty officers into classes, the 1886 uniform instructions established a new series of rating badges. That for first-class petty officers was a chevron of three stripes, points down, with a spread eagle above the chevron. The specialty mark was placed on a red lozenge, and was set between the eagle and the interior angle of the lozenge. An exception to this design was made to indicate masters-at-arms, the principal first-class petty officers: he had the same three-stripe chevron, but with an arch consisting of three stripes of cloth connecting the upper ends of the chevron, and the spread eagle placed on the arch. The red lozenge of the other first-class petty officers was omitted, and the specialty mark, a large five-pointed star, was placed between the eagle and the inner angle of the chevron. Petty officers second class were identified by the same badge as first-class petty officers—the three-stripe chevron and eagle—without the lozenge under the specialty mark. Petty officers third class wore the same badge, with only two stripes in the chevron. On both blue and white uniforms the chevrons, the arch of the master-at-arms, and the lozenge of first-class petty officers were in red. The eagle and specialty marks were in white cloth on blue clothing, and in blue on white.

Rating badges of this pattern were worn until General Order No. 431 of September 24, 1894 made provision for the rating of chief petty officer. Under the 1894 change, the rating badges were similar to those used in 1962, except that the eagle faced to the left, instead of to the right as it does today. The arch, originally worn only by masters-at-arms,

The tailed-body coat, the special full dress, of the 1886 Uniform Regulations is eleven uniform regulations removed from the first blue and gold full dress coat of 1802, but is similar in many respects. All officers from rear admirals to ensigns wore sleeve lace of the same arrangement as the current instructions; but today, the colored corps-cloth has been replaced by a corps device above the upper stripe. The admiral and vice admiral wore the live-oak embroidery of 1869 on the cuffs and collar instead of lace in special full dress.

The frock coat of 1886 was similar to that of 1852 with minor changes in cut to follow the tailoring styles of the middle eighties. The frock coat was the multi-purpose coat of the Navy as it had been during the Civil War. It was worn with epaulets, cocked hat, and gold-laced trousers for full dress; with epaulets, plain blue or white trousers, and either a cocked hat or a white helmet for dress; and with shoulder straps, blue or white trousers, and cap or white helmet for undress.

The white service-coat of 1886 was patterned on the blue service-coat of 1877 and trimmed with white braid. Rank was indicated by means of white-braid sleeve-stripes. The embroidered devices of the collar of the blue coat were omitted. Since the colored cloth of the staff corps was omitted from the sleeves and corps devices from the collar, there was no way to determine an officer's specialty.

PLATE I

Only first-class petty officers were permitted to wear double breasted sack coats, the predecessors of the current chief petty officer's coats. Only the master-at-arms wore the rating badge of first-class petty officers, with the arch of three stripes connecting the upper ends of the chevron. The location of the badge on the right arm indicates that the petty officer is assigned to the starboard watch. The open figure-eight knot indicates that the wearer was formerly an apprentice seaman. The cap device is the same pattern as the buttons, a spread eagle perched on the stock of a horizontal anchor, surrounded by a circle of thirteen stars.

The second-class boatswain's mate is wearing the white uniform of all enlisted men except first-class petty officers, bandsmen, and mess men. The uniform was like the blue frock and trousers, but the white overshirt was worn outside the trousers instead of being tucked in. The petty officer's badge on the left sleeve indicates a member of the port watch. The three chevrons of a second-class petty officer were red, and, on whites, the eagle and the crossed-anchor specialty mark were blue. The ex-apprentice mark for all men, below first-class petty officers, was worn below the neck-opening of the jumper. The three stripes of white braid indicate second- and third-class petty officers and seamen second-class. The white canvas hat was the warm-weather head piece of all enlisted men.

PLATE XIV

FIG 1

FIG 2

In 1886 only a master-at-arms had an arch of three stripes, connecting the upper ends of the chevron of the petty officers' badge. When the rating of chief petty officer was established in 1894, the arch became the mark of chiefs. The lower figure shows the badge of other first-class petty officers, the three striped chevron without the arch but with the rating mark placed on a red lozenge. Petty officers second class wore the same badge, without the lozenge. Third-class petty officers had only two stripes in the chevron and no lozenge under the specialty mark.

David Dixon Porter, who became admiral of the Navy upon the death of Admiral Farragut in 1870, is shown in the full dress uniform of his rank as prescribed in 1869 for Admiral Farragut. The only difference between Porter's and Farragut's uniforms is that the latter wore his personal star, two inches in diameter with the steam frigate *Hartford* in silver in the center. Porter's star is one inch in diameter, the same as worn by all other line officers. Although partially obscured by the beard, the standing collar was decorated with gold embroidery similar to that of the sleeves and full dress belt.

(Army Signal Corps Photo, Brady Collection, National Archives.)

was reduced to a single strip of cloth, and prescribed for all chief petty officers. The stripes of the chevron were separated by a quarter of an inch instead of being side by side as in 1886. The current petty officers' devices are shown in the vignette.

Petty officer rating badges, 1962, Chief, First class, Second class, Third class.

All first-class petty officers were directed to wear dark, Navy-blue double-breasted sack coats with rolling collars, and rows of five gilt buttons. Prior to the creation of three classes of petty officers, principal or leading petty officers had, from time to time, been permitted to wear coats or jackets in contrast to the frocks of other enlisted men. In line with the authorization of a white service dress for officers, first-class petty officers were permitted to wear white duck sack coats in summer. With blue uniforms, a visored blue cap was worn, and with whites a canvas hat was permitted. The device for the blue cap was a bronze disk showing a spread eagle perched on the stock of a horizontal anchor, the whole surrounded by a circle of thirteen stars and edged with a cable.

Other petty officers wore the same blue overshirt or white jumper, —the "frocks" of earlier orders—as other enlisted men. The blue overshirt was worn tucked inside the waistband of the trousers, the white jumper hanging loose. The collar and cuffs of the white jumper were covered with thin Navy-blue flannel. The collar of both the blue overshirt and the white jumper were banded with three rows of white tape and had a white-embroidered star in the corners. Three stripes of white tape on the cuffs indicated second- and third-class petty officers and seamen first class; two strips of tape, second-class seamen; and a single tape, seamen third class.

Chaplains, after being permitted to wear a Navy uniform under the 1876 order, were again ordered to wear civilian clothing. The 1886 regulations read, "Chaplains shall wear the dress commonly worn by clergymen, consisting of black or dark navy-blue cloth, and black, low-crowned soft felt hat." It must have been somewhat expensive to serve as a chaplain of the United States Navy. Under one order he had to buy a uniform, and often under the next, once again, to buy civilian clothing.

CHANGES TO THE UNIFORM REGULATIONS OF 1886

When the new rating of chief petty officer was established in 1894, General Order No. 431 of September 24, 1894 was issued to modify the rating badges of petty officers. The stripes of the red chevron were to be separated by a quarter of an inch instead of being side by side as in 1886, and above these chief petty officers now wore one stripe joined with the ends of the upper stripe to form an arc of a circle. The spread eagle rested on the center of the top of the arch. The specialty mark was placed between the angle of the upper chevron and the eagle. This rating badge is still employed by the Navy. Petty officers first class had three stripes in the chevron; those of the second class, two stripes; and those of the third class, one stripe. These class marks for petty officers are still in use.

Under the 1886 regulation, all commissioned officers wore the same cap and cap device. On June 12, 1897 Circular No. 79 introduced embroidered visors for senior officers, similar to those worn today. The visors of the caps of rear admirals, commodores, captains, and commanders were to be covered with dark blue cloth. All other commissioned officers were to wear caps with black patent leather visors. The visors of caps of line rear admirals and commodores were to be embroidered "all around"—actually, all over—with oak leaves and acorns. Staff officers of corresponding relative rank had a band of gold embroidery half an inch wide around the front edge and back of the visor, the blue of the background showing in between. Line captains and commanders had a border of oak leaves and acorns on the front edge of the visor only, and staff officers of corresponding relative rank had a half-inch band around the front. The oak-leaf and acorn motif had its origin in the decoration prescribed for the full-dress body coat of 1830. In the visor ornamentation, the change elaborated the methods of differentiating between Line and Staff.

The 1897 change modified the service coat, for now the sleeve decoration of the blue coat was changed from black braid to the same gold lace worn on full-dress and frock coats. Officers of the Line displayed the star; those of the Staff, the colored cloth of their corps between

The men of the U.S.S. *Maine* are shown in a variety of dress of the pre–Spanish-American War period. Chief petty officers can be identified by the double-breasted sack coats and visored caps; Marines by their kepis. Although most of the men are in blues, some are wearing pea jackets, and others are in working dress. The two men center and the man seated in the right foreground are in the originally unbleached but now dirty overall jumpers.

(*Detroit Photographic Company Collection, the Library of Congress.*)

apt. Clark,
and Naval Cadet Overstreet
atching a successful shot fired by
e Oregon at the Colon.

Captain Clark, skipper of the U.S.S. *Oregon*, and some of his staff are watching the effect of the ship's fire on the Spanish battleship *Cristobal Colon*, at Santiago. The service whites were the only uniform suitable for warm-weather wear, but in this photograph, they look anything but military. None of the officers is wearing the shoulder straps prescribed for the white service coat, so there is no way to identify rank. The bill of the captain's cap does appear to have the gold embroidery introduced in June, 1897, but a white cap-cover has covered the cap device.

(*Official Navy Photo.*)

the stripes. The white service coat as introduced in 1883 had used white braid for sleeve lace, and no collar insignia. Now, shoulder straps were to be worn on the white coat to indicate an officer's rank and corps.

Another section of this order concerned chief petty officers. The bronze cap device of 1886 was changed to a gilt foul anchor, with the letters *U.S.N.* in silver. A chief petty officer today wears a similar device.

UNIFORM REGULATION OF 1897

"Regulations governing the Uniform of Commissioned Officers, Warrant Officers, and Enlisted Men of the Navy of the United States," approved by Secretary John D. Long on July 1, 1897, brought the 1886 instructions up to date and, as usual, introduced some new material. Throughout the order the words "for all commissioned officers, except chaplains" appear again and again. As in 1886, chaplains were to wear the dress of clergymen, but now they were permitted a "navy cap with black buttons and strap, and without ornaments . . ." This certainly had little Navy connotation, for the same sort of cap might be worn by merchant seamen or yachtsmen. Where the restricting phrase might have been overlooked in sections of the order, chaplains were governed by the general clause which denied them the privilege of wearing the Navy's uniform.

Since there were no fundamental changes in the uniform to be worn by officers, the 1897 instruction contained no illustrations of officer personnel. It did contain colored plates of the clothing and accessories to be worn by enlisted men, including the petty officers' rating badges authorized in 1894. Among these were fifteen specialty marks, more than were needed in the period of transition from sail to steam of 1866, but still far fewer than those required to handle the complicated weapons, machinery, and equipment of the atomic-age Navy.

CHANGES TO 1897 REGULATIONS

When the Hospital Corps was created by an Act of Congress on June 17, 1898, a uniform change was necessary. General Order No. 493 of June 25, 1898 changed the rating of apothecary to that of hospital steward, and that of bayman to hospital apprentice. Hospital stewards, rated as chief petty officers, replaced the caduceus of the apothecary with a Geneva cross in silver. Hospital apprentices first class, who rated as petty officers third class, used a red Geneva cross as a specialty mark, placed between the single red chevron and the spread eagle. Other hospital apprentices were classed with seamen second class, and wore a red cross on the left arm of the blue overshirt or white jumper. Pharmacists were directed to wear the uniforms of warrant officers, with a Geneva cross in gold as a collar device.

The "Addenda to Uniform Regulations, 1897," dated December 23, again allowed chaplains to wear a dress which indicated their affiliation with the United States Navy. The general proviso which had been used in most earlier uniform instructions—"while performing divine services, chaplains may wear the dress worn by clergymen of their respective churches"—was restored. Chaplains were not permitted to wear the special full-dress body coat, but were permitted to possess frock and service coats. The frock coat did not have the double-breasted cut, with Navy buttons, of other officers, but was single-breasted, with black covered buttons. Chaplains had not worn such frock coats since the early part of the Civil War.

The sleeve ornaments for the frock and service coats of chaplains were strips of lustrous black braid instead of the gold lace of other commissioned officers. The corps device to be worn on the standing collar of the blue service coat was the silver cross, in an inclined position, specified by Secretary Welles in 1863. Even the visor decorations reflected the unique status of chaplains. Those of the relative rank of captain or commander wore a border of black mohair instead of the gold lace of other staff officers. The chin strap was black in lieu of gold. Since chaplains could not wear epaulets, cocked hats, or shoulder straps, they were in effect "second class" naval officers where their dress was concerned.

UNIFORM INSTRUCTIONS OF 1899

The rather sweeping uniform modifications of May 1899 do not represent a new uniform regulation, but are rather a revision of the existing 1897 order. Secretary Long's forwarding letter of May 8, 1899 reads: "Make the following changes in regulations governing the uniform of commissioned officers, warrant officers, and enlisted men of the Navy of the United States, 1897, to go into effect as soon after the receipt of this circular as officers are able to provide themselves with the uniform required." The changes covering the dress of the Admiral (for this rank had been newly reinstated with the appointment of George Dewey), chaplains, and warrant officers (since the rank of chief warrant officer had been established), all required modifications of the original text in so many places that the order of 1897 was revised and reprinted. As a result of this reprinting, a Uniform Regulation of 1899 has evolved. Although it might more properly be given the title of "Uniform Regulations, 1897 (Revised)," for simplicity it will be referred to hereafter as the 1899 regulation.

In the revision, pages 5 through 18 of the 1897 order were reprinted and pages 18a, 18b, 18c, and 19 were added. The changes in the section on enlisted men were minor, so only page 36 was reprinted. In the illustrations of specialty marks, the caduceus was replaced by the newly authorized Geneva cross.

The 1899 regulation incorporated the changes ordered between July 1897 and May 1899, and made some further modifications. For Admiral Dewey, sleeve insignia consisting of two strips of two-inch lace with a one-inch strip between them, and the standard star of the Line was prescribed. This was the same lace worn formerly by Admiral Porter. On the shoulder ornaments the four silver stars, with a gold foul anchor under each of the two outer stars, were reinstated.

Another change concerned all officers other than chaplains, chief warrant and warrant officers, mates, and clerks. Instead of shoulder straps for the shoulders of the white service coat and the overcoat, shoulder marks were authorized. The shoulder marks of 1899 were similar to those worn today and known unofficially as "shoulder boards." The 1899 shoulder marks were made of blue cloth, stiffened with hair cloth and lined with black silk. They extended from the top of the sleeve seam to the base of the collar, ending in a triangular peak fastened with a small button. They were practically identical with those of 1962, except for the stiffening. The marks of flag officers were covered with gold lace, with a one-eighth-inch border of blue cloth. Staff officers of the relative rank of rear admiral or commodore had a similar border around the shoulder marks, made, however, of the colored cloth designating the corps. The devices of the shoulder marks were identical to those worn on the epaulets and shoulder straps.

The shoulder marks to be worn by officers from the rank of captain to ensign displayed the same arrangement of lace strips as worn on the arms of blue coats. Line officers wore a star above the upper lace strip; staff officers showed the colored cloth of their corps between strips.

The creation of the commissioned grade of chief warrant officer in 1899 was reflected in the 1899 order. Chief boatswains, gunners, carpenters, and sailmakers were directed to show a single strip of half-inch lace, woven with dark blue silk thread at intervals of two inches, the width of the blue portion being half an inch. This is the sleeve lace now worn by commissioned warrant officers. The collar devices for the frock and service coats of chief warrant officers were to be of silver, as prescribed for warrant officers of more than twenty years' service in 1883. The devices for junior warrant officers were still to be in gold embroidery.

CHANGES TO 1899 REGULATIONS

"Addenda to Uniform Regulations No. 1" of July 12, 1899 directed that the word "relative" be stricken from the 1899 edition of the uniform instructions. This of course was in line with the ruling of 1899 giving staff officers rank instead of relative rank. Another change, effective January 5, 1900, reflected the amalgamation of members of the Engineer Corps into the Line. The cross of four oak leaves was deleted from the uniform regulations and removed from the sleeves, collars, and shoulder ornaments of engineers. They now wore the devices of the Line—the star on the sleeves and shoulder marks, and the anchor on the collar of the service coat, the epaulets, and the shoulder straps. Now the device of the officers who, when the *Fulton* was being fitted out in 1836, had become a somewhat unofficial part of the Navy, could be worn only by officers of the Engineer Corps who had retired prior to the 1899 act.

GENERAL ORDER NO. 48

For all intents and purposes, General Order No. 48 of June 6, 1901, was a new uniform instruction. The promulgating letter read in part:

The following regulations are established for uniforms for officers and enlisted men of the United States Navy.

The Department has in preparation plates illustrating these regulations, and at an early date will republish these regulations with plates in book form. References herein to numbered plates refer to the uniform regulations of 1897, other references to plates are to those to be published when these regulations are reissued in book form.

The new instructions were to become effective on July 1, 1902, but on February 27, 1902 General Order, No. 48 (Revised) was issued, making some minor changes in the original instructions. The effective date was still to be July 1, 1902. These instructions actually remained in effect until 1905, when a new uniform regulation was published.

The innovations of General Order No. 48 and the subsequent re-vision were comparatively few. The style of the white service coat was changed from the fly-front, braid-decorated one of 1883 to that worn at present. The general cut of the coat and the standing collar were to be retained, but the coat was to be fastened with five gilt buttons and the white braid decoration was eliminated. The coat was to be worn with shoulder marks as under the previous order. The white coat when worn by chaplains was to have five white composition buttons instead of the Navy buttons, and the shoulder marks were to be omitted.

As a result of the Spanish-American War, the United States now controlled territory in the Caribbean and the southern Pacific, where blue evening dress uniforms would have been most uncomfortable. Ac-cordingly, a white mess jacket was introduced for "ordinary social oc-casions in the evening to which officers are invited in their official capacity, and where hot weather or other circumstances make it appropri-ate." The jacket was to be worn with either white or blue trousers, and with shoulder marks, except by chaplains.

The same order permitted chief warrant officers to wear the cap device of commissioned officers, a practice still in effect. Enlisted men were authorized to wear blue denim jumpers and trousers as a working suit for such duties as would soil the blue or white uniforms.

A correction to General Order No. 48 (Revised), of October 22, 1902, did permit chaplains to wear shoulder marks on the white-buttoned mess jacket and white service coat, the "same as for line officers with whom they rank, but without the stars, and stripes to be of lustrous black mohair braid, instead of gold lace." Black braid on dark blue shoulder marks would not go far in the way of identification, since there was no contrast; but at least chaplains were now distinguished from mess at-tendants, who wore a similar white coat with a fly front.

UNIFORM REGULATIONS OF 1905

The "Regulations Governing the Uniform of Commissioned Officers, Warrant Officers, and Enlisted Men in the Navy of the United States, 1905" when finally approved on January 21, 1905, were basically those of General Order No. 48 with the various revisions. Shoulder straps were abolished, and have not been worn by the Navy since then. For dress uniforms the Army still employs shoulder straps to replace the pin-on shoulder ornaments of service uniforms. This procedure is not necessary in the Navy, for sleeve lace is employed to show both rank and corps when blue or forestry green aviation uniforms are worn. Shoulder marks are used to show rank and corps on whites and khakis, since these uniforms are without sleeve lace. Another change concerned the device of the Civil Engineer Corps. The insignia was changed to "two crossed silver sprigs, each composed of two live oak leaves, and an acorn." It would appear certain that the device was designed by a civil

Device of the Civil Engineer Corps, 1905.

engineer, for the crossed sprigs look more like a pair of crossed dividers than anything botanical! The stylized oak leaves, with an acorn at the end, closely resemble the legs of dividers, with the acorn taking the place of an adjusting screw. The device was worn on epaulets, on shoulder marks, and behind the rank device on the blue service dress collar. With the abolishment of the original *C.E.* insignia, all officers of the staff corps except chaplains wore devices based on oak leaves and acorns.

CHANGES TO THE 1905 REGULATIONS

The only notable changes in the 1905 uniform regulations are No. 3, of March 24, 1908, and No. 4, of October 12, 1908. The first permitted chaplains to wear gilt Navy buttons instead of the flat white or black buttons of the original order, and the second directed them to wear the same double-breasted frock coat as other officers in lieu of the single-breasted coat of 1905. Little by little, the distinctions between Line and Staff, and between classes of officers, were being abolished.

UNIFORM REGULATIONS OF 1913

New uniform regulations approved on January 25, 1913 by Secretary of the Navy G. von L. Meyer were basically those of the previous order, with comparatively few innovations. Again, chaplains were required to wear a single-breasted frock coat. It is to be hoped that chaplains had not disposed of the single-breasted frock coats of the 1905 order when they acquired the double-breasted coats ordered by the 1908 change. There

Rear Admiral Mordecai T. Endicott, who was appointed Chief of the Bureau of Yards and Docks on April 4, 1898, was the first officer of the Civil Engineer Corps to hold this position. From the creation of the Bureau in 1842, a line officer had served as Chief. The white service uniform displays the shoulder marks of a rear admiral with the 1905 device of the Civil Engineer Corps replacing the foul anchor of line rear admirals. The gold lace on the visor was typical of all staff flag-officers, the border of gold lace replacing the oak-leaf and acorn embroidery of the Line.

(Courtesy of the Bureau of Yards and Docks.)

As an illustration of the special full-dress uniform of 1913, a photograph of Admiral George Dewey is used. The uniform is similar in style to that first prescribed in 1802, and in decoration to the full dress coat of 1852. Special full dress was not worn during World War I and was not reinstated after the war, it thus disappeared from the Navy's wardrobe.

The frock coat as pictured and described in the 1913 Uniform Regulations is typical of the coat from 1913 until it was omitted from the regulations of 1947. Generally, it follows the pattern of the undress coat introduced in 1852 except that it was longer and had five buttons in each row instead of the original nine. The frock coat was worn with epaulets, laced trousers, and cocked hat for full dress; epaulets, plain trousers, and cocked hat for dress; and as shown for undress.

The lieutenant (junior grade) in the blue service uniform of 1913 was an aide to the Secretary of the Navy or a senior naval officer, for the aiguillettes are over the left shoulder. If they had been on the right side, he would have been assigned to the White House. The service coat is that introduced in 1877, with the sleeve lace as prescribed in 1897 instead of the black braid of the original order. A staff officer wore the same coat but showed the distinctive colored cloth of his corps between the sleeve stripes, without the star, and with the corps device on the collar in lieu of the anchor of the Line.

The rating badge of the chief petty officer on the left is the type introduced in 1894, and the specialty mark is the star of a master-at-arms. The open figure-eight knot indicates that the chief is an ex-apprentice. The two stripes on the left sleeve mean that he has served two enlistments and is on the third. The uniform of the first-class boatswain's mate on the right is typical of the blues of all enlisted men. His petty-officer badge shows the mark of a boatswain, two crossed anchors. Three strips of braid on the cuffs indicated petty officers, first, second and third class; ship's cooks, first and second class; seamen, hospital apprentices, and bakers, first class. Two strips of braid were used to identify seamen second class; ship's cooks, third and fourth class; hospital apprentices, and bakers second class. Seamen third class and mess attendants had a single strip.

The uniform worn by Lieutenant Commander John Codman Soley of the Massachusetts Naval Militia is very similar to that of the regular Navy after 1897, when the black braid sleeve stripes were replaced by gold lace. The cap device has the coat of arms of Massachusetts on the crossed anchors, as recommended by the 1913 Navy uniform instructions, instead of the shield and spread eagle of the Navy cap device. The visor of the cap is entirely different from that of the Navy, for only officers of the rank of commander and above had gold embroidery (Line officers) or flat gold lace (Staff officers).

(*Official Navy Photo.*)

were to be six black covered buttons in a single row in contrast to the two rows of five Navy buttons on the frock coats of other officers. Here we have a twentieth-century example of the rank-by-buttons system used in the nineteenth. The inclined cross was displayed on either side of the collar in the same manner as the devices worn by warrant officers. Rank was indicated by stripes of black braid on the sleeves of blue coats.

A new but short-lived feature appeared in the 1913 order. Shoulder marks were abolished; in their stead, rank was to be shown on the sleeves of the overcoat by means of black braid. On the shoulders of white service coats and mess jackets, metal devices were to be employed to show both rank and corps. White coats were to be made with a cloth strap of the coat material, let in at the sleeve head seam, and fastened near the collar by a button. Eyelets were to be provided to receive the pin-on devices. This is the first use of the metal insignia now worn on shirts of khaki, on tropical uniforms, and on raincoats by officers of the Navy.

The section of the General Regulations concerned with "working dress," which preceded the detailed description of the 1913 uniform, is worth a review. It was during the life of the 1913 regulations that the Navy's first working uniform came into being. The dungarees of earlier orders could be worn by both officers and men as a complete suit, with the cap or hat of the day. Officers and men aboard submarines could wear dungarees, and those engaged in work which would damage a regular uniform were permitted to wear dungarees under limited circumstances. In general the suits could be worn only in the engine rooms, in turrets, or in machinery spaces below decks.

Chapter 9 of the 1913 regulations was devoted to "General Regulations Governing the Uniforms of the Naval Militia." In January 1913 the Navy Department had no control of the naval militias of the states such as the War Department did of the land militia forces. As a result, the instructions read: "It being desirable that the same practice shall be followed by both the Navy and the Naval Militia in all matters of service, the Department *recommends* that the regulations contained herein governing naval uniforms shall be followed as closely as possible by the several Naval Militia organizations, subject to the modifications *recommended* in this and the two following chapters." (Italics supplied.) Incidentally, there were no "two following chapters"!

The exceptions recommended to the dress of officers and men of the Navy were attempts to differentiate between regular and non-regular components of the Navy. Line officers of the militia were to replace the star of the Navy Line with a gold foul anchor. Militia staff officers were to wear the colored cloth of their corps, but the cloth was to show a break of an inch and a quarter at the center of the sleeve. The cap device was to be that of commissioned officers of the U. S. Navy, with the Navy's shield replaced by a shield bearing the coat of arms of the wearer's state. Enlisted men of the militia were to be identified by a lozenge —blue bordered with white for blue clothes, and white bordered with blue for white. In the center of the lozenge was to be a foul anchor, the color of which was to be either white or blue, to contrast with the background. The militia mark was to be worn on the sleeve opposite the branch mark or rating badge. The cap ribbon was to bear the words "Naval Militia," followed by the name of the state. When a ship had been assigned to the state, the cap ribbon was to show the name of the vessel, with a lozenge on either side.

 U. S. S. TOPEKA.

The vignette shows the cap ribbon to be worn by members of the Naval Militia according to the 1913 Uniform Regulations. The same lozenge was to be worn on the uniform of all enlisted men.

Officers of the new Dental Corps were directed to wear orange velvet cloth between the gold sleeve stripes, and to display a "gold spread oak leaf with silver acorn on either side of the stem." The spread oak leaf is the basic device used by all corps under the control of the Bureau of Medicine and Surgery, and is like the device prescribed for medical officers in 1883. The Dental Corps device is in use today. A leaf with no acorn is used for the Nurse Corps, and a plain leaf with a twig is now the device of the Medical Service Corps. Officers of the Medical Reserve wore the insignia of officers of the Medical Corps, but with the leaf in silver and the acorn in gold—the reverse of the device of medical officers of the regular Navy. Their sleeve cloth was crimson instead of dark maroon, to distinguish them from regular surgeons.

The 1913 uniform regulations thus introduced a system of distinctions between the regular Navy and the reserve and militia arms, in addition to carrying forward the earlier means of indicating Line and Staff. The next decade, which would include a major war, was to abolish these attempts to set apart the officers of the Line of the regular Navy from all others who wore the uniform.

CHANGES TO THE 1913 REGULATIONS

"Changes in Uniform Regulations, 1913, No. 1" of June 24, 1913 did away with the metal devices for white coats, and restored the use of shoulder marks for overcoats, as well as for the service coat and mess jacket. The same lace and insignia were specified for shoulder marks as in the 1905 order. Again, chaplains were restricted to black braid stripes.

Change No. 5 of May 29, 1915 covered the dress of the naval militia. Now that the naval militias of the states came under Navy jurisdiction, as a result of the Naval Militia Act of February 16, 1914, the "recommended" of the 1913 instructions was changed to "prescribed." The means of differentiating between regular and non-regular officers was modified. The corps devices of officers of the naval militia—including the star, which was again permitted on the sleeves of line officers—were to be surrounded by a gold circle. The colored corps cloth of the sleeves and shoulder marks of staff officers was to show the break in the center. The same lozenge, but now with the letters *N.M.*, was to be worn by enlisted men, other than chief petty officers, on the breast of the overshirt or jumper, just below the neck opening. Chief petty officers were to wear the device on the sleeve. The cap device for all officers was that of the regular Navy.

The serious possiblity that the United States would become involved in the European war led to a change providing uniforms for the Naval Reserve Force authorized by Congress on March 3, 1915. "Changes in Uniform Regulations, United States Navy, 1913, No. 10" added a tenth chapter entitled "General Uniform Regulations, United States Naval Reserve Force." It separated the Naval Reserve into classes, as follows:

Class I.—The Fleet Naval Reserve, both officers and men, same as for the Navy for such uniforms as are required.

Class II.—The Naval Reserve.

Class IV.—The Naval Coast Defense Reserve.

Class V.—The Naval Reserve Flying Corps.

Officers:—Same as for officers of the Navy for such uniforms as are required for active duty, except that the Naval Reserve device shall be worn on the collar in lieu of corps device, and metal buttons shall be the design adopted for the Naval Reserve Force.

Men.—Same as for the Navy, except that the cap ribbon shall bear the words U.S. Naval Reserve Force.

Class III.—The Naval Auxiliary Reserve.

Officers.—In time of peace the uniform of the steamship line or company in which serving, with the Naval Reserve device on the collar of the military coat or on the lapels of the box coat. On active service or in war the uniform cap of a commissioned or warrant officer of same rank shall be worn.

Men.—In time of peace, uniform required by the steamship line. In time of war, same as for the Navy corresponding rating, with cap ribbon bearing the words U.S. Naval Reserve Force. . . ..

The Naval Reserve Force device was a miniature of the commissioned officers' cap device, in metal. The Reserve Force button displayed a plain anchor, with the letters *U.S.* on either side of the shackle above the stock, and with the letters *N.R.* on either side of the shank, between the stock and flukes.

Naval Reserve Force devices, 1915.

Here again the Navy prescribed sufficient differences from the basic uniform to indicate that the wearer was not a "regular."

To provide a uniform for the rapidly expanding aviation branch, the Navy on June 22, 1917 issued Change No. 11. This order was long overdue, for although the Navy had begun to train officers for flying duties in 1910, and had purchased planes as early as 1911, the need for a special dress for the new service had not been recognized. The first officers were trained at the facilities of the pioneer builders of aircraft. In the absence of a suitable official uniform—for one can hardly regard dungarees as such—they assumed the dress of civilian aviators. Old clothing, riding breeches, jackets, Norfolk coats, caps or helmets—in short, anything that was protective and comfortable was worn. The officers were far away from Navy activities and so were not constantly inspected for compliance with uniform regulations.

The first special, although unofficial, uniform for officers flying or working with aircraft, was worn when the Navy's small aviation detach-

The dress of Naval aviators worn during the winter of 1912-1913 was unofficial, but most suitable for duties involving flying. The two officers seated on chairs second and third from the left are Marines and are shown in the campaign dress of the current Marine Corps uniform instructions.

(*Courtesy of the National Archives.*)

A photograph of aviators at Pensacola in March, 1914, shows a close similarity between the unofficial dress of naval officers and the authorized campaign uniform of Marines. The Marine Corps officers, Lieutenant McIlvain second from left and Lieutenant Smith third from right have metal rank and corps insignia on the collars and the device of the Corps on the head pieces. The naval officers are wearing, in effect, a khaki copy of the white service coat, with Marine Corps breeches and puttees. The buttons are Navy gilt instead of the bronze buttons of the Marine officers. Rank is indicated by the same shoulder marks worn with service whites.

(*Official Navy Photo.*)

ment operated with the fleet during maneuvers off Guantanamo Bay, Cuba in the winter of 1912–1913. Photographs of the unit show all officers, Navy and Marine, in khaki uniforms. The "Regulations of the Uniform Dress . . . of the Marine Corps, 1900" had included a khaki campaign uniform, which consisted of a single-breasted coat, with standing collar, to be worn with trousers. A new Marine uniform instruction of 1912 permitted breeches and leather puttees in campaign dress. The photographs show the Marine officers in the authorized dress, and the naval officers in a khaki copy of the Navy's white service coat, with the breeches and puttees of the Marine Corps, and a cap with a khaki cover. The Marines wore their insignia on the standing collar; the naval aviators wore the shoulder marks prescribed by the current Navy uniform regulations. This same serviceable and appropriate dress was worn by the unit when it moved to the new aviation station at Pensacola, Florida, and during the Mexican affair of 1914 at Veracruz.

The first official uniform for aviation duty was authorized by Change 11 of June 22, 1917, shortly after the United States entered World War I. The uniform prescribed was identical with the unofficial uniform of 1912, except that the breeches were to be worn with leggings of drab woven wool—those most unsatisfactory leg coverings of the period. The instruction tied the uniform directly to that of the Marine Corps, for it was to be made of "khaki material as prescribed in Uniform Regulations, United States Marine Corps . . ." for summer wear. Officers could wear either breeches or trousers, and also were permitted to wear khaki flannel shirts. As working dress, a one-piece overall suit of khaki canvas could be worn to protect the uniform. This was a more suitable garment than the blue denim dungarees of the 1913 order.

As in the Civil War, the Navy Department issued instructions suspending dress uniforms. On October 10, 1917 Secretary Daniels issued General Order No. 328, which read:

SPECIAL FULL-DRESS UNIFORMS

1. During the continuation of the present war, officers commissioned in the Regular Establishment, and those receiving temporary commissions in the same, shall be required to furnish themselves only with service-dress uniforms, including overcoat. Similar orders have already been issued relative to Reserve Officers.

The body coat and the frock coat, with their accessories, were not required. The orders on the dress of the Naval Militia and other non-

The photograph of aviation personnel of World War I shows two of the methods used by the Navy to distinguish between regulars and non-regulars. The officer in the center of the front row has a circle around the star of his shoulder marks, indicating he was either a member of the National Naval Volunteers (ex-Naval Militia), who wore the encircled star from January to June, 1918, or a member of the Naval Reserve Force, who wore this device from July, 1918, to November, 1919. The officer in service blues is a member of the Naval Reserve Force, for under Change #10 to the 1913 regulations of January 18, 1917, the miniature cap devices was to be used as a corps device in lieu of corps insignia. The two officers on the extreme left are warrant officers. The one seated is a warrant carpenter and the standing officer is a boatswain. Both the wrap leggings of 1917 and the leather puttees of 1918 are shown.

(Official Navy Photo.)

The right hand figure is Rear Admiral Robert E. Peary, Civil Engineer
Corps, United States Navy in the flying suit of the latter part of World
War I and the early 1920's. The lieutenant commander is wearing the forestry
green overcoat with brown sleeve lace and shoulder marks introduced in
October, 1917.

(Courtesy of the Bureau of Aeronautics.)

regular components of the Navy had made only service dress uniforms mandatory. Actually, this order was continued until new uniform regulations were issued in 1922.

Since cotton khaki was satisfactory only for summer wear, a warmer dress was soon required. Change No. 12 of September 7, 1917 directed that the winter uniform be of the forestry green cloth of the Marine Corps. Forestry green is the color of the current winter aviation working uniform. Change No. 14 of October 12, 1917 added a green overcoat, with flat brown buttons and brown sleeve rank stripes. This order also authorized the wearing of the aviation uniform by officers other than aviators who were attached to air commands. This same proviso is in effect today.

"Change in Uniform Regulations, . . . No. 15"—undated, but issued between Change 14 of October 12th 1917 and Change No. 16 of January 10, 1918—made provision for "Enrolled Women of the Naval Reserve Force," the "Yeomanettes" of World War I. The legislation of 1915 establishing a Naval Reserve Force had placed no restriction on the sex of reservists. The uniform coat for enlisted women was single-breasted, styled somewhat like the Norfolk coat of the period, and was to be blue in winter and white in summer. The skirts were cut full at the bottom and almost reached the ground, in the style of 1917–1918. White shirtwaists were worn in summer and winter. The whole uniform was topped off with a straight-brimmed sailor hat, of Navy blue felt with the winter uniform, and of white straw in summer. Black shoes and stockings were to be worn with blues, and white shoes and hose with whites. The class mark of male yeomen of the Navy was to be worn on the sleeves, with rating badges for petty officers.

Change No. 16 of January 10, 1918 again modified the uniforms of the non-regular components of the Navy. Chapter 9 of the regulations was completely revised. One section referred to the "United States National Naval Volunteers"—that is, those officers and men of the naval militias who had been sworn into Federal service—and to the naval militia. The volunteers assumed the distinctions previously displayed by the naval militia, except that the men's cap ribbons were to bear the words "U. S. National Naval Volunteers." Officers of the naval militia were to substitute for the star on the sleeves and shoulder marks the letters *N.M.* in gold embroidery. Staff officers were to show the break in the cloth between the gold sleeve lace just as did staff officers of all the non-regular groups, and to place the letters *N.M.* above the sleeve strips in the same manner as militia line officers. All militia line and staff officers were to use the *N.M.* in lieu of a corps device on epaulets and on the service

A uniform change of late 1917 provided a uniform for women of the Naval Reserve Force. A white uniform of the same pattern as the blue costume shown was prescribed for summer wear. The practice of wearing a white hat or cap with blue uniforms is still followed.

(*Courtesy of the Library of Congress.*)

dress collar. Instead of the lozenge formerly worn, men of the naval militia were to wear the *N.M.* on the front of the overshirt or on the sleeves, and "Naval Militia" followed by the name of the state on cap ribbons. For the casual observer a book of rules was needed to distinguish between the regular Navy and the three non-regular components.

A change of April 1, 1918—No. 18—covered only the "service aviation uniform." Both the summer and winter uniforms were to be of forestry green cloth—wool in winter, cotton or lightweight wool in summer. The coat was modified slightly: the upper pockets were pleated to provide more room, and two lower bellows pockets were added. Officers who had coats made according to earlier instructions could continue to wear them; so there was a green and khaki aviation service throughout the war. Officers flew combat missions with leather jackets over their shirts, and thus had no rank insignia. The change directed that "shoulder marks may be attached to the shirt and shall be worn if the coat is omitted when making flight where liable to capture." Today, this condition is met by having metal insignia on the collar of the khaki shirt.

Chaplains, after many years of black braid sleeve lace, were permitted by an order of June 26, 1918, to wear gold lace. As a corps color, lustrous black cloth was to be worn between the lace on the sleeves and shoulder marks. For Jewish chaplains, a shepherd's crook was substituted for the cross.

Once again the dress of non-regular officers of the Navy was modified. Change No. 20—undated but issued between Change 19 of June 26 and Change 21 of July 2, 1918—completely revised Chapter 10, on the Naval Reserve Force. The devices of all officers of Class II, Naval Reserve Force, were to be within a gold circle. This method was used to indicate the naval militia in 1915, and in January 1918 became the mark of the National Naval Volunteer. Staff officers continued the practice prescribed for all non-regulars, of having a break in the colored cloth indicating their corps on the sleeves and shoulder marks. Officers of Class V, the Naval Reserve Flying Corps, wore the uniform of the flying officers of the regular Navy, but replaced the star with a miniature aviation device, the winged foul anchor.

A week after the Armistice ending World War I was signed, the Navy Department took the final step required to bring about uniformity in the dress of officers of the regular Navy. The "Change in Uniform Regulations, No. 25" of November 16, 1918 removed the cloth of the various staff corps from between the gold lace rank stripes of the sleeves and shoulder marks of all staff officers, and directed that the corps devices be worn above the upper strip of lace in the same position as the star of the Line. All corps devices were to be reduced in size so that they could be contained in a circle an inch and an eighth in diameter, and were to be shown in gold embroidery. The present system of using the same arrangement of gold lace to indicate the rank of all officers, with an appropriate corps device, had at last been prescribed.

The standing collar of the blue service coat, and the epaulets, both carried the staff corps devices in gold, superimposed on a silver foul anchor, the device of the Line. The shoulder marks carried a gold corps device on an anchor worn above the upper stripe, in the same position as the star of line officers.

Change No. 25 authorized chaplains to wear the gold lace and gold device in the same manner as all other staff officers. All officers of flag rank, and also captains and commanders, were directed to wear the oak-leaf and acorn embroidery on the visors of the cap, removing one more distinction between Line and Staff. The coats of warrant officers were brought into line with those of commissioned officers. Chief warrant officers, of both Line and Staff, wore the corps device above the gold and blue strip of lace, and warrant officers displayed the corps device four inches from the edge of the cuff.

The Navy's present double-breasted blue coat was introduced by Change No. 27, of March 17, 1919. The new service coat was described as of "dark navy-blue cloth or serge, double-breasted, with rolling, turn-down collar; length of lapel to be from 9 to 10 inches on the roll . . ." The coat was very similar to that worn by the British Navy of World War I, but with two rows of three buttons each instead of the four of the Royal Navy. The coat was patterned on civilian clothing of the period, a switch from the service coat of 1877 which had been tailored like the then popular military tunic. It is only natural that the service coat of the United States Navy should be influenced by the British Navy, for the two services had worked closely together since the entry of the United States into the war in April 1917. With a change in coat style, a change in shirt pattern was required. The shirt with the stiff standing collar of earlier periods was replaced by one having a stiff turndown collar, to be worn with a black four-in-hand tie.

In another move toward uniformity, Change No. 28, of November 13, 1919, directed that warrant officers wear a strip of quarter-inch lace on the sleeves, with the same blue breaks at two-inch intervals as those of chief warrant officers. Now all classes of warrant officers, except mates, had sleeve stripes with gold corps devices above them. The system of sleeve lace and devices now applied to both commissioned and warrant officers.

Although the dress and insignia of officers of the regular Navy had reached uniformity, the Navy still considered it necessary to continue to distinguish between regular and non-regular officers. Paragraph 6 of Change No. 28 described corps devices, and section (q) directed that officers of the Naval Reserve Force wear the "sleeve markings prescribed for officers of the regular Navy of the same corps and rank, with the addition of a distinguishing mark consisting of a geometrical figure surrounding the corps device." The modifications assigned the various classes of the Reserve were:

Class 1—A semi-circle surrounding the lower half of the device the ends being turned in to meet the body of the device.

Class 2—A circle.

Class 3—An equilateral triangle with the base parallel to the stripes of lace and apex pointing up.

Class 4—A rhombus with longer diagonal perpendicular to the stripes of lace.

Class 5—A pentagon with one side parallel to the stripes of lace and opposite angle pointing up.

Class 6—A hexagon with an angle pointing directly down.

The same modified insignia were worn on the epaulets and shoulder marks of reserve officers. One had to be able to recognize the corps devices, and to have some basic knowledge of geometry, to determine the class to which a reserve officer belonged.

The Bureau of Navigation, by Circular Letter No. 49–22 of October 13, 1922, advised all personnel that a new uniform instruction was being printed, and summarized the principal changes to be made to the much-amended 1913 regulations. The special full-dress coat, the last direct descendant of the first "blue and gold" uniform of the Navy, was to be abolished and replaced by the full dress of the 1913 edition of the regulations—the frock coat with epaulets, cocked hat, and laced trousers. In effect, the full dress of 1862 was to be restored, using a frock coat which had been slightly modified over the years. The body coat which was being replaced had served as the full-dress coat of the Navy since its introduction in 1802—a life of 120 years, less the periods during the Civil War and World War I when its wear was suspended. No other coat has has had such a long life in the United States Navy.

The other important change was the abolishment of the special aviation uniform. The letter of October 13, 1922 announced: "Uniform for aviators same as for other Naval officers; doing away with the green and khaki, which may be worn until June 1, 1923, but only at air stations." It had taken officers in the aviation branch of the Navy many years to convince the Department that a special dress was required for work connected with aircraft. Blues and whites were certainly not suitable for working on engines or for manning the controls in flight. It is true that the Navy had provided special protective clothing, but flight gear has never been considered part of the Navy's uniform.

It is difficult at this late date to think of good reasons for abolishing the only "working uniform" for special service. Naval Aviation had acquired considerable stature during World War I, and all nations were convinced that the air arm would play a major role in any future wars. The aviators who had served in Europe had had a more or less independent status, and considered themselves somewhat different from other branches of the Navy. With the return of peace, and the need to reduce the over-all strength of the Navy, it was necessary to absorb the greatly increased number of aviation personnel into the Navy structure. Many aviators believed that a separate corps should be established within the Navy for flyers. Others believed that an air force independent of both the Navy and the Army was the proper solution. Possibly the Navy considered the way to discourage these separatist tendencies was to integrate the aviation personnel into the Navy and require the same dress for all.

UNIFORM REGULATIONS OF 1922

The new uniform instructions approved by Secretary of the Navy Edwin Denby on September 20, 1922 contained no provision for an aviation dress. The only working dress for officers of the Navy was the dungaree suit of blue denim. The special full-dress body coat was omitted, as explained in the letter of October 1922, but the frock coat with epaulets, cocked hat, full-dress sword belt, sword, and gold-laced trousers, made a quite adequate full-dress uniform.

The 1922 edition of the uniform regulations made no real change in the dress of the Navy over and above that prescribed by the revised 1913 regulations. Chaplains were still prohibited from wearing the full-dress uniform, but in other respects (except for the appropriate devices in lieu of the star and foul anchor, the distinctive marks of the Line), officers of the Staff were dressed like their line contemporaries. On epaulets, however, staff officers continued to display the corps device, superimposed on the silver anchor of the Line. The device of the Civil Engineer Corps was modified in design, although the written description remained basically that of 1905. Now the crossed sprigs "of two live-oak leaves" were to be embroidered in gold, but the acorns were to be in silver, following the pattern of the oak-leaf and acorn motif devices of the Medical, Dental, and Supply Corps. The device of naval constructors, the "sprig of two live-oak leaves, spreading with an acorn on the stem between the leaves," continued to be entirely in gold embroidery. The pattern of the Civil

Civil Engineer Corps device, 1922.

Engineer Corps insignia was modified so that it no longer looked like a pair of dividers.

The various methods employed during the life of the 1913 uniform regulations to indicate members of the Naval Reserve and the Naval Militia were abolished by the 1922 order. Article 6 of Chapter 1 directed:

> Uniform for Naval Reserve Force and Naval Militia.
> (a) Officers and men of the Naval Reserve Force and officers and men of the Naval Militia shall wear the uniforms prescribed for officers and men of corresponding rank and rating in the Regular Navy.
> (b) They will not be required to possess other than the following: Service dress blue, service dress white, overcoat, sword, sword knot (if commissioned), and undress belt.
> (c) All other uniforms prescribed for officers of the U.S. Navy are optional for officers of the Naval Reserve and Naval Militia, but such uniforms must be of regulation pattern.

The Navy had finally abolished the distinctions between regulars and non-regulars. During World War I the reserve component of the United States Navy had proved its worth. Some 30,000 officers and over 300,000 men had come into the Navy through reserve channels to supplement the small regular Navy. Most of these non-regular personnel were released after the Armistice, but many continued on active duty. The dress of the Navy had now become truly "uniform."

CHANGES TO THE 1922 REGULATIONS

In 1925 a "working uniform" was authorized for the use of "Naval Aviators, Observors [sic], and all other Naval Officers detailed to duty involving flying . . ." Bureau of Navigation Circular Letter No. 23–25, of April 8, 1925, reinstated an up-to-date copy of the 1917 aviation uniform. The cut of the coat reflected the change in the style of the blue

The aviation working dress introduced in 1925 was forestry green in winter and cotton khaki in summer. On both uniforms, rank was indicated by means of black braid sleeve stripes, with the star in black silk embroidery. In 1929, either breeches and puttees or trousers were permitted.

(Official Navy Photo.)

service coat at the end of World War I. Instead of the single-breasted coat with a standing collar, the new coat was single-breasted, with a roll collar and notched lapels. It was very similar to the familiar khaki of the present, but with bronze buttons instead of the gilt ones currently worn. As during the war, the summer uniform was khaki and the winter one of forestry green wool. Breeches, to be worn with leather puttees, were prescribed. Rank was to be indicated by means of black mohair sleeve stripes, with the stars in black silk on both summer and winter uniforms. The order of April 1925 was covered by a uniform change, No. 2 of October 7, 1925. A change of May 1, 1929, permitted aviators to wear either breeches or trousers.

Change No. 7 of March 31, 1931 authorized a khaki working uniform for submariners—but with trousers instead of breeches, which would have been out of place in a submarine. This same order brought back the metal pin-on devices which had had such a short life in 1913. In both the aviation and submarine service, coats were frequently removed, leaving an officer without any indication of rank. Pin-on rank devices were to be worn on the collar tabs of khaki uniform shirts. From these changes of 1925 to 1931, the working uniform for all officers in World War II was developed.

After the creation in 1915 of the Naval Reserve Force, and the incorporation of officers and men of the state naval militias into Federal units during the war, the importance of the naval militia units diminished. A change of September 5, 1935 rewrote Article 6 of the 1922 uniform regulations, omitting the naval militia entirely, and directing that "officers and men of the Naval Reserve shall wear the uniform prescribed for officers and men of corresponding rank and rating in the Regular Navy."

Although the story of the changes in the dress of the Navy and final development of a single uniform, with standard systems for rank and corps designation, could end in 1922, it may be of interest to bring the story up to date by reviewing the changes made prior to, during, and since World War II; for with changing times, military dress also changes.

As the Navy prepared for possible involvement in World War II, bases were built in the Atlantic and Pacific area, and naval stations in the United States were expanded to support a growing fleet and enlarged air power. The need for a serviceable and distinctive working uniform for all officers, not just those in aviation and submarines, was indicated. An "ALNav" (a message to all hands of the Navy) of February 21, 1941 authorized the wearing of the khakis of aviators and submariners by all officers, at the discretion of the commanding officer. This order was a boon to officers of the Civil Engineer Corps, both the comparatively few regulars and the many reserves who had volunteered for active duty, for a major construction program was under way in the many corners of the globe. Neither blues nor whites are a satisfactory costume for construction men and engineers. A message of April 25, 1941 directed that the khaki working coat be worn with gilt buttons and shoulder marks. The greens of aviators retained the black sleeve stripes and star of the 1925 order, as they do today.

UNIFORM REGULATIONS OF 1941

The uniform regulations, approved by Secretary of the Navy Frank Knox on May 31, 1941 were a revised edition of the earlier order and its many changes. In order to indicate their rank when the khaki coat was removed, all officers were to wear metal collar devices. Line officers were to display a rank device on either side of the collar, and staff officers a rank device on the right collar tip, with a corps insignia on the left. With the prospect of being involved in a global war, requiring service in many climates, tropical uniforms were permitted but not mandatory. Either white or khaki shorts, with matching short-sleeved, open-necked shirts were to be worn. As a headpiece, either a cap, with the proper cover, or a white or khaki helmet was to be worn. Shoes—white, black, or brown —were to be worn with white socks or anklets. Rank and corps affiliation were to be indicated by pin-on devices in the same fashion as on the khaki shirts of the working uniform. Some articles suitable for cold-weather wear were specified; but it was only after the United States had entered the war, and many actions had taken place in the frigid zones, that the list of protective clothing was greatly expanded.

The "Uniform Regulations, United States Navy" approved by Secretary Knox on May 31, 1941, was the first publication to include the dress of the Navy Nurse Corps. From the creation of the Nurse Corps in 1908 until 1941, the uniforms to be worn by nurses had been prescribed by the Chief of the Bureau of Medicine and Surgery, subject to the approval of the Secretary of the Navy. These instructions were directed solely to the Nurse Corps, and were distinct from any regulation which covered the dress of men of the Navy.

Originally, the Navy's nurses were not uniformed in a military sense, for they wore the white duty costume and cap of the civilian nursing profession. When off duty, Navy nurses wore civilian clothes. A photograph of the first twenty nurses enrolled in the Navy shows them in a white, ward costume like their civilian counterparts.

There is little information presently available on the dress of Navy

Admiral Ben Moreell was Chief of the Bureau of Yards and Docks, Chief of Civil Engineers during World War II, and "father" of the Seabees. The uniform is aviation green and the four stars on the shoulder marks and collar are those of an admiral of the United States Navy. Admiral Moreell is the only civil engineer to hold this rank. The corps device is seen on the left collar tip and superimposed on the anchor of the shoulder marks.

(Courtesy of Admiral Moreell.)

The twenty nurses in this group were the first enrollees in the Navy Nurse Corps after its creation in 1908. They have been dubbed "The Sacred Twenty" by the Corps. It is to be noted that the uniform is the one generally worn by the nursing profession of the period, a ward uniform and white cap. There is no visible sign that this group was associated with the Navy, for there is no form of insignia or device. For many years, the uniform instructions listed a watch as part of the uniform.

(Navy Department Photo.)

nurses during the early years of the Corps. A distinctive device was introduced in 1913 for identification purposes. It was a pin, approximately the size of a quarter dollar. The edge of the device was bordered with gold oak leaves, the background of the center was in blue enamel, in the middle was a gold foul anchor on which was superimposed a shield of red and white stripes, with a blue field. The letters *U.S.N.* were located at the bottom of the pin, in blue enamel. The device was to be worn below the V of the neck of the indoor uniform, or on the shirtwaist of civilian clothes.

The original Nurse Corps device was of gold with the background in dark blue enamel. The stripes of the shield are alternately red and white, and the field blue. At the bottom of the pin, showing faintly, are the letters, *U.S.N*

The style of a new device introduced in 1917 bore a resemblance to that of the Medical Corps, for the oak leaf and acorn worn by doctors was superimposed on a gold foul anchor. The letters *N.N.C.* were placed on the leaf and acorn. Various modifications of this insignia were worn by Navy nurses until World War II.

No definite information has been found to indicate that the Navy prescribed a "street" or outdoor uniform for nurses in World War I. However, a picture of the second Director of the Navy Nurse Corps, Lenah H. Intcliffe Higbee, who served in this capacity from 1911 to 1922, shows her in a coat which is definitely of the First World War. The standing-collared coat is like that worn by both the Army and Navy of the period, and the "sailor" hat adds a nautical touch. The device worn on either side of the collar is similar to that ordered in 1917, but without the letters *N.N.C.*

The first complete description of the uniforms of the Navy Nurse Corps, that has been located, is contained in the "Uniform Regulations, United States Navy Nurse Corps", 1924. From the General Regulations of this instruction, it is evident that some uniform regulations had been issued prior to 1924, for a statement is made that "Uniform Regulations as herein revised supersede all other uniform regulations of the Navy Nurse Corps. . . ." It is unfortunate that these early instructions can not now be located. The white cap, worn with the white indoor or ward uniform, was to have a band of black velvet across the front, with stripes to show the nurses' classifications. For the Superintendent of the Nurse Corps, two quarter-inch gold stripes, with a band of one-eighth-inch-wide

This portrait of Lenah H. Intcliffe Higbee, Superintendent of the Navy Nurse Corps from January, 1911, to November, 1922, shows the corps device introduced in 1917, but without the letters *N.N.C.* While no regulation covering the outdoor uniform has been located, the cut of the coat is typical of those worn by American military personnel in World War I.

(Official Navy Photo.)

The type of protective outer clothing worn by the two Navy nurses aboard the *U.S.S. George Washington* in December, 1918, was also used by the American Red Cross and the Army Nurse Corps. The only basic difference was in the collar insignia. The device of the Nurse Corps, the anchor with the leaf and acorn on it, is plainly visible. Although no official order has been found which prescribes a street uniform for nurses, contemporary correspondence indicates that a blue coat of the norfolk style and a full skirt were authorized. The sleeves of the coat can be seen under the cape of the coat-cape.

(Army Signal Corps Photo, National Archives.)

lace between them were employed; for the Assistant Superintendent, two one-quarter-inch wide stripes; principal chief nurses displayed one stripe a quarter-inch-wide, with an eight-inch-wide stripe above it; assistant chief nurses, a single quarter-inch stripe, nurses, an eighth-inch stripe and nurses who had not completed their probationary period wore only a black band, one-half inch wide.

The instructions made provision for both blue and white outdoor uniforms. In both cases, the coats were double breasted, of the semi-fitting sack type, with rolling collars and peaked lapels. Nurses' coats followed the style of the double-breasted blue coat for officers intro-duced in 1919 to replace the single-breasted standing-collared blue service coat of World War I. As an indication of grade, nurses wore the same arrangement of stripes on their sleeves as they did on their indoor caps, but the stripes were one-half and one-quarter inch wide, in lieu of the cap band stripes of one-quarter and one-eighth inches. On the blue uniform the sleeve stripes were of black silk braid; on the whites, white linen braid. A metal, pin-on Nurse Corps device, which was similar to that of 1917, was worn on either side of the collar of the white indoor uniform and the white outdoor coat. Embroidered corps devices were worn on either side of the collar of the blue coat.

The outdoor hats were wide-brimmed with a flat top; blue-black velvet in winter and white straw in summer. No device was worn on either hat. The portrait of Josephine B. Bowman, Director of the Nurse Corps, 1922–1935, shows the hat of the period and the corps device.

When the Nurse Corps uniform instructions were revised and re-printed in 1929, few new features were introduced. One change indicates the relationship between civilian and military styles. The 1924 instruction had required that skirts be 10″ above the floor. The 1929 instruction made this 12″. The major change was in the style of the outdoor hat. The wide-brimmed hat of 1924 was replaced by a tight-fitting headpiece similar to the cloche worn by women in the 20's. The hat was blue for wear with both blue and white uniforms, and employed the Nurse Corps device as a cap device.

Chapter XVII of the 1941 uniform instructions specified the uniform for nurses and included only the ward uniform and outer protective clothing. No provision was made for an outdoor uniform. The order stated that the prescribed uniforms were to be worn at all times when on duty. Civilian clothes were to be worn when off duty or on leave. For wear out of doors, a hat similar to that of 1929, a blue sweater, a cape and a blue rain coat were provided. Shortly after the United States entered World War II, the outdoor uniforms were reinstated.

The third Superintendent of the Navy Nurse Corps, Josephine B. Bowman, 1922-1935, is wearing the blue outdoor uniform prescribed in 1924. The corps device shows plainly the letters *N.N.C.* on the oak leaf and acorn, which in turn are superimposed on a gold foul anchor. As an indication of grade, the Superintendent wore two stripes of one-half-inch black braid with a one-quarter-inch-wide stripe between them on the sleeves.

(Official Navy Photo.)

The blue outdoor uniform is typical of the 1924 to 1941 period. The hat is the one specified in 1929 and modified slightly in 1941. The cut of the coat and skirt was modified from time to time as the clothing of civilian women changed.

(*Official Navy Photo.*)

The 1941 regulations prescribed two devices for chaplains: the inclined Latin cross and "the Star of David above and attached to the top center of the Tablets of the Law." The shepherd's crook of 1918 had been omitted from the uniform regulation of 1922. In 1932 the shepherd's crook was authorized as the device for the Naval Reserve chaplains of Jewish faith, although a change in uniform regulations does not appear to have been issued.[2]

CHANGES TO THE 1941 REGULATIONS

Many changes to the 1941 Uniform Regulations were issued during World War II, but only those which had a major effect on the dress of the Navy will be reviewed. The broadened use of the khaki working uniform had provided a comfortable, military dress for wartime use, and one which was liked by most Navy personnel. The Bureau of Naval Personnel, by a letter of April 16, 1943, directed that the color of the working uniform be changed to slate gray, of the same pattern as the khaki uniform. "Grays" were to be worn with blue-black plastic buttons, gray shoulder marks, and a gray-covered cap with a black braid chin strap. The indications of rank and corps were to be in black braid and embroidery. In general, this change was not very favorably received, for it was a break with tradition. Gold lace and embroidery and gilt buttons had been part of the Navy's dress since the introduction of the first "blue and gold" uniforms of 1802. It was remarked that the new gray uniform bore a close resemblance to that of the Post Office Department, and that the Navy was to be dressed in "Confederate" gray.

It was originally proposed that the wearing of khakis would be permitted only so long as the existing stocks of cloth and uniforms lasted. However, the khakis were never completely replaced by the grays. Tradition dies hard; and a Bureau of Personnel Circular Letter of August 11, 1943 permitted the wearing of standard shoulder marks, dark blue with gold lace rank stripes and gold-embroidered corps devices. The gold chin strap of the cap was restored, and senior officers were permitted to wear the gold embroidery on the visors. An ALNav, No. 406 of October 15, 1946, reversed the decision of 1943, and reinstated khakis as the working uniform of the Navy. "Grays" could be worn only until October 1948, with the exception that personnel aboard ships at sea and members of the Naval Reserve, during training periods, could continue their use until October 1949. As is the general rule, the uniforms abandoned during a war are restored in time of peace. Tradition plays a part in every decision effecting the dress of the military.

With the United States at war, some form of outdoor military dress for the Nurse Corps was necessary. The 1941 uniform instructions had prescribed a costume similar to that of civilian nurses, with a minimum indication of membership in the United States Navy. By a letter to the Chief of the Bureau of Medicine and Surgery of March 20, 1942, the Chief of the Bureau of Navigation authorized new uniform items for the Nurse Corps: both blue and white service dress, a blue overcoat, and both blue and white caps. A uniform instruction issued to members of the Nurse Corps on December 1, 1942 described the uniforms in detail, modified the sections of Chapter 17 of the 1941 regulations, and added new illustrations to supplement the original five showing the very limited clothing of the 1941 order.

The instructions for the white indoor uniform and cap, the cape, and the raincoat were unchanged. The new blue service coat was double-breasted, with two rows of three gilt buttons each. The rolling [sic] collar, lapelled coat was to be worn buttoned, on the left—a concession to the feminine sex. Grade was shown by means of gold or yellow silk sleeve lace: two strips of half-inch lace with a quarter-inch strip between them for the Superintendent; two strips for the Assistant Superintendent; a strip and a half for chief nurses; and a single half-inch lace for all others. No corps device was to be worn above the sleeve lace, but a metal corps device—the oak leaf and acorn superimposed on a gold foul anchor, with the letters *N.N.C.* raised above the oak leaf—was to be worn on either side of the collar.

The white service coat was single-breasted, with three gilt buttons, a rolling [sic] collar, and notched lapels. No sleeve insignia was worn. Grade was indicated by shoulder marks which had the same stripe arrangement as the blue coat-sleeves, but no corps device. The metal corps device was worn on the left side of the collar of the white shirt, and a rank device on the right side, in the same manner as the devices worn on khaki shirts by male officers. The Superintendent of the Nurse Corps wore the gold oak leaf of a lieutenant commander; the assistant superintendent, the two silver bars of a lieutenant; chief nurses, the silver bar of a lieutenant (junior grade) ; and all others, the gold bar of an ensign.

The outdoor cap, either blue or white to match the uniform, had a vague resemblance to that of male officers. The band of the cap was an inch and a quarter wide in front and three-quarters of an inch wide in back, and was covered with a band of black mohair. The crown of the cap flared up into a circular shape, the slant in front being about half an inch

In 1942, members of the Navy Nurse Corps displayed the gold lace of their grade on the sleeves of the blue service coat but omitted the corps device worn by male officers. Corps affiliation was indicated by a metal pin-on device on either side of the collar. The corps device also served as a cap ornament

(Courtesy of Lieutenant Commander Eleanore M. Gallagher.)

A uniform change of March 20, 1942, reinstated outdoor or service dress uniforms for the Nurse Corps. The white braid sleeve stripes which had been used to indicate grade prior to 1941 were omitted. Grade was indicated by the gold stripes on the shoulder marks and by a rank device on the right shirt collar point. Corps affiliation was indicated by the Nurse Corps device on the left collar tip and on the cap in lieu of the standard officer's cap device. In this photograph, Commander Danyo had the grade of chief nurse and wore the stripe and a half on the shoulder ornaments and a silver bar on the right side of the collar.

(Courtesy of Commander Anna Danyo.)

longer than in back. This visorless cap was worn with gold lace chin strap half an inch wide, fastened at either side with small gilt buttons. In lieu of the male officer's cap device, the Nurse Corps device was fastened to the front of the cap, above the chin strap.

The order of December 1942 thus provided nurses with a coat similar to that of male officers, a cap which could be recognized as that of the Navy, and rank and corps identifications closely related to those of men.

The modification of the 1938 Reserve Act in July 1942 to permit enrollment of women in the Naval Reserve posed a new problem to the Navy Department, the design of a proper dress for women. On March 20, 1943 the Bureau of Naval Personnel issued "Uniform Regulations, Women's Reserve, United States Naval Reserve, 1943 . . .", which made no mention of the current 1941 uniform regulations. Until 1948, the instructions for dress of the WAVES were separate and distinct from those of the regular Navy. It would appear that during that period the employment of women in the uniformed Navy was considered temporary, and that it was regarded as less complicated to have the instructions for their dress separate from those of male officers and men, and of the Nurse Corps.

There was little precedent for female costume in the United States Navy, the only uniform for women having been that of the "Yeomanettes" of World War I. The uniform authorized in 1917 did not conform to military or civilian styles of the 1940's. Times had changed, and so had women's dress. The matter was studied not only by the Navy, but by a board of fashion experts. The result was a smart and distinctive combination of military dress and civilian style.

The uniforms for all WAVES consisted of a blue or white single-breasted jacket, a matching skirt, and a hat with either a blue or a white cover. The uniforms designated for officers were as follows:

1. Service Dress, Blue, A.—Navy blue jacket, Navy blue skirt, Navy blue hat, black gloves, and black shoes. Navy blue or Reserve blue [a light blue] shirts for work, white shirts and white gloves for dress.

2. Service Dress, Blue, B.—Same as Service Dress, Blue A, but with white cap cover and gloves.

3. Service Dress, White.—White jacket, white skirt, (long sleeved) white shirts, white hat cover, white shoes, white gloves.

4. Working Uniform.—Navy blue jacket, Navy blue skirt, short-sleeved white shirt, white hat cover, white gloves.

The jackets were easy-fitting, single-breasted, with four gilt buttons. The WAVE device, a three-bladed propeller with a foul anchor superimposed on it, was worn on the rounded ends of the collars. On blue jackets, the propeller was in Reserve blue embroidery, the anchor in white, and the background in Navy blue. On the white jacket, the background was white, the propeller Navy blue and the anchor Reserve blue. Rank was indicated by Reserve blue braid on Navy blue jackets, and by Navy blue on white coats. (Reserve blue is much lighter in color than navy blue.) The hat was made so that either blue or white covers could be used, by the same general method as the men's combination caps. The officer's hat had a stiffened oval crown, and the brim was rolled up at the sides and straight at front and back. The cap device was that of commissioned officers—the crossed anchors, the shield, and spread eagle. The uniform was very similar to that of male officers, but if the gilt buttons were replaced, the sleeve stripes removed, and another hat worn, the costume might suitably be worn by a business woman.

There was a greater degree of uniformity in the dress of officers and enlisted persons of the Women's Reserve than there was between the uniforms of male officers, chief petty officers, and men. All enlisted women wore coats of the same pattern as officers, but with dark blue pastic buttons. Chief petty officers wore the same hat as commissioned officers, with the hat device used by their male associates—the vertical foul anchor in gold, with the letters *USN* in silver on it. The hat for other enlisted women was to have the brim turned up in back and down in front. The hat was trimmed with a dark blue cap ribbon, marked "U. S. Navy" in gilt letters. Rating badges and specialty marks like those for male enlisted men were used.

Special uniforms were prescribed for working dress: a coverall of medium blue cotton for work in aviation; slacks of same material as the jackets with which they would be worn, for use when the wearing of a skirt was not suitable; and a smock of Reserve blue to protect the uniform when required.

On October 15, 1943 new "Uniform Regulations, Women's Reserve . . ." were released. superseding those of March 1943. It was specifically noted that the uniforms described could not be worn by nurses. The revised instruction reflected some of the changes which had taken place in the dress of male officers and men. A gray working uniform was prescribed; a shirtwaist dress of gray seersucker with a matching collarless jacket, and a gray hat cover. The buttons were to be blue-black plastic like those of the gray uniform which was to replace the khakis. Provision was made for identification of women officers of the staff corps. The devices of the Medical, Dental, Supply, Civil Engineer, and Hospital Corps were to be worn above the sleeve stripes, but not in gold. On the

This photograph, taken at the former Naval Hospital in Brooklyn, shows all the uniforms prescribed for the Nurse Corps in 1944. From left to right, they are: service dress, blue C; service dress, blue A, with raincoat; indoor duty uniform; service dress, blue A; service dress, blue B, with overcoat; service dress, white; indoor duty uniform, with cape; working uniform gray; indoor uniform, with blue sweater; service dress, blue B.

Although the change of December 15, 1944, had specified a beige stocking for use with the blue uniforms, nurses were permitted to wear the formerly authorized black hose during the transition period.

(Official Navy Photo.)

The arrangement of sleeve ornaments prescribed for the Nurse Corps on December 15, 1944, is identical with that of male commissioned officers of the United States Navy. The white cap cover indicates that the uniform of the day was service dress, blue B.

(Courtesy of Commander Anna Danyo.)

The uniform change of December 15, 1944 reflected the granting of rank to members of the Nurse Corps and brought their uniforms into conformance with that of male officers. The Nurse Corps device which had been worn as a cap ornament was replaced by the cap device worn by male commissioned officers. The shoulder marks were now the same for all officers, stripes of gold lace to indicate rank, with the corps device above them. Commander Danyo at the time this picture was taken held the rank of lieutenant, as indicated by the two stripes on the shoulder marks and the two silver bars on the right collar tab.

(Courtesy of Commander Anna Danyo.)

All nurses are wearing headgear authorized by the 1944 order, either the cap with the cap device of all commissioned officers of the Navy, or the overseas cap with a miniature cap device on the left and a rank device on the right. The nurse in the front row at the left is wearing the blue coat of the 1942 order which omittd the corps device on the sleeves and placed the device on the collar. It has generally been Navy practice to permit the wearing of an older uniform during a period of transition after a new instruction had been issued.

(Courtesy of Commander Mary W. Galindo.)

blue service jacket and overcoat, the oak leaves and caduceus were to be Reserve blue and the acorns white. On white uniforms and the gray service jacket, the oak leaves and caduceus were to be Navy blue, the acorns Reserve blue. A change in the regulations for the dress of WAVES of September 15, 1944 permitted line members of the Women's Reserve to wear the star, in Reserve blue on Navy blue garments, in Navy blue on whites or grays.

The granting in July 1942 of relative rank to nurses is reflected in a uniform change of June 30, 1944. By a Bureau of Naval Personnel order the letters *N.N.C.* were to be removed from the corps device, leaving the spread oak leaf and acorn of the Medical Corps superimposed on a gold foul anchor. The device was to be worn on the sleeves of the blue service coat, in the same position as the star of the Line, and on the shoulder marks of the white service coat. As a cap device, nurses were directed to wear that of male commissioned officers: a silver shield mounted on crossed foul anchors, the whole surmounted by a silver spread eagle. This was one more step toward uniformity of dress, for now the Nurse Corps, a permanent component of the regular Navy, was dressed in uniforms that closely resembled those of male officers, and displayed the indications of rank and corps in the same manner as for men.

The instructions for the dress of members of the Nurse Corps were brought up to date by a Bureau of Naval Personnel letter of December 15, 1944, and became Chapter 14 of the 1941 uniform instructions. The changes of December 1942 and June 1944 were incorporated in this revision. For the first time, nurses were designated by their rank, not as Superintendent, Assistant Superintendent, and so on. Provision was made for ranks up to and including that of captain, and the same sleeve lace and metal rank devices were employed as for men.

UNIFORM REGULATIONS OF 1947

The "Uniform Regulations, United States Navy, 1947," approved by Secretary of the Navy James Forrestal on May 2, 1947, carried forward, for the most part, the wartime dress of the Navy. The full-dress uniform of 1941 was abolished, so that only the "service" uniforms were available for formal wear. The frock coat—which had served as full dress since the special full-dress body coat was dropped after World War I—the gold-laced trousers, epaulets, and cocked hats, all disappeared from the uniform regulations. With the elimination of the evening dress coat and the white mess jacket, the blue service coat with a black bow tie was to serve for evening social dress. A male officer's wardrobe was reduced to the uniforms worn during the war—blue, white, khaki service, khaki and gray working uniforms, and the green winter uniform for naval aviators. The headpieces were caps with covers to match the uniform, garrison caps, and tropical helmets. Of course there were overcoats, raincoats, and tropical dress. The uniforms for nurses were those of the 1944 change, and no mention was made of a dress for WAVES, for these instructions were still being covered by separate orders. The dress of women of the Navy followed the same pattern as that for male officers—service and working dress.

UNIFORM CHANGES SINCE 1947

"Change No. 3" of October 21, 1948, announced "Uniforms for all women of the naval service have been standardized and new regulations are published herein. Uniform Regulations for the Women's Reserve, U.S.N.R., approved 15 October 1943, and Chapter XI, U. S. Navy Uniform Regulations, 1947, are hereby cancelled." The blue jacket of the WAVES was prescribed for all women, to be worn with gilt buttons, and by nurses without the WAVE insignia. All commissioned officers were to wear sleeve lace of Reserve blue, with corps devices in the same colored embroidery, except that acorns were to be white. The white uniform of the WAVES was to be worn without collar insignia, with white braid sleeve stripes and yellow silk corps devices. The WAVE cap was to be worn with appropriate cap covers. Commissioned women officers were to wear the same cap device as male officers; warrant officers and chief petty officers the devices of their male counterparts; enlisted women the anchor-propeller device of the WAVES. Nurses were to retain their special clothing—indoor duty whites, caps, and capes. A dress of gray and white seersucker, slacks, dungarees, raincoats, overcoats, and an exercise suit (light blue denim shorts, skirt of the same material, and chambray or white shirt) were authorized for all women. The dress of women in the Navy had reached uniformity.

The pattern established for the dress of the United States Navy during World War II, and carried forward by the regulations of 1947, was reflected in the uniform instructions of August 17, 1951 and April 6, 1959. The dress of women officers has come closer to that of men, for now the sleeve lace on blue uniforms is gold, and the corps devices are identical to those worn by male officers. The only difference is that on whites, women show white braid with yellow embroidered corps insignia.

Here complete agreement with male officers is not possible, since the men's whites are worn with shoulder marks.

Although a full-dress uniform has not been reinstated, and probably never will be in this era of "cold" and "brush" wars, appropriate evening dress has been provided. For male officers a tail coat similar to a civilian full-dress coat is worn, with the same sleeve lace as the blue service coat, a white vest, and a white tie. For women, "evening dress" consists of a blue single-breasted jacket with three buttons on either side, a rounded collar, and half-peaked lapels; a shirt of white silk or similar material, a black tie, a full skirt, and a dark blue cumberbund. For evening dress only a small crescent-shaped diadem of dark blue felt, with an officer's cap device on the turned-up brim, is worn. The outfit is definitely military and at the same time feminine.

The uniform for social occasions has been extended to include special dinner dress uniforms for male officers. For such occasions, dinner dress for women of the Navy consists of either dress blues or whites. Two uniforms are provided for male officers. One consists of a blue jacket with the sleeve ornaments of the service coat, high-waisted trousers, a gold cumberbund, and a white dress shirt with a turned-down collar. The other, for warm climates, consists of a white mess jacket with blue trousers, black cumberbund, and shoulder marks. Both are most attractive uniforms.

CONCLUSION

As the weapons and methods of war have become more and more complicated in this age of electronics and atomic energy, the dress of the Navy of the United States has been simplified and standardized. Today's dress is, with the few exceptions noted earlier, the costume of the last war. The accent is now on comfort and serviceability rather than the ostentatious decoration of earlier periods. The Navy has not gone back to lace-trimmed full-dress uniforms, cocked hats, and epaulets as it did after both the Civil War and World War I. The present dress is definitely military, without the gaudiness of earlier periods. Wars have long since lost an aura of pageantry and romanticism. In today's world, war is a grim and unglamorous business.

From this review of the changes in the uniforms of the Navy, it is evident that the Civil War, the first really major war in which the United States was involved, set a pattern of uniformity which has been the basis for changes in the instructions for the dress of the Navy. As we have seen, attempts were made from time to time to restore systems which distinguished Line from Staff, or regular from reserve, but each succeeding conflict has tended to minimize these distinctions. The urgencies of the Civil War left their mark on the uniforms of the United States Navy, for the betterment of the service.

NOTES

[1] Jarrett, Dudley, *British Naval Dress* (London, J. M. Dent and Sons, Ltd., 1960), p. 102.
[2] Drury, Clifford M., *The History of the Chaplain Corps, United States Navy, 1778–1939* (Washington, Bureau of Naval Personnel, NavPers 1580), p. 230.

Lieutenant
Service Dress

Flag Officers
Full Dress

Warrant Gunner
Full Dress

SEA OR LINE OFFICERS, 1861

Master's Mate
Service Dress

Commander
Summer Service Dress

Rear Admiral
Full Dress

SEA OR LINE OFFICERS, 1862—1864

Rear Admiral
Service Dress

Warrant Boatswain
Service Dress

Captain
Sack Coat

SEA OR LINE OFFICERS, 1864–1866

Commodore's Secretary
Undress

Chief Engineer
Service Dress

Passed Assistant Surgeon
Full Dress

CIVIL OR STAFF OFFICERS, 1861

Surgeon (Commander)
Service Dress

Third Assistant Engineer
Service Dress

CIVIL OR STAFF OFFICERS, 1864–1866

Gunner's Mate   Boy   Seaman

ENLISTED PERSONNEL, 1864—1866

Appendix A
Uniform Regulations, United States Navy, 1852

REGULATIONS

FOR THE

UNIFORM & DRESS

OF THE

NAVY AND MARINE CORPS

OF THE

UNITED STATES.

From the Original Text and Drawings in the Navy Department.

PHILADELPHIA:
PRINTED FOR THE NAVY DEPARTMENT,
BY T. K. AND P. G. COLLINS.
1852.

REGULATION.

UNIFORM AND DRESS

OF THE

NAVY OF THE UNITED STATES.

FULL DRESS.—[Sea Officers.]

Coat.

For a Captain—shall be of Navy blue cloth, double-breasted, lined and faced with white silk serge; two rows of large Navy buttons on the breast, nine in each row, placed four inches and a half apart from eye to eye at top, and two inches and a half at bottom. Stand-up collar, to hook in front at bottom, and to slope thence upwards and backwards at an angle of twenty-five degrees on each side, and to rise no higher than will permit a free movement of the chin over it; to have a strip of Navy gold lace, one inch and a half wide around the top and down the front, with a strip of gold lace one-half of an inch wide around the bottom, as per pattern. The cuffs to be two inches and a half deep, with one strip of gold lace three-quarters of an inch wide below the seam, but joining it, and two strips of lace of the same width on the sleeves, above the cuffs, separated by a space of half an inch from each other, and a like strip of lace from the lower button to the end of the cuff, on the upper side of the opening, and four small size Navy buttons in the opening.

The waist of the coat to descend to the top of the hip bone; the skirts to begin about one-fifth of the circumference from the front edge and descend four-fifths from the hip bone towards the knee, and to be lined with white silk serge, with one button behind on each hip and one near the bottom of the skirt in each fold. The pocket-flaps to be pointed and laced all around with three-quarter inch lace, lined with white serge, to show the edge of the lining, and to have four large Navy buttons underneath, showing one-half of their diameter. Coat to be worn fully buttoned, unless otherwise permitted by the officer in command.

For a Commander—the same in all respects as for a Captain, except that it shall have lace one inch and a quarter wide around the top and down the front of the collar—one strip of gold lace three-quarters of an inch wide on the upper edge of the cuff, touching the seam, and one of the same width on the sleeve above the cuff, the two separated by a space of one-half of an inch, and a like strip from the lower button to the end of the cuff. The pocket-flaps to be without lace, with but three large buttons underneath them, and but three small buttons in the opening of the cuff.

For a Lieutenant—the same in all respects as for a Commander, except that it shall have lace one inch wide around the top and down the front of the collar, and but one strip of lace three-quarters of an inch wide around the upper edge of the cuff, touching the seam.

For a Master—the same in all respects as for a Lieutenant, except that, instead of lace, it shall have around the cuffs three medium size Navy buttons, and three small ones in the opening.

For a Passed Midshipman—the same in all respects as for a Master, except that there shall be no lace around the bottom of the collar, and no buttons around the cuffs.

For a Midshipman—the same in all respects as for a Passed Midshipman, except that the collar, instead of lace, shall have embroidered on each side, in gold thread, a foul anchor three inches long, and two inches from bill to bill.

For a Boatswain, Gunner, Carpenter, and Sailmaker—shall be of Navy blue cloth, lined with the same; rolling collar, double-breasted, two rows of large Navy buttons on the breast, eight in each row; pointed pocket-flaps, with three large buttons underneath each, showing one-half their diameter; three medium size buttons around each cuff, and two small ones in each opening; one button behind on each hip, one in the middle of each fold, and one in each fold near the bottom of the skirt. On each side of the collar to have one loop of three-quarters wide gold lace, to show one inch and a half wide, and four inches long, with a small size Navy button in the point of each loop.

FULL DRESS.—[Civil Officers.]

Coat.

For a Surgeon—the same in all respects as for a Commander, except that, instead of the lace on the collar, it shall have embroidered on each side, in gold thread, three sprigs of live oak, as per pattern: and instead of the lace on the cuff, three embroidered sprigs of live oak, smaller than those on the collar, according to pattern.

For a Passed Assistant and Assistant Surgeon—the same in

all respects as for a Surgeon, except that the cuffs of a *Passed Assistant Surgeon* shall have three medium size Navy buttons on the upper edge, and those of an *Assistant Surgeon* shall be plain with three small buttons in the opening.

For a Purser—the same in all respects as for a Surgeon, except that the collar shall be embroidered, in gold thread, with a wreath of live oak on the upper edge and front, and the cuffs be embroidered around their upper edges with a wreath of the same three-quarters of an inch wide, as per pattern.

For a Chaplain—the same in all respects as for a Surgeon, except that it shall be single-breasted, with one row of nine large Navy buttons in front, and the collar and cuffs of black velvet, without embroidery.

In performing Divine Service, the Chaplain may, at his discretion, wear the black gown, or the uniform prescribed in the Regulations.

For a Professor and Commodore's Secretary—shall be of Navy blue cloth, rolling collar, single-breasted, with one row of eight large Navy buttons in front, three under plain pocket-flaps, one on each hip behind, and one in each fold of the skirt, near the bottom, with three small size Navy buttons in the opening of the cuff. Coat to be lined on the skirts, but not faced with white silk serge.

For a Clerk—shall be of Navy blue cloth, rolling collar, single-breasted, with one row of seven large Navy buttons in front, one behind on each hip, two in each fold of the skirt, near the middle, and one in each fold near the bottom of the skirt, and three small buttons in the opening of the cuffs. Coat to be lined with black silk serge.

For a Chief Engineer—the same in all respects as for a Surgeon, except that it shall be single-breasted, with one row of nine large Navy buttons in front, and the collar shall have on each side an embroidered device, two inches high and three inches long—the anchor in silver, and the wreath in gold, as per pattern. The cuffs to have three large size Navy buttons around the upper edge, with three small ones in the opening. Skirts to be lined with black silk serge.

For a First Assistant Engineer—the same in all respects as for a Chief Engineer, except that the cuffs shall have three medium size Navy buttons around the upper edge.

For a Second Assistant Engineer—the same in all respects as for a First Assistant, except that the cuffs shall have no buttons on their upper edges.

For a Third Assistant Engineer—the same in all respects as for a Second Assistant.

Pantaloons.

For all Officers—shall be of Navy blue cloth, or white drill, made loose to spread well over the foot, and to be worn over the boots or shoes. Blue pantaloons will have a stripe of Navy gold lace down the outer seam, one inch and a half wide for *Captains*; one inch and a quarter wide for *Commanders*; and one inch wide for *Lieutenants:* gold cord, three-eighths of an inch in diameter, will be worn on the outer seam of blue pantaloons by *Masters*, and one-fourth of an inch in diameter by *Passed Midshipmen*.

Within the tropics, white pantaloons will be worn at all seasons, unless otherwise permitted by the officer in command.

North of the tropics, blue cloth pantaloons will be worn from the first of October to the fifteenth of May, and the white from the fifteenth of May to the first of October.

South of the tropics, blue will be worn from the fifteenth of May to the first of October, and the white from the first of October to the fifteenth of May, unless otherwise directed by written order of the Commander-in-chief of a Squadron or of a vessel acting singly.

Vest.

For all Officers—if worn, to be white, single-breasted, standing collar, with nine small Navy buttons in front, and not to show below the coat.

Cocked Hat.

Captains, Commanders, Lieutenants, Pursers, Surgeons, Passed Assistant and Assistant Surgeons, Masters, Passed Midshipmen, Midshipmen, Secretaries, Chief Engineers, and *First Assistant Engineers,* when in full dress or in undress, will wear black cocked hats, of the following description, viz.: Not more than eight nor less than six inches and a half high on the back, (or fan,) nor more than eight nor less than five inches in front, (or cock,) and not more than nineteen nor less than seventeen inches long, from point to point, the curve to be one inch and one-tenth at the back; the hat to be bound with black silk lace, to show one inch and a quarter on each side; in the fold at each end of the hat a tassel, formed of five gold and five blue bullions, and on the cock, a black silk cockade five inches wide. *Captains and Commanders* to wear over the cockade a loop of six gold bullions, half an inch in diameter, the two inner bullions to be twisted together, with a small Navy button in the lower end of the loop.

All other Officers entitled to wear cocked hats, will wear over the cockade a loop formed of four gold bullions, three-eighths of an inch in diameter, not twisted, with a small button in the lower end of the loop.

Epaulettes.

Captains, Commanders, Lieutenants, Pursers, Surgeons, Passed Assistant and Assistant Surgeons, Masters in the line of promotion, and *Chief Engineers,* will wear two gold epaulettes, of the dimensions, bullion, and finish shown in the patterns, and with the following devices in silver on the frog, viz.: for *Captains,* an eagle and anchor, two inches and five-eighths long, with a silver embroidered star above, one inch and one-eighth in diameter. The senior Captain in the Navy and the Commander-in-chief of a Squadron will have on the strap an additional star, one inch in diameter—the centres of the stars to be separated one inch and a half.

Commanders will have two crossed foul anchors, two inches long from crown to ring.

Lieutenants—one foul anchor, two inches long.

Masters' epaulettes will be plain, and of the same pattern as Lieutenants.

Surgeons, Passed Assistant Surgeons, and Assistant Surgeons' epaulettes will have solid smooth crescents, with the letters 𝕸. 𝕯. in old English characters, embroidered in silver, in the middle of the frog. The senior Surgeon of the Navy and the "Surgeon of the Fleet," will have a silver embroidered rosette on the strap above the letters. The senior and other Pursers, the same as senior and other Surgeons, with the letters 𝕻. 𝕯. in old English characters, embroidered in silver in the middle of the frog.

Chief Engineers—the same as Masters, except that the strap shall be of silver lace, with the letter 𝕰. three-quarters of an inch long, in old English character, embroidered in gold on the frog, and the crescents to be smooth and solid.

Sword and Scabbard.

For all Officers—shall be cut-and-thrust blade, not less than twenty-six inches, nor more than twenty-nine inches long, half-basket hilt, grip white: Scabbards of black leather. Mountings of yellow gilt; and all as per pattern.

Sword-Belt.

For all Officers—Shall be of plain black glazed leather, not less than one inch and a half, nor more than two inches wide, with slings of the same not less than one-half nor more than three-quarters of an inch wide, and a hook in the forward ring to suspend the sword. Belt-plate of yellow gilt in front, two inches in diameter, as per pattern. The belt to be worn over the coat.

Sword-Knot.

For a Captain and Commander—shall be blue and gold cord, twenty-four inches long, including the tassel; gold and blue slide; tassel of twelve gold bullions, one inch and three-quarters long, inclosing five blue bullions, with basket-worked head.

For all other Commissioned Officers—a strap of gold lace, half an inch wide, and eighteen inches long, including the tassel; gold slide; tassel of twelve gold bullions, one inch and three-quarters long, with basket-worked head—all as per pattern.

Cravat or Stock.

For all Officers—shall be of black silk, or satin, without any tie in front, for full dress; a white shirt collar to show above it.

UNDRESS.—[Sea Officers.]

Coat.

For a Captain—shall be a frock-coat of Navy blue cloth, faced with the same, and lined with black silk serge; double-breasted; with two rows of large Navy buttons on the breast, nine in each row, placed four inches and a half apart from eye to eye at top, and two inches and a half at bottom.

Rolling collar, skirts to be full, commencing at the top of the hip bone and descending four-fifths thence towards the knee, with one button behind on each hip, and one near the bottom of each fold. Cuffs, the same as for full dress.

For a Commander—the same in all respects as for a Captain, except that the cuffs shall have but two strips of gold lace around them, half an inch apart, one above and the other below the seam, but joining it, and three small buttons in the opening.

For a Lieutenant—the same in all respects as for a Commander, except that the cuffs shall have but one strip of gold lace around the upper edge.

For a Master—the same as for a Lieutenant, except that the cuffs shall have, instead of lace, three medium size Navy buttons around the upper edge.

For a Passed Midshipman—the same as for a Master, excepting the buttons around the cuffs.

For a Midshipman—the same as for a Passed Midshipman, except that medium buttons shall be substituted for the large buttons.

UNDRESS.—[Civil Officers.]

For a Surgeon, Passed Assistant, and Assistant Surgeon—shall be a frock-coat of Navy blue cloth, faced with the same, double-breasted, rolling collar, two rows of large Navy buttons on the breast, nine in each row; proportion for body and skirts the same as for a Captain; skirts lined with black silk serge; one button behind on each hip and one near the bottom of each fold of the skirt. Cuffs plain, with three large size Navy buttons around the upper edge, and three small ones in the opening.

For a Purser—the same as prescribed for a Surgeon.

For a Chaplain—the same as for a Surgeon, except that it shall be single-breasted, with one row of nine large Navy buttons on the breast, the cuffs plain, with three small buttons in the opening only.

For a Professor and a Commodore's Secretary—the same as for a Chaplain, except that there shall be but eight buttons on the breast.

For a Clerk—the same as for a Secretary, except that there shall be but six buttons on the breast.

Engineers.

For a Chief Engineer—the same as for a Surgeon except that it shall be single-breasted, with one row of nine large Navy buttons on the breast, three large size buttons around the upper edge of the cuff, and three small ones in the opening.

For a First Assistant Engineer—the same as for a Chief Engineer, except that the cuffs shall have three medium size buttons around the upper edge.

For a Second and Third Assistant Engineer—the same as for a First Assistant, except the buttons around the upper edge of the cuff.

Vests.

For all Officers—the same pattern as for full dress, and to be white or of blue cloth, according to the season for blue or white pantaloons.

Pantaloons.

For all Officers—the same style and pattern as for full dress, but without lace or cord.

Cocked Hats.

The same as for full dress; but the regulation cap may be worn when permitted by the officer in command.

Shoulder-Straps.

Every officer entitled to epaulettes, shall wear above the shoulder-seam of the undress-coat, shoulder-straps, made according to pattern, as follows: *For a Captain*—of blue cloth, four inches long and one inch and three-eighths wide, bordered with an embroidery of gold, one-quarter of an inch in width, with the same device as prescribed for the frog of the epaulette, (except the star,) embroidered in silver on the centre of the strap. The senior Captain in the Navy, and the Commander-in-chief of a Squadron, will wear in addition, a silver star, seven-tenths of an inch in diameter, on each end of the strap. *For a Commander*—the same as for a Captain, except that the device shall be the same as that directed for the epaulettes. *For a Lieutenant*—the same as for a Commander, except that the device shall be the same as that directed for the epaulettes.

For a Master—the same as for a Lieutenant, without any device. *For a Passed Midshipman*—a gold lace strap, one-half of an inch wide and four inches long. *For a Surgeon*—the same as for a Lieutenant, except that they shall be one inch wide. Those of more than twelve years' standing, to have the letters **M. D.** in old English characters, embroidered in silver in the centre, and on each end a gold acorn—and, those of less than twelve years, the same, without the acorn.

For a Passed Assistant Surgeon—the same as for a Surgeon, except that the straps shall be three-quarters of an inch wide, and the embroidery around, one-eighth of an inch wide, with an embroidered gold bar on each end. *For an Assistant Surgeon*—the same as for a Passed Assistant Surgeon, without the bars.

For a Purser—of more than twelve years, the same as for a Surgeon, except that they will have the letters **P. D.** in old English characters, embroidered in silver in the centre, with a single oak leaf in gold at each end.

For a Purser—of less than twelve years, the same, without the leaf.

For a Chief Engineer—the same as for a Master, except that, in the centre of them, there shall be embroidered, in silver, the letter **E.** in old English character.

Shoulder-straps to be always worn as distinctive marks, when the epaulettes are not worn.

Buttons.

Shall be of three sizes; large, medium, and small; and all of the same device, as per pattern.

SERVICE DRESS.

The "Service Dress" of all officers shall be the same as the undress, with caps instead of cocked hats, and with or without swords, and with or without epaulettes, for all officers entitled to wear them.

Caps.

Cap of blue cloth, to be not less than three inches and a half nor more than four inches in height, and not more than ten, nor less than nine inches and a half in diameter on the top, with patent-leather visor, to be worn by all officers in service dress.

For a Captain—the same device as on the epaulette, without the star, in silver embroidery, surrounded by a gold embroidered wreath of oak and olive leaves, as per pattern, on the front of the cap, above a band of gold lace, one inch and a half wide.

For a Commander—the same as for a Captain, except that the device shall be two crossed foul anchors in silver, similarly disposed and embroidered, above a band of gold lace, one inch and a quarter wide.

For a Lieutenant and Master—one silver foul anchor, similarly disposed and embroidered, above a band of gold lace, one inch wide.

For a Passed or other Midshipman—the same as for a Lieutenant, except the band of gold lace.

For a Boatswain, Gunner, Carpenter, and Sailmaker—a gold embroidered anchor, in front, without the wreath.

For a Surgeon, Passed and Assistant Surgeon, and Purser—a gold embroidered wreath of oak leaf, as per pattern, inclosing the letters **M. D.** and **P. D.** in old English characters, in silver, respectively.

For a Professor, Secretary, and Clerk—the same wreath, without any device.

For all Engineers—an embroidered device and wreath, as per pattern; the wheel embroidered in gold and the anchor in silver, similarly placed above a band of gold lace, one inch wide.

Summer Frock-Coat.

In summer or in tropical climates, officers may wear frock-coats and pantaloons of dark blue summer-cloth, of the style and pattern herein prescribed, with medium size Navy buttons.

Jackets.

May be worn as "Service Dress" by all officers *when at sea,* except when at general muster, or in charge of the Deck. To be of Navy blue cloth, or white drill, lined with the same, double-breasted, rolling collar, same number of small size buttons on breast as for full dress-coat; open fly-sleeve, with four small buttons in the opening. With shoulder-straps for the appropriate grades—but without epaulettes.

Straw Hats.

In summer or in tropical climates, officers may also wear, on shipboard, under similar circumstances, white straw hats —the body of the hat to be six inches in height, and the rim three and a half inches in width.

Over-Coats.

For all Officers—shall be of dark blue Pilot Cloth, double-breasted, rolling collar, skirt to descend three inches below the knee. The same number of Navy buttons, and similarly arranged, as for undress-coat—no buttons to be worn on the cuffs or pocket-flaps.

Officers entitled to shoulder-straps, will wear the same on their over-coats, as directed for undress-coats.

Blue cloth cloaks may be used in boats, or when epaulettes are worn, if it be rendered necessary by cold or wet weather.

Dress for petty Officers and Crew.

Boatswain's Mates, Gunner's Mates, Carpenter's Mates, Sailmaker's Mates, Ship's Steward, and *Ship's Cook,* will wear, embroidered in white silk, on the right sleeve of their blue jackets, above the elbow in front, an eagle and anchor, of not more than three inches in length, with a star of one inch in diameter, one inch above. The same device, embroidered in blue, to be worn on the sleeves of their white frocks, in summer.

All other petty officers, except officers' stewards, and yeomen, will wear the same device on their left sleeves.

The outside clothing for *Petty Officers, Firemen,* and *Coal-heavers, Seamen, Ordinary Seamen, Landsmen,* and *Boys,* for muster, shall consist of blue cloth jackets and trousers, or blue woollen frocks, with white duck cuffs and collars: black hats; black silk neckerchiefs, and shoes, or boots in cold weather—in warm weather, it shall consist of white frocks and trousers; black or white hats, as the Commander may for the occasion direct, having proper regard for the comfort of the crew: black silk neckerchiefs, and shoes; the collars and cuffs to be lined with blue cotton cloth, and stitched round with thread. Thick blue cloth caps, without visors, may be worn by the crew at sea, except on holidays or at muster.

APPROVED:

WILL. A. GRAHAM,
Secretary of the Navy.

NAVY DEPARTMENT,
March 8, 1852.

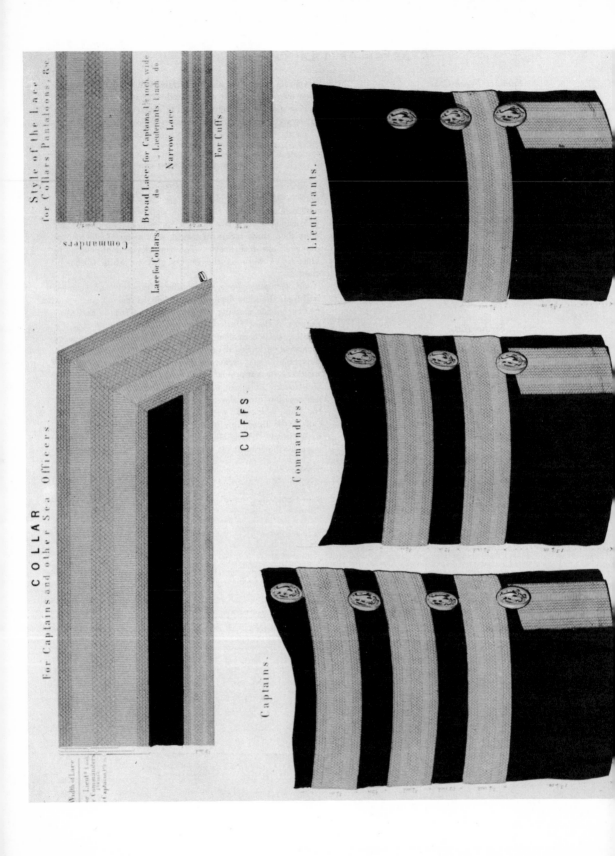

Style of the Lace
for Collars Pantaloons &c

Broad Lace: for Captains 1¼ inch wide
do Lieutenants 1 inch do
Narrow Lace

For Cuffs

(Commanders)

Lace for Collars

COLLAR
For Captains and other Sea Officers.

Lieutenants.

CUFFS.

Commanders.

Captains.

COLLARS AND CUFFS. FULL DRESS.

Surgeons.
Pursers.
Chief Engineers.

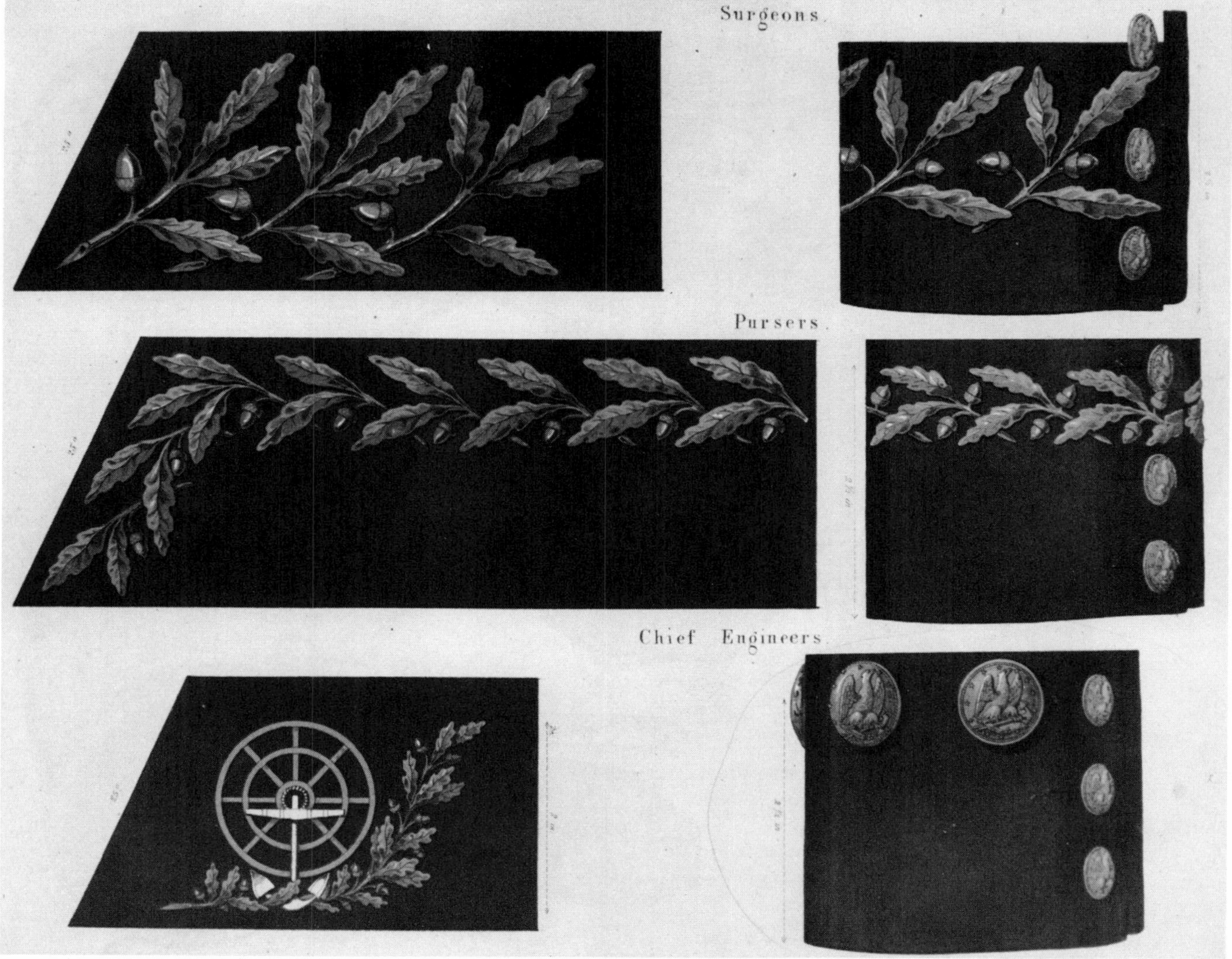

EPAULETTES.

Captains.

Sizes of Bullion.

Captains 3½ inch long ⅝ inch diam
Commanders, 3 in. „ „ ½ „ „
Lieutenants 3 in „ „ ⅜ „ „

Surgeons

Passed Assist
& Assist. Surgeons

Pursers

Masters

A Silver wreath
worn by the Senior

Embroidered Centre and
Sheared border

Rosette by
Junior Surgeon

Profile of Rosette.

Surgeons & Pursers
of more than 12 years

Surgeons & Pursers
of less than 12 years

Bullion 3 in. long
and 2 in diam.

Bullion 3 in long
and 3.8 in diam

Bullion 3 in. long
and 3.8 in diam

Bullion 3 in long
and 3.8 in diam

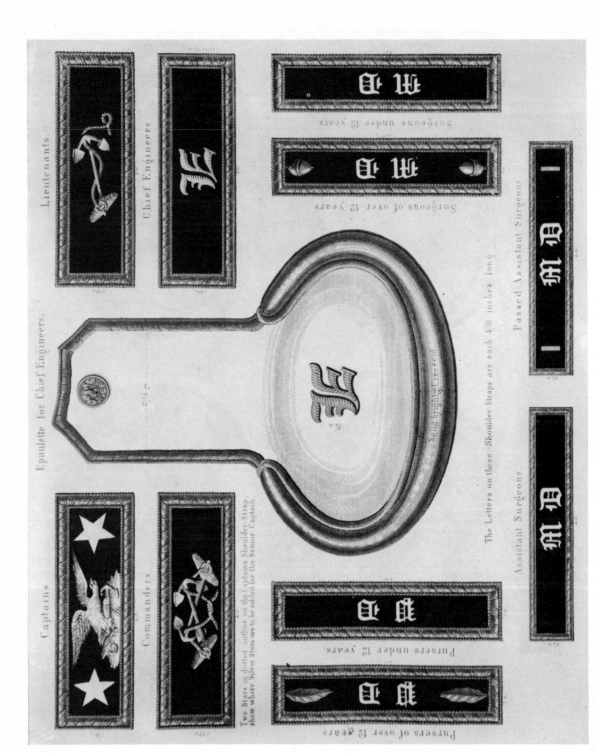

Lieutenants

Chief Engineers

Surgeons under 12 years

Surgeons of over 12 years

Passed Assistant Surgeons

Epaulette for Chief Engineers.

The Letters on these Shoulder-Straps are each 4/10 inches long.

Assistant Surgeons

Captains

Commanders

Two Stars in dotted outline on the Captains Shoulder-Strap, show where Silver Stars are to be added for the Senior Captain.

Pursers under 12 years

Pursers of over 12 years

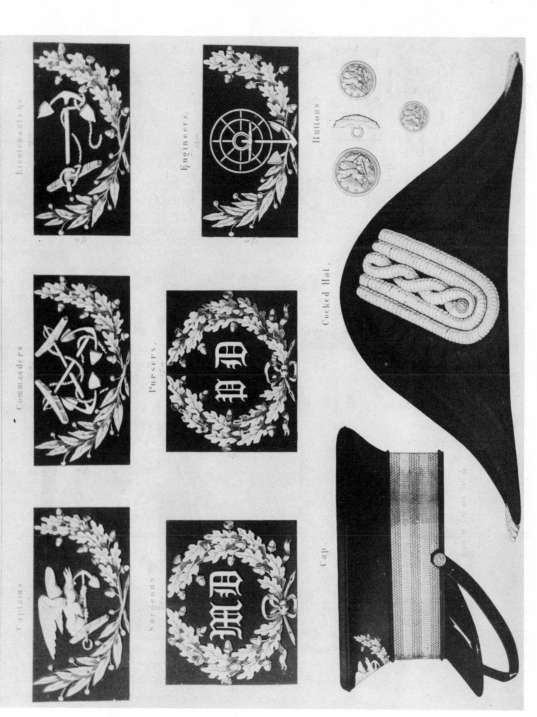

Lieutenants.

Engineers.

Buttons.

Commanders.

Pursers.

Cocked Hat.

Captains.

Surgeons.

Cap.

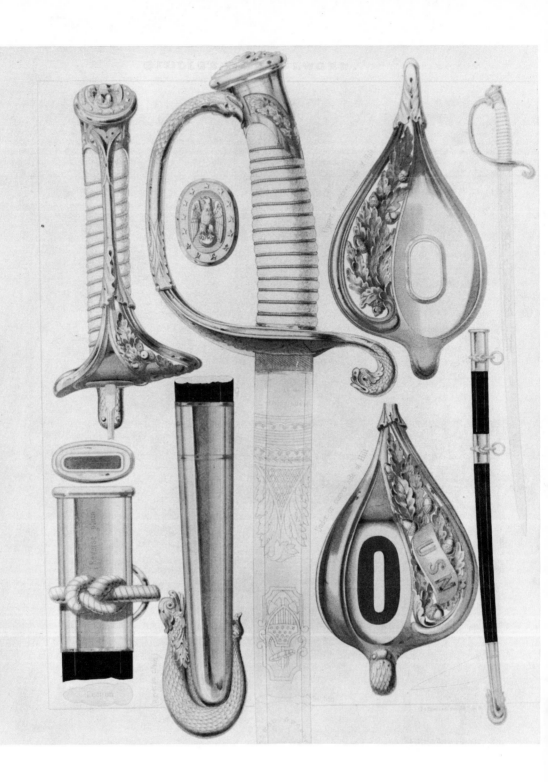

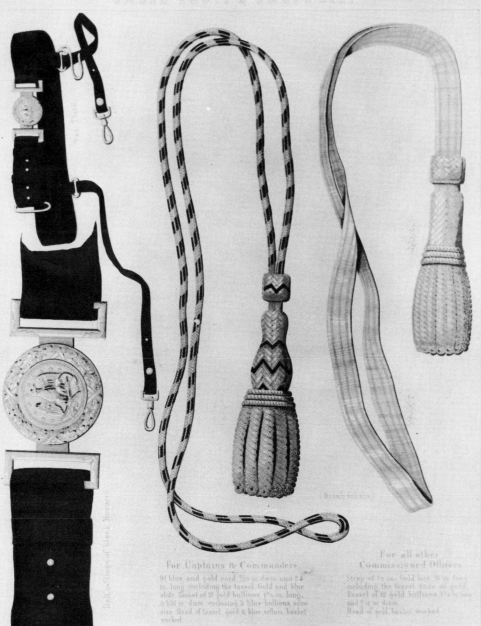

SWORD KNOTS & SWORD BELT

For Captains & Commanders

Of blue and gold cord ⁵⁄₁₆ in. diam. and 2 ft. in. long, including the tassel. Gold and blue slide, tassel of 2½ gold bullions 1¼ in. long, ⁷⁄₁₆ in. diam. enclosing 5 blue bullions same size. Head of tassel, gold & blue velvet, basket worked.

For all other Commissioned Officers

Strap of ⅝ in. Gold lace 26 in. long, including the tassel. Slide of gold. Tassel of 2½ gold bullions 1¼ in. long, and ⁷⁄₁₆ in. diam. Head of gold basket worked.

Belts, Straps of black Morocco.

FULL DRESS.

Chief Engineer   Purser   Surgeon   Captain

FULL DRESS.

Master   Passed Midshipman   Midshipman   Lieutenant

UNDRESS

Captain.   Master.   Passed Midshipman.   Midshipman.   Surgeon.

SERVICE DRESS.

Captain   Midshipman   Surgeon.   Purser

SERVICE DRESS.

Commander. Passed Midshipman Chief Engineer. Master.

Appendix B

Uniform Regulations, United States Navy, 1959

The best way to describe the various uniforms, devices, and insignia now worn by Navy personnel is to reproduce pertinent illustrations from the current uniform regulations.

The service blue and khaki uniforms, and the tropical and working dress of male officers and petty officers are identical except for devices and insignia. However, two types of white uniforms are worn: the single-breasted, standing-collar coat by officers and a double-breasted, roll-collared coat by petty officers. The dress of male enlisted personnel below the rating of chief petty officer has little similarity to that worn by officers and chief petty officers. Women of the Navy, both officer and enlisted, wear identical uniforms, with very few exceptions. Rank, rate, and grade are shown by distinctive devices or insignia.

For a better understanding of the captions shown under the illustrations of blue uniforms, a definition of the Navy's terminology is required:

Blue A uniform—blue coat, blue trousers or skirt, black shoes, and blue cap-cover or hat.

Blue B uniform—blue coat, blue trousers or skirt, black shoes, and white cap-cover or hat.

Blue C uniform (officers only)—blue coat, white trousers or skirt, white shoes, and white cap-cover or hat.

EVENING DRESS BLUE B UNIFORMS

**EVENING DRESS
WHITE JACKET UNIFORM**

Evening dress uniforms are worn at official formal evening functions which civilian women normally wear evening dress and civilian men we evening clothes (white tie). Evening dress uniforms are worn with miniatu medals. Only commissioned and warrant officers may wear evening dre Male officers have an evening dress for less formal occasions consisting white mess jacket, blue high-waisted trousers, white vest, dress shirt, wing collar, and black tie.

Dinner dress is authorized for all officers, male petty officers, and all e listed women. It is worn at ordinary official social functions at which civili men would normally wear dinner dress (black tie). There are two other dinn dress uniforms for officers which are not shown. Both men and women m wear dinner dress blue C, the blue coats shown, with white skirt or trouse and white shoes. The other is for male officers only, the white evening me jacket, worn with a black cumberbund and a stiff turn down collar.

Full dress is worn by all personnel on occasions of state, ceremony, a solemnity. The uniform is basically the blue or white service dress wi large medals. Only male commissioned and commissioned warrant office except chaplains, wear a sword in full dress.

**DINNER DRESS
BLUE JACKET UNIFORM**

DINNER DRESS BLUE B UNIFORMS   FULL DRESS WHITE UNIFORM

EVENING DRESS WHITE UNIFORMS   FULL DRESS BLUE UNIFORM

Male officer   Male chief petty officer

SERVICE DRESS BLUE
B UNIFORMS

Enlisted man below
chief petty officer   Enlisted woman

Male officer

Woman officer

Male chief petty officer

SERVICE DRESS WHITE

UNIFORMS

Enlisted man below
chief petty officer

Enlisted woman

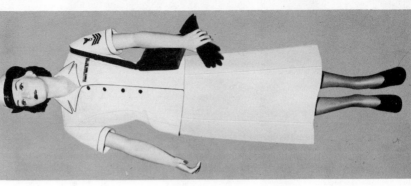

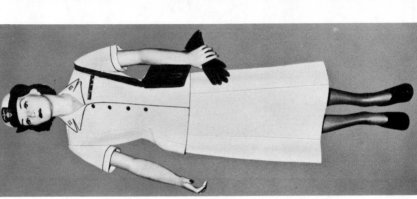

Woman officer

Enlisted woman

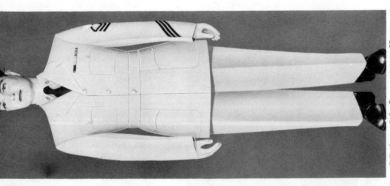

Male officer

Male chief petty officer

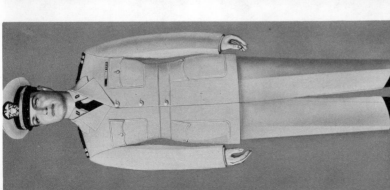

The service dress khaki uniform is worn by male officers and chief petty officers. The uniform is made of tropical worsted, gabardine, or a similar light-weight tropical fabric. There is no similar uniform for enlisted men below the rating of chief petty officer.

The women's service dress light blue uniforms are the counterpart of men's khakis. The material is a light, blue-and-white striped, corded, dacron-wool material.

The khaki working uniform is worn by male officers and petty officers, and by Navy nurses when engaged in duties with or around aircraft. The uniform is of cotton cloth, and a coat like that worn in service dress khaki is prescribed. Nurses also are permitted to wear khaki slacks.

The gray working uniform is the women's equivalent of the khaki working uniform. It is a one-piece shirtmaker-style of gray and white seersucker, and

Male officer   Woman officer   Male chief petty officer

HAKI WORKING UNIFORMS

GRAY WORKING UNIFORMS

Enlisted woman

Woman officer

Male officer

Woman officer

Enlisted man
below chief petty officer

BLUE WORKING UNIFORMS

AVIATION GREEN
WORKING UNIFORMS

Male officer

Woman officer

| Male officer | Woman officer | Enlisted man below chief petty officer |

DUNGAREE WORKING UNIFORMS

WHITE WORKING INDOOR DUTY UNIFORM

(Nurses only)

The aviation green working uniform is worn by male officers, chief petty ~~ers~~, and Navy nurses assigned duty in or around aircraft. The material is ~~stry~~ green, woolen or worsted. Men wear a khaki shirt and nurses wear ~~same~~ shirt as prescribed for the khaki working uniform. Slacks can be ~~n~~ instead of the skirt.

No coat is prescribed for the blue working uniform. Male chief petty ~~ers~~ wear the same shirt and trousers as officers. The head piece is blue ~~vhite~~ for men, according to the order of the day, and a blue garrison cap ~~women~~. Women wear a white shirt.

All personnel wear blue chambray shirts when in the dungaree working ~~orm~~.

Male officer

Male chief petty officer

Enlisted man below
chief petty officer

TROPICAL WHITE UNIFORMS

TROPICAL WHITE
LONG UNIFORM

Male officer

Enlisted man below
chief petty officer

SERVICE DRESS BLUE C UNIFORMS

TROPICAL KHAKI UNIFORMS

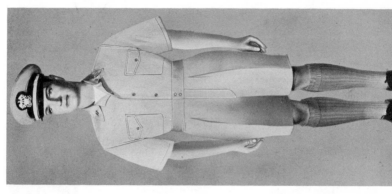

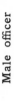

Male officer

Woman officer

Male officer

Enlisted man below chief petty officer

Chief petty officers wear the same tropical white long uniform as officers, with the cap device of their rating, a gold foul anchor with the letters *U.S.N.* in silver, superimposed on it. Instead of an officer's shoulder marks, chiefs wear the anchor-letter device on the collar tips but no sleeve rating badge.

Service dress blue C uniforms are worn by officers only.

Both officers and chief petty officers wear the same uniform, except that chiefs display their cap device, and pin-on devices on the collar. This same uniform is called tropical khaki long when worn with long trousers by officers and chief petty officers.

OFFICER GRADE STRIPES

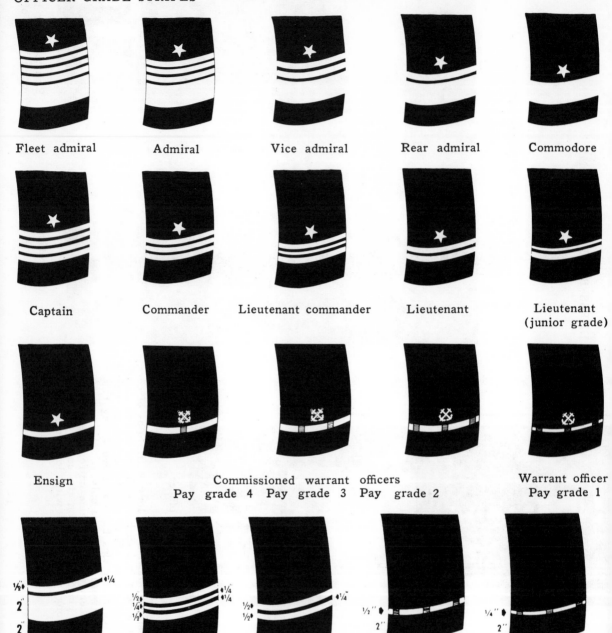

Fleet admiral	Admiral	Vice admiral	Rear admiral	Commodore
Captain	Commander	Lieutenant commander	Lieutenant	Lieutenant (junior grade)

Ensign

Commissioned warrant officers
Pay grade 4 Pay grade 3 Pay grade 2

Warrant officer
Pay grade 1

MANNER OF WEARING

Staff corps officers wear the same sleeve lace as officers of the Line, but substitute the corps devices for the star. Although the device of a boatswain is shown in the illustrations of the sleeve lace of commissioned warrant officers and warrant officers, each officer displays the device of his specialty.

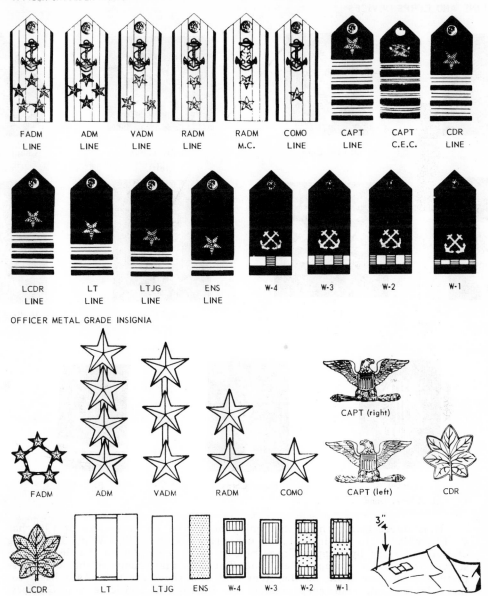

OFFICER SHOULDER MARKS

| FADM LINE | ADM LINE | VADM LINE | RADM LINE | RADM M.C. | COMO LINE | CAPT LINE | CAPT C.E.C. | CDR LINE |

| LCDR LINE | LT LINE | LTJG LINE | ENS LINE | W-4 | W-3 | W-2 | W-1 |

OFFICER METAL GRADE INSIGNIA

| FADM | ADM | VADM | RADM | COMO | CAPT (right) | CAPT (left) | CDR |

| LCDR | LT | LTJG | ENS | W-4 | W-3 | W-2 | W-1 |

Staff officers wear the shoulder marks shown, replacing the star of the Line by a corps device, as shown in the cut of the marks of a captain, Civil Engineer Corps (top row, second from right) for ranks from captain to ensign. A rear admiral, staff corps, places the device of his corps on the foul anchor of the Line, as the center illustration, top row.

The metal pin on devices are the size to be worn on the shoulder straps of blue and khaki raincoats and on the forestry green overcoat of aviators. Similar devices of a smaller size are worn on collar points of khaki, blue flannel, and tropical-khaki shirts. Line officers wear the grade insignia on both collar points. Staff corps officers and warrant officers wear the grade device on the right collar point only, with a corps or specialty device on the left point.

OFFICER LINE AND CORPS DEVICES

Line	Medical Corps	Supply Corps (left)	Chaplain Corps (Christian)
Chaplain Corps (Jewish)	Civil Engineer Corps	Dental Corps	Medical Service Corps (left)
Leader U. S. Navy Band	Nurse Corps	ENS	

It is interesting to note, that only one of the corps devices of 1962 has a resemblance to an insignia in use prior to the Civil War. The sprig of live-oak worn by Supply Corps officers is very similar to the device prescribed for pursers in September, 1852. The only real change is that originally there was but one acorn on the stem, and now there are two. As a basis for their devices, all staff corps under the Bureau of Medicine and Surgery, employ the spread oak leaf prescribed for medical officers in 1883. Medical officers use the 1883 insignia, a gold leaf and silver acorn; dental officers, the spread leaf with an acorn at either side of the stem; the Nurse Corps, the leaf only; and the Medical Service Corps, a plain leaf with a slanting twig. All staff corps follow the oak leaf or oak leaf and acorn motif except chaplains and the leader of the United States Navy Band.

The cut of the sleeve ornaments of an ensign indicates how the corps devices are placed with reference to the gold-lace sleeve stripes.

Boatswain or Operations Technician

Surface Ordnance Technician or Control Ordnance Technician

Mine Warfare Technician or Underwater Ordnance Technician

Ship's Clerk

Electronics Technician

Machinist

Ship Repair Technician

Electrician

Aviation Operations Technician

Aviation Ordnance Technician

Aviation Maintenance Technician

Aviation Electronics Technician

Aerographer

Photographer

Bandmaster

Supply Clerk

Civil Engineer Corps

Medical Service or Dental Service

Communications Technician (left)

Most of the devices worn by warrant officers are similar to the specialty marks worn by petty officers, for warrant officers normally come up through the ranks. Some are based on the insignia of the staff corps while others can be traced back to the insignia of warrant officers as prescribed by earlier uniform regulations. A wide range of skills is covered by these devices, indicative of the complexity of modern naval matters.

Chief
Petty Officer

Petty Officer
First Class

Petty Officer
Second Class

Petty Officer
Third Class

ENLISTED SPECIALTY MARKS (an integral part of the rating badge)

GENERAL RATINGS

Aerographer's Mate

Air Controlman

Aviation Boatswain's Mate

Aviation Electrician's Mate

Aviation Electronics
Technician

Aviation Fire Control
Technician

Aviation
Machinist's Mate

The rating badges of all petty officers, male and female, are worn on the left sleeve, half way between elbow and shoulder. The specialty marks are shown between the eagle and the inner angle of the upper chevron. This type of petty officer rating badge was instituted in 1886 and brought into the present form in 1894.

Enlisted specialty marks are an integral part of a petty officer's rating badge. From the small beginning of eight distinctive marks in 1866, the number has grown to sixty-three. The large number of marks now employed indicates the complexities of the modern Navy—in the air, on the land, and on and under the sea. Many of the specialty marks are used to identify men of the construction battalions who build the Navy's shore facilities overseas and in combat areas in time of war.

iation Ordnanceman   Aviation Storekeeper   Aviation Structural Mechanic   Boatswain's Mate

Boilermaker   Boilerman   Builder   Commissaryman   Communications Technician

Construction Electrician   Construction Mechanic   Damage Controlman   Dental Technician   Disbursing Clerk

Electrician's Mate   Electronics Technician   Engineering Aid   Engineman   Equipment Operator

Fire Control Technician   Gunner's Mate   Hospital Corpsman   Illustrator Draftsman   Interior Communications Electrician

Instrumentman   Journalist   Lithographer   Machine Accountant   Machinery Repairman

Machinist's Mate

Mineman

Missile Technician

Molder

Musician

Nuclear
Weaponsman

Opticalman

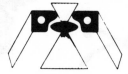
Parachute Rigger

Patternmaker

Personnel Man

Photographer's
Mate

Photographic
Intelligenceman

Postal Clerk

Quartermaster

Radarman

Radioman

Shipfitter

Ship's Serviceman

Signalman

Sonarman

Steel Worker

Steward

Storekeeper

Torpedoman's Mate

Tradevman

Utilities Man

Yeoman

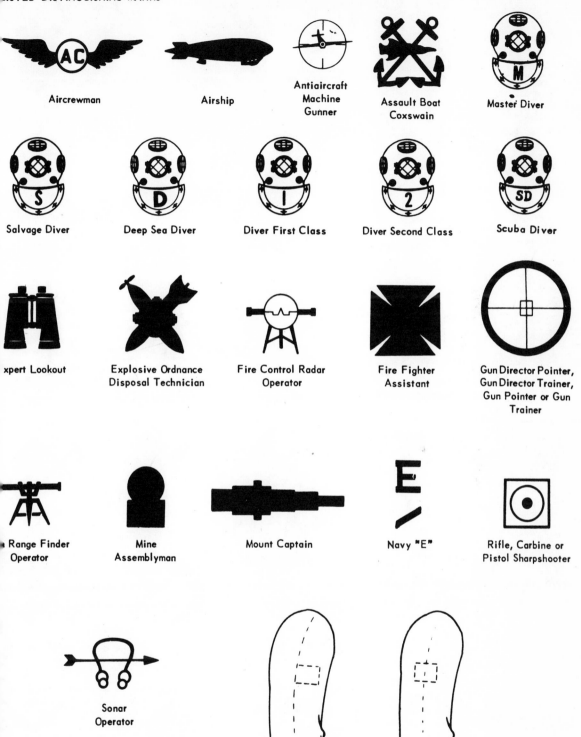

Aircrewman

Airship

Antiaircraft
Machine
Gunner

Assault Boat
Coxswain

Master Diver

Salvage Diver

Deep Sea Diver

Diver First Class

Diver Second Class

Scuba Diver

xpert Lookout

Explosive Ordnance
Disposal Technician

Fire Control Radar
Operator

Fire Fighter
Assistant

Gun Director Pointer,
Gun Director Trainer,
Gun Pointer or Gun
Trainer

Range Finder
Operator

Mine
Assemblyman

Mount Captain

Navy "E"

Rifle, Carbine or
Pistol Sharpshooter

Sonar
Operator

Jumper

Coat

The Navy uses a system of embroidered devices to indicate a man's special qualifications, in addition to those which are required for the general ratings indicated as part of the petty officer's device. The distinguishing marks are worn on the right sleeve between the elbow and shoulder as indicated in the cut.

Appendix C
Insignia and Devices of the Civil War Period

SEA OR LINE OFFICERS, 1861–JULY 31, 1862

FULL DRESS   SERVICE DRESS

RANK	SLEEVES	COLLAR	TROUSERS	EPAULETS	COCKED HAT	SHOULDER STRAPS	CAP DEVICE
Flag Officer*							
Captain*							
Commander*							
Lieutenant*							
Master*							

Passed Midshipman*			NONE			
Midshipman*			NONE		NONE	
Boatswain† Gunner Carpenter Sailmaker			NONE		NONE	
Master's Mate§			NONE		NONE	
Shipped or Rated Master's Mate‡			NONE		NONE	

* FULL DRESS COAT—Navy blue cloth, double breasted, lined and faced with white serge; two rows of nine large Navy buttons. Standing collar.
UNDRESS COAT—Navy blue frock coat, double breasted, faced with blue cloth and lined with black silk serge; two rows of nine large Navy buttons. Rolling collar.

† FULL AND UNDRESS COAT—Navy blue cloth, double breasted, lined and faced with blue cloth; two rows of eight large Navy buttons. Rolling collar.

§ UNDRESS COAT ONLY—Blue cloth or flannel, single breasted, rolling collar; single row of nine large Navy buttons.

‡ UNDRESS COAT ONLY—Blue cloth or flannel jacket, double breasted, rolling collar; two rows of six medium size Navy buttons.

CIVIL OR STAFF OFFICERS, 1861–JULY 31, 1862

	SERVICE DRESS		FULL DRESS				
RANK	CAP DEVICE	SHOULDER STRAPS	COCKED HAT	EPAULETS	TROUSERS	COLLAR	SLEEVES
Surgeon over 12 years*							
Surgeon under 12 years*							
Passed Assistant Surgeon*							
Assistant Surgeon*							
Paymaster over 12 years*							

Paymaster under 12 years*						
Assistant Paymaster*						
Chief Engineer over 12 years*						
Chief Engineer under 12 years*						
First Assistant Engineer*				NONE		

CIVIL OR STAFF OFFICERS, 1861–JULY 31, 1862
FULL DRESS

RANK	SLEEVES	COLLAR	TROUSERS	EPAULETS	COCKED HAT
Second Assistant Engineer*				NONE	
Third Assistant Engineer*				NONE	
Chaplain†				NONE	NONE
Professor of Mathematics§				NONE	NONE
Commodore's Secretary§				NONE	NONE
Clerk‡				NONE	NONE

SERVICE DRESS

SHOULDER STRAPS	CAP DEVICE
N O N E	
N O N E	
N O N E	
N O N E	
N O N E	

* FULL DRESS COAT—Navy blue cloth, double breasted, lined and faced with white serge; wo rows of nine large Navy buttons. Standing collar.

UNDRESS COAT—Navy blue frock coat, double breasted, faced with blue cloth and lined vith black silk serge; two rows of nine large Navy buttons. Rolling collar.

FULL DRESS—Single breasted black coat with a standing collar and nine black cloth-covered buttons. No insignia. Blue cloth cap.

SERVICE DRESS—Black frock coat, single breasted, nine black cloth-covered buttons.

FULL AND UNDRESS COATS—Navy blue frock coat, single breasted, rolling collar. One ow of eight large Navy buttons.

FULL AND UNDRESS—Navy blue frock coat, single breasted, rolling collar. One row of even Navy buttons.

LINE OFFICERS, JULY 31, 1862–JANUARY 28, 1864

FULL DRESS

SERVICE DRESS

RANK	SLEEVES	EPAULETS	COCKED HAT	SHOULDER STRAPS	CAP DEVICE
Rear Admiral					
Commodore					
Captain					
Commander					
Lieutenant Commander					

Lieutenant					
Master					
Ensign					
Midshipman			NONE	NONE	
Boatswain* Gunner Carpenter Sailmaker		NONE	NONE	NONE	

LINE OFFICERS, JULY 31, 1862–JANUARY 28, 1864

FULL DRESS
SERVICE DRESS

RANK	SLEEVES	EPAULETS	COCKED HAT	SHOULDER STRAPS	CAP DEVICE
Master's Mate †		NONE	NONE	NONE	
Shipped or Rated Master's Mate §		NONE	NONE	NONE	NONE

All officers, except where noted, wore a double breasted blue frock coat, with two rows of nine buttons, and rolling collar, for both full and service dress. In full dress, the coat was worn with epaulets, cocked hat, sword and sword knot. In service dress, shoulder straps and cap were worn, the sword being optional.
The exceptions were:
* Rows of eight buttons on each breast.
† Single breasted Navy blue frock coat, row of nine buttons.
§ Instead of frock coat, a double breasted jacket, with two rows of six buttons was worn.

| RANK | FULL DRESS | | | | SERVICE DRESS | |
	SLEEVES	EPAULETS	COCKED HAT	SHOULDER STRAPS	CAP DEVICE
Surgeon over 12 years					
Surgeon under 12 years					
Passed Assistant Surgeon					
Assistant Surgeon					
Paymaster over 12 years					

RANK	SLEEVES	EPAULETS	COCKED HAT	SHOULDER STRAPS	CAP DEVICE
Paymaster under 12 years					
Assistant Paymaster					
Chief Engineer over 12 years					
Chief Engineer under 12 years					
First Assistant Engineer		NONE			
Second Assistant Engineer		NONE			

Rank				
Third Assistant Engineer		NONE		NONE
Chaplain*		NONE	NONE	NONE
Professor of Mathematics†		NONE	NONE	NONE
Commodore's Secretary†		NONE	NONE	NONE
Clerk§		NONE	NONE	NONE

All officers, except where noted, wore a double breasted, blue frock coat, with two rows of nine buttons, and rolling collar, for both full and service dress. In full dress, the coat was worn with epaulets, cocked hat, sword and sword knot. In service dress, shoulder straps and cap were worn, the sword being optional.

The exceptions were:

* Black single breasted frock coat, rolling collar, single row of nine black-covered buttons.
† Single breasted Navy blue frock coat, single row of eight large Navy buttons.
§ Single breasted Navy blue frock coat, single row of seven large Navy buttons.

LINE OFFICERS, JANUARY 28, 1864—1866
SERVICE DRESS

RANK	SLEEVES	SHOULDER STRAPS	CAP DEVICE
Rear Admiral			
Commodore			
Captain			
Commander			
Lieutenant Commander			
Lieutenant			
Master			

RANK	SLEEVES	SHOULDER STRAPS	CAP DEVICE
Ensign			
Midshipman*		NONE	
Boatswain			
Gunner			
Carpenter			
Sailmaker			
Master's Mate*		NONE	

CIVIL OR STAFF OFFICERS, JANUARY 28, 1864—1866
SERVICE DRESS

RANK	SLEEVES	SHOULDER STRAPS	CAP DEVICE
Chief of Bureau of Medicine and Surgery			
Fleet Surgeon and Surgeon over 15 years			
Surgeon over 5 years			
Surgeon under 5 years			
Passed Assistant Surgeon			
Assistant Surgeon			
Chief of Bureau of Provisions and Clothing			

RANK	SLEEVES	SHOULDER STRAPS	CAP DEVICE
Fleet Paymaster and Paymaster over 15 years			
Paymaster over 5 years			
Paymaster under 5 years			
Assistant Paymaster			
Chief of Bureau of Steam Engineering			
Fleet Engineers and Chief Engineer over 15 years			
Chief Engineer over 5 years			

CIVIL OR STAFF OFFICERS, JANUARY 28, 1864—1866
SERVICE DRESS

RANK	SLEEVES	SHOULDER STRAPS	CAP DEVICE
Chief Engineer under 5 years			
First Assistant Engineer			
Second Assistant Engineer			
Third Assistant Engineer*		NONE	
Chief of Bureau of Constructions			
Naval Constructor over 20 years			
Naval Constructor over 12 years			
Naval Constructor under 12 years			

RANK	SLEEVES	SHOULDER STRAPS	CAP DEVICE
Assistant Naval Constructor			
Chaplain over 12 years			
Chaplain under 12 years			
Professor of Mathematics over 12 years			
Professor of Mathematics under 12 years			
Secretary			
Clerk*		NONE	

ll officers wore a Navy blue frock coat with rolling collar, double breasted, with two rows
" large Navy buttons except where noted. Only the service dress was permitted, the coat with
oulder straps and the blue cloth cap, with corps device, when authorized.
xception in the style of the coat:
Two rows of medium-sized Navy buttons, instead of the large buttons.

Index

Acts of Congress
March 27, 1794, first naval armament, established ranks and ratings, pay, 19, 20, 22
April 20, 1796, authorized completion of three frigates, 22
July 1, 1797, authorized manning of frigates; listed ranks, rates and pay, 22
April 27, 1798, provided for additional vessels, 23
April 30, 1798, created Navy Department, 23
February 25, 1799, funds for two drydocks, 32
February 25, 1799, pay of captains and commanders, 24
March 3, 1801, reduced Navy, limited officers, 25
April 21, 1806, authorized officer strength, rank of master commandant, 27
February 7, 1812, created Board of Navy Commissioners for Navy management, 28
March 30, 1812, appropriations, pursers to be commissioned, 27
June 2, 1813, appropriations, authorized schoolmasters, 34
March 9, 1814, funds for first steam vessels, 34
April 29, 1816, additional steam vessels, 35
April 4, 1818, prescribed American flag, 64
March 3, 1827, funds for two drydocks, 32
May 24, 1828, for better organization of Medical Department, 32
March 3, 1835, provision for professors of mathematics and secretaries, 33
March 3, 1837, changed titles, master commandant to commander, sailing master to master, 34
March 3, 1839, additional steam vessel, 38
August 31, 1842, created Bureau System of management, 39, 165
August 31, 1842, clarified status of professors of mathematics, 41
August 31, 1842, pay and appointment of engineers, classes, uniform, 41, 97
June 17, 1844, status, naval constructors, pay, 42

March 3, 1847, first appropriations for Naval Academy, 44
August 3, 1848, commissioned rank for professors of mathematics, 47
March 3, 1853, directed that a naval constructor be chief of Bureau of Construction, Equipment, and Repair, 41
August 5, 1854, confirmed relative rank of surgeons and pursers, 47, 111
January 16, 1857, created rank of Flag Officer, 47
March 3, 1859, confirmed relative rank, engineers, 48
June 22, 1860, changed title of pursers to paymasters, 48, 165
July 17, 1861, established grade of assistant paymaster, 49
July 24, 1861, provided for temporary officers and men, Navy, 180
July 31, 1861, created position of Assistant Secretary of the Navy, 49
July 5, 1862, modified bureau system, changed to eight bureaus, 49
July 16, 1862, modified and enlarged ranks of line officers, 50
December 21, 1864, authorized rank of Vice Admiral, 52, 131
July 25, 1866, authorized transfer of some volunteer officers to Navy, 158
March 2, 1867, gave civil engineers commissioned rank, 158
March 3, 1871, relative rank, star officers, created Pay Corps, 161, 165, 201
March 31, 1872, relative rank, professors of mathematics, 161
March 3, 1883, changed masters to lieutenant (junior grade), 174
March 2, 1891, first funds for Naval Militia, 180
July 19, 1892, changed name of Provisions and Clothing to Supplies and Accounts, 165
August 3, 1894, assistance to state naval militias, 180
June 17, 1898, established Hospital Corps, 177, 220
March 3, 1899, Personnel Act, rank, etc., 163, 177, 178
January 21, 1903, placed or-

ganized land militia under War Department, 181
May 13, 1908, established Nurse Corps, 178
August 22, 1912, authorized dental surgeons, 179
February 14, 1914, gave Navy responsibility for state naval militias, 181
June 30, 1914, abolished Bureau of Equipment, 165
March 3, 1915, created Naval Reserve, office of Naval Operations, 167, 181, 183, 241
August 29, 1916, changes, Naval Reserve, Engineering Duty Only officers, restored rank of Admiral, abolished Professors' Corps, 167, 178, 181, 183
July 1, 1918, changes, Naval Reserve, Naval Volunteers, 182
June 4, 1920, changes Naval Reserve, Naval Militia, 182
June 20, 1920, changes Naval Reserve, Naval Militia, 182
July 12, 1921, established Bureau of Aeronautics, 167
February 28, 1925, Naval Reserve, Naval Militia, 182
July 1, 1938, Naval Reserve, 182
June 20, 1940, established Bureau of Ships, 170
May 13, 1942, changed name of Bureau of Navigation to Bureau of Naval Personnel, 173
July 3, 1942, relative rank for nurses, 178
July 30, 1942, Naval Reserve, 183, 263
February 28, 1944, actual rank for nurses, 178, 179
April 18, 1946, established Medical Service Corps, 185
April 16, 1947, Nurse Corps to be a regular staff corps, 179
August 4, 1947, Medical Service Corps, 185
June 12, 1948, regular status, Waves; Officers, commissioned, 183
August 18, 1959, established Bureau of Naval Weapons, 173

Adams, John, appointed Stoddert, first head of Navy Department, 1798, 23
Aeronautics, Bureau of: established

1912; combined with Bureau of Ordnance in 1959 to form Bureau of Naval Weapons, 173

Airplane, Navy's first interest, 167

AlNav, Navy message: February 21, 1941 authorized khaki uniform for all officers, 249; October 15, 1946, abolished gray uniform and reinstated khakis, 259

Anchor, as indication of officers of the Line, 75, 89, 100, 102, 127, 187, 189, 207, 220, 244, 246; see also Devices, Line

Annapolis, Maryland: site of Naval Academy, 42, 44; aviation camp, 1911-1913, 169

Army, U.S.: National Guard, 181; shoulder straps, 224

Army and Navy Journal, November 21, 1863, Navy uniform instructions, 126

Assimilated rank, 44, 45, 46, 47, 86, 107, 124, 178; see also Relative rank

Assistant engineers: appointed by ship's captain, 1837, 38; authorized by Congress, 1842, 41; relative rank, 1859, 48; uniform prescribed by Capt. Perry, 1837, 86, 89; device, 104, 113, 127; relative rank, 159, 160; device, 192; see also Engineers

Assistant paymasters, rank established 1861, 49; see also Paymasters, Pay officers, Pursers

Assistant Pursers; see Pursers

Assistant Secretary of the Navy, position authorized, 1861, 49

Assistant Surgeons, title authorized, 1828, 32, 33; relative rank, 45, 46; device, 79, 83, 92; relative rank, 99, 100; device, 104; relative rank, 120, 159, 160; see also Uniforms, Medical Officers, see also Surgeons, Medical Officers

Aviation; see Naval Aviation

Aviation Camp: San Diego, 1910, 167; Annapolis, 1911, 169

Aviation Device, 243

Aviation uniform; see Uniform, Aviation

Baldwin, Loammi, civil engineer under Navy Board, 32

Bancroft, George, Secretary of the Navy; established Naval Academy, 1845, 42; gave relative rank to surgeons, 1846, 46

Barbary Powers, American troubles with, 19, 25, 60, 64

Barton, Surgeon W.P.C., first Chief of the Bureau of Medicine and Surgery, 41

"Blue and Gold" uniforms, 56, 60, 245, 259

Board of Navy Commissioners: responsibilities, 23; Board created 1815, 28; duties, membership 29; directed to prepare plans for a steam vessel, 1835, 35; superceded by Bureau System, 1842, 39; Sanger, W.P.S., civil engineer under Board, 1836, 158

Boards, Navy management; Navy Board, 1815, 39; Chief of Bureau Board, 1877, 164; Construction Board, 1889, 164; General Board, 1900, 165; present management, 173

Boatswain: warrant rank authorized, 1794, 20; pay, 22; relative rank, 45; considered Line officer, 1863, 51; see also Warrant Officers; Uniforms, Boatswain

Body coat, 56, 60, 63, 64, 65, 75,

89, 93, 107, 113, 187, 188, 196, 201, 202, 238, 245, 246, 269

Borie, Adolph P., Secretary of the Navy: served under President Grant, 158; directed that all Bureau Chiefs clear thru Admiral Porter, 159; relative rank, 159

Bowman, Josephine B., Superintendent, Nurse Corps, 256, photo, 257

Branch, John, Secretary of the Navy, uniform instructions, 1830, 74

Breeches, 58, 63, 79, 81, 249

British uniforms: seamen, 59; use of colored sleeve cloth for Staff, 1863, 194

Bureau, Chief of: qualifications, 1842, 40, 41; rank, 52, 126; devices, 127; on Construction Board, 1889, 164; report to Chief of Naval Operations, 173

Bureau System: established 1842, 39; functions, 39, 40; modified, 1862, 49; dispute with Secretary of the Navy, 1869, 159; changes in, 165, 167; responsibilities for aeroplane development, 169; modifications of, 170, 173

Bureaus: five established 1842, 39; responsibilities, 40; number increased to eight, 49; changes in, 165, 167, 170, 173 see also Aeronautics; Construction, Equipment and Repair; Construction and Repair; Engineering; Equipment and Repair; Medicine and Surgery; Naval Personnel; Naval Weapons; Navigation; Navy Yards and Docks; Ordnance; Ordnance and Hydrography; Ships; Steam Engineering; Yards and Docks, Bureaus of

Buttons, Navy types, 59, 64, 74, 241, 245, 250, 259, 264

Cabot, George, nominated to be Secretary of the Navy by President Adams, 1798, 23

Cadet, engineer, graduate of Naval Academy, 1883, 174, 204

Cadet, Midshipman, graduate of Naval Academy, 1883, 174, 204

Cap, bands, 82, 86, 94, 97, 101, 108, 110, 111, 115, 119, 127

Cap, cloth, enlisted, 1852, 108

Cap, device, 94, 97, 108, 110, 113, 119, 120, 121, 126, 127, 128, 134, 189, 196, 199, 200, 207, 217, 220, 234, 263, 264, 269

Cap, nurses, 253, 259

Cap, officers, 82, 86, 108, 110, 113, 115, 117, 119, 126, 127, 128, 134, 188, 200, 201, 217, 221, 238, 250, 259, 270

Cap, petty officers, 193, 194, 202, 216

Cap, ribbon, enlisted, 233, 241

Captain: rank established 1794, 19; increased pay, 1799, 24; of "Five Years Standing," 1820, 69, 72; see also Uniforms, Captain

Carpenter: warrant rank authorized, 1794, 20; pay, 22; relative rank, 45; staff officers, 1863, 51, 52; see also Uniforms Carpenter

Chambers, Capt. W. I., in charge of aviation in early stages, 167

Chandler, B. F., civil engineer, 161

Chaplain: rank authorized, com-

missioned, 1794, 33; as teachers, 34; duties, 38, 39; at Naval Academy, 44; relative rank, 45, 51, 52, 159, 160, 194; see also Uniforms, Chaplains

Chaplain Corps: Corps device, 128; titles, 163; under Bureau of Personnel, 173; device, 232, 243, 259

Chesapeake, frigate, 1794, 21, 22

Chief Engineer: first employed, 35, 38; authorized, 1842, 41; see also Engineers

Chief of Naval Operations: senior officer of the Navy, 29; office established 1915, 167; authority of, 169, 170; relationship to Bureaus, 171; rank of Admiral authorized for, 177

Chief Petty Officer, rating established 1894, 208; see also Uniforms, Chief Petty Officers

Chief Warrant Officers, commissioned status, 1899, 178; see also Uniforms, Warrant Officers

Circular, Navy Department, 1863, directs compliance with uniform instructions, 126

Civil Engineers: first employed 1802, 30; drydock construction, 32; commissioned, 1867, 158; relative rank, 161, 163; duties in World War II, 183, 184; women officers, 264; see also Uniforms, Civil Engineers

Civil Engineer Corps: Sanger, W.P.S., "Father of," 32; officers commissioned, 1867, 158; device, 205, 225, 246, 247; working uniform, 1941, 249, 250

Civil Officers, 53, 65, 75, 120; see also noncombatant, and staff officers

Clerks: warrant officers, 1835, 33; relative rank, 1863, 51; see also Uniforms, Warrant Officer

Cocked hats, 56, 58, 63, 65, 69, 72, 81, 82, 86, 94, 100, 110, 117, 119, 128, 187, 188, 189, 200, 205, 207, 208, 221, 245, 246, 269, 271

Colored cloth, worn on sleeve as indication of Staff, 194, 199, 201, 205, 207, 217, 222, 233, 241, 243

Commander, rank established 1837, 34; see also Uniforms, Commander

Commander-in-Chief, U.S. Fleet, duties combined with Chief of Naval Operations, 1942, 170, 173

Combatant officers, 21, 44; see also sea and line officers

Commissioned officers, list of such, 1794, 19

Commodore, rank authorized 1862, 50; see also Uniforms, Commodore

"Commodore," as courtesy title for an "Officer in Command of a Squadron" prior to 1862, 47, 64, 72, 93, 100, 107; see also Uniforms, "Commodore"

Congress, Continental: a "Resolve," 1775, government of the Navy, 22; "Resolve," 1776, relative rank between officers of the Army and Navy, 20

Congress, frigate, 1794, 21, 22, school aboard, 1802, 34

Congress, Joint Resolution of, U.S. Naval Auxiliary Naval Force, 1898, 180

Constellation, frigate, 1794, 21,

22, service during "Quasi-War" with France, 24
Constitution, frigate, 1794, 21, 22
Constitution, sections concerning Navy, 18, 179
Construction Battalions, commanded by Civil Engineer Corps officer, 184
Construction Board, Navy management device, established in 1889, 164
Construction and Repair, Bureau of: created 1862, 49; Bureau Chief served on Construction Board, 164, assisted in early aeroplane development, 169; combined with Engineering, Bureau of, to form Ships, Bureau of, 1940, 170; *see also* Ships, Bureau of
Construction, Equipment and Repair, Bureau of, created 1842, 39; duties of, 40; naval constructor to be Chief of, 41; split into three bureaus, 1862, 44; *see also* Construction and Repair; Equipment; Steam Engineering; Bureaus of
Continental Navy, status of at end of Revolution, 17
Corporal, Marine, rate authorized, 1794, 20
Corps, term first used when Congress established the Engineer Corps in 1842, 41; *see also* Chaplain, Civil Engineer, Dental, Engineer Medical, Paymaster, Naval Constructors, and Professors of Mathematics, Corps
Corps devices; *see* Devices, Corps
Crowninshield, Benjamin, Secretary of the Navy, conflict with Navy Board over responsibilities, 1815, 29
Curtiss, Glenn, pioneer aircraft builder,, 167
Daniels, Josephus, Secretary of the Navy: order establishing rank for Staff officers, 1918, 163; abolished Naval Aide system, 165; uniforms for World War I, 238
Decatur, Lt. Stephen, destroyed *Philadelphia*, Tripoli, 1804, 25
Delaware, frigate, docked Norfolk, 1833, 32
Denby, Edwin, Secretary of the Navy, issued Uniform Regulations, 1922, 246
Dental Corps: established 1912, 179; under Medicine and Surgery, 185; device, 233; reserve authorized, 1913, 179; device, 247
Devices
Aviation, 243
Cap, 94, 97, 108, 110, 111, 113, 115, 119, 120, 121, 126, 127, 128, 131, 134, 192, 196, 199, 200, 233, 234, 244, 263, 264, 269, 270
Chaplain Corps, 128, 221, 232, 243, 259
Civil Engineer Corps, 205, 225, 246, 247, 264
Collar, 63, 104, 134, 189, 202, 203, 204, 207, 223
Commodore (courtesy rank) 64, 72, 93, 100, 107
Colored sleeve cloth (as an indication of Staff Corps), 194, 196, 201, 205, 207, 217,

222, 233, 241, 243
Corps; *see* individual corps
Dental Corps, 233, 247, 264
Engineer Corps, 104, 127, 178, 223
Epaulets, 93, 97, 99, 107, 108, 113, 119, 189, 199, 201, 204, 222, 245, 246
Executive Officers, 1861, 114
Hospital Corps, 220, 264
Line officers: Foul anchor, 75, 89, 100, 119, 120, 127, 189, 207, 222, 223, 244, 246, 269; Gold star, 121, 124, 126, 130, 187, 188, 189, 194, 196, 201, 204, 217, 222, 243, 244, 246, 250, 269
Medical Corps, 79, 100, 107, 127, 207, 247, 264, 269
Medical Corps, Reserve, 233, 253
Medical Service Corps, 233
Metal, 93, 232, 249, 250, 256, 260, 264, 270
Midshipmen, 89, 97
Naval Constructors, 128, 201, 247
Nurse Corps, 233, 253, 256, 260, 263, 269
Pay Corps, 127; *see also*, Pursers, Supply Corps
Petty officers, 96, 130, 192, 193, 200, 205, 208, 216, 217, 220, 221, 222, 264
Professors of Mathematics, 128, 183, 187, 201, 204, 205
Pursers, 79, 104, 107, 121
Rank, 72, 75, 93, 94, 97, 100, 103, 107, 108, 119, 127, 128, 130, 131, 134, 189, 204, 207, 222, 250, 260
Secretary, 128, 199
Sleeve lace, indication of rank, 103, 111, 117, 119, 120, 121, 124, 126, 131, 134, 187, 188, 189, 193, 194, 196, 199, 201, 202, 203, 204, 205, 217, 220, 224, 233, 243, 244, 249, 256, 269, 270, 271
Shoulder marks, 222, 224, 234, 245, 259
Shoulder straps, 93, 97, 99, 100, 107, 108, 110, 113, 114, 119, 127, 130, 189, 199, 201, 204, 205, 217, 222
Supply Corps, 247
Warrant Officers, 130, 207
Waves, 263, 264, 269, 270
Dewey, Adm. George: head General Board, 1900, 165; ranks established for, 1899, 177; uniform, 221, 222
Dickerson, Mahlon, Secretary of the Navy, directed construction of steam vessels, 185, 35
Dirks, 74
Dress uniform, 104, 117
Drydocks, construction of, 1827, 32
Dungarees, 232, 270
Education: chaplains as teachers, 34; professors authorized, 33; rating of schoolmaster authorized, 1813, 34; educational duties of professors, 1841, 38; schools set up ashore, 39; establishment of the Naval Academy, 1845, 42, 44; professors to instruct midshipmen at the Academy and on board ship, 47

Ellyson, Lt. T. G., first Naval aviator, 167
Ely, Eugene, civilian pilot for Curtiss, 167
Engineer Corps: established 1842, 41; no official uniform prescribed, 1841, 97; device, 1852, 104, 108; new device, 1861, 113; modified device, 1863, 127; officers of, to be amalgamated with Line, 177, 178, 185; colored cloth sleeve lace prescribed as device, 1869, 194; device, 201, 223
Engineer Department: ratings for, 42; assistants in, 49; relative rank for officers, 51
Engineers (steam): first employed 1836, 35; appointed by ship's captain, 38; authorized by Congress, 1842; classes, 41; relative rank, 46, 48, 51, 52, 111, 113, 114, 126, 158-161; transferred to Line 1899, 177, 178; relative rank, 194, 199, 201; *see also* Uniforms, Engineers
Enlisted personnel: authorized by Congress, 1794; ratings established, 20; schooling, 33, 38, 39; ratings, 42; recruiting of, 49, 50; beards, 96, 97; ratings, 176; enlisted women, WWI, 183; rating badges, 192, 193, 194, 200, 205, 208; Naval Militia, Naval Reserve, 233, 234, 235; yeomanettes, 241; Waves, 263, 264, 269, 270, 271; *see also* Uniforms, Enlisted
Ensign: rank established 1862, 50, 117; rank Ensign (junior grade) for passed midshipmen created, 1883, 174; *see also* Uniforms, Ensign
Enterprise, American schooner, "Quasi-War" with France, 24
Epaulets, 58, 60, 64, 65, 72, 92, 93, 97, 99, 106, 107, 110, 111, 113, 114, 117, 119, 120, 128, 187, 188, 189, 199, 201, 204, 221, 222, 241, 245, 269, 271
Evening dress, 202, 224, 269, 270, 271
Executiive Officer, device for, 1861, 114
Farragut, David Glasgow: first Vice Admiral, 1864, 52; Admiral, 1866, 158, 177; special sleeve star, 189
Flag Officer: rank established by Congress, 1857, 51; collective designation, 48, 196, 201, 202, 208
Fleet Reserve, established, 1915, 181, 182
Forrestal, James, Secretary of the Navy, approved uniform instructions, 1947, 269
Foul anchor, as a Line device, 75, 89, 100, 119, 120, 127, 187, 189, 207, 220, 222, 223, 244, 246
France, "Quasi-War" with, 1798-1801, 24, 25
Frigates, first authorized in 1794, construction of, 21
Frock coat, 59, 82, 92, 97, 107, 114, 117, 130, 188, 200, 202, 204, 217, 221, 223, 225, 232, 238, 245, 246, 269
Full dress, 65, 69, 72, 100, 103, 104, 110, 117, 128, 187, 188,

196, 200, 201, 205, 217, 221, 245, 246, 269, 271
Full Dress, coats, 65, 68, 72, 89, 103, 104, 108, 117, 188, 217, 245
Full dressed, cocked hats, 58
Garrison cap, 82, 93, 270
General Board, Navy management, 1900, 165
General Orders: Navy, 1820, uniform regulation, 69; 1821, uniform change, 74; 1830, uniform regulations, 74; 1846, relative rank, medical officers, 46; 1847, relative rank, pursers, 47; 1832, change medical officers' device, 83; 1834, change, medical officers' uniform, 86; 1838, modify uniform, midshipmen, 86; 1852, uniform regulations, 103; 1856, uniforms, surgeons and pursers, 111; 1859, January, relative rank, engineers, 111, 112; 1859, March, change, enlisted uniform, 111; 1861, relative rank staff officers, device for Executive Officers, 114; 1862, major change to 1852 uniform regulations, 50, 127; 1863, relative rank staff officers 51, 126, 159; 1869, March, uniform regulations, 194, 196, 199, 202; 1869, April, relative rank, 159, 200; 1869, uniform changes, 196; 1876, changes, enlisted dress, 203; 1881, relative rank, Civil Engineers, 161; 1894, badges for chief petty officers, 208, 217; 1898, changes in Medical Department, 220, 221; 1901, uniform regulation, 223, 224; 1902, revisions in uniform instruction, 223, 224; 1917, uniforms required during World War I, 238
Gold lace, indication of rank; see Devices
Gold sleeve star; see Devices
Grant, U.S., President, appointed Borie, A. P., Secretary of the Navy, 158
Gray working uniform, 259, 264, 270
Green, aviation uniform, 225, 241, 243, 245, 249, 250, 270
Gunner: warrant rank authorized, 1794, 20; pay 22; relative rank, officer, 1863, 51; see also Warrant Officers, Uniforms, Warrant Officers
Hartford, steam frigate Flagship, Admiral Farragut, device on his sleeve star, 189, 196
Haswell, C. H., first steam engineer, Navy, 35
Hats, canvas, 216
Hats, round, 69
Hats, straw, 97
Hats, women, 241, 253, 256, 260, 263, 264
Headquarters Construction Companies, construction units, World War II, 183, 185
Helmet, 82, 207, 235, 250, 270
Higbee, Lenah Incliffe, Superintendent of Nurses, 253, photograph, 254
Hospital Corps: established 1898, 177; under Bureau of Medicine and Surgery, 185; device, 220, 264
Hospital Surgeon, 65, 68; see also Medical Officers
Humphreys, Joshua, naval constructor, 1794, 22; assistant to

Secretary of the Navy, 23, 30
Humprheys, Samuel, naval constructor, under Navy Board, 30
Insignia, see Devices
Inspection, Aide for, Naval Aide System, 1909, 165
Jacket, enlisted, 94, 115, 193, 194; mess, 224, 232, 234, 269, 271; officers, 64, 83, 92, 131, 134, 188, 189, 200; women, 263, 264
Khaki, Marine Corps cloth, 238
Khaki uniforms, 63, 229, 238, 241, 243, 245, 249, 250, 259, 270
Knee breeches, see Breeches
Knox, Commo. Dudley W. *A History of the United States Navy*, 53f, 185f
Knox, Frank, Secretary of the Navy, approved 1941 Uniform Regulations, 250
Latrobe, Benjamin Henry, architect, employed by Navy, 1802, 30
Letter, Secretary of the Navy to Captain M. C. Perry, 1837, uniform for engineers, 86
Lieutenant: rank established 1794, 19; pay, 24; allowance for 25, 27; rank status, 44, 45; number allowed, 1862, 50; as Executive Officers, 114; *see also* Uniforms, Lieutenant
Lieutenant, Commandant, 1820, 69, 72, 74
Lieutenant, junior grade, title established 1883 to replace that of Master, 174
Lieutenant, Line of Battleships, 1820, 69, 72, 74
Lieutenant, Marines, rank authorized, 1794, 19, pay, 22
Lieutenant-commander, created in 1862, 117; *see also* Uniforms, Lieutenant-commander
Live oak and acorn, embroidery, 75, 79, 82, 92, 93, 100, 104, 196, 201, 202, 203, 217
Long, John D., Secretary of the Navy, established General Board, 1900, 165, approved 1897 1897 Uniform Regulations, 220
Madison, James, President, nominated members, Board of Navy Commissioners, 1815, 29
Marine Corps, Commandant reports to Chief of Naval Operations, 173; uniforms, 238
Marine Corps, corporals, authorized 1794, 20; sergeants, authorized, 1794, 20
Marine Detachment, frigates, 1794, 20
Mason, J. T., Secretary of the Navy, relative rank, pursers, 1847, 47, 99
Master: rank established 1837 to replace "Sailing Master," 34; title changed to Lieutenant junior grade, 1883, 174; *see also* Uniforms, Master
Master Commandant: rank established 1837, rank abolished, 1801, 25; rank restored, 1806, 27; title changed to commander, 1837, 34; *see also* Uniforms, Master Commandant
Masters' Mates, warrant officers, 1794, 20; *see also* Warrant Officers
Material, Aide for, Naval Aide System, 1909, 165
Medical Corps: device, 79, 86, 92, 104, 108, 110, 127, 199,

205, 207, 247, 253, 264, 269; Medical Corps Reserve, device, 1912, 233; *see also* Medical Department, Medical Officers, Bureau of Medicine and Surgery
Medical Department: established, 1794, 20, 21; reorganized, 1828, 32, 33; Device, 1863, 51; Bureau of Medicine and Surgery, 177; Hospital Corps, 1898, 177; Nurse Corps, 1908, 178; Dental Corps, 1912, 179; Medical Service Corps, 1947, 185
Medical Officers: commissioned status, 1794, 20, 21; classes increased, 1828, 32, 33; Relative Rank, 45, 46, 47, 48, 51, 52, 120, 126, 158, 159, 160, 163, 194, 201
Medical Service Corps, created 1947, 185; device, 233
Medicine and Surgery, Bureau of: created 1842, 39; duties of, 40, 41; Hospital Corps part of, 1898, 177; Nurse Corps established, 1908, 178; Dental and Medical Reserve Corps added, 1912, 179; sections of, 185; oak leave and acorn basis device of all Medical corps, 233; prescribed nurses uniforms, 250, 260
Merchant Marine Reserve, created 1938, 182
Mess Jacket; *see* Jackets
Metal Corps insignia: authorized 1913, 232; abolished, 1913, 234; reinstated, 1931, 249; khaki uniforms, 250; nurse device, 1944, 269
Metal Naval Reserve device, 1915, 235
Meyer, George von L., Secretary of the Navy, established Naval Aide System, 1909, 165; approved 1913 Uniform Regulations, 225
Michigan, steam man-of-war, 1839, 38
Midshipmen: warrant rank established, 1794, 20; education of, 33, 34, 38, 39; 42, 44; relative position on Naval rank structure, 45; education, 47; cadet engineers, naval cadets, 1883, 174; *see also* Uniforms, midshipmen
Mississippi, steam man-of-war, 1839, 38
Missouri, steam man-of-war, 1839, 38
National Guard, authorized, 1903, 181
National Naval Volunteers, established 1916, 182, uniforms, 241, 243
Naval Academy: established 1845, 43; appropriations and staff for, 44; uniform devices, 75; under Bureau of Navigation, 1941, 173; graduates of, 174; uniform, 204, 207
Naval Agents, employed in 1794, 21, 22
Naval Aide System, 1909 under Secretary Meyer, 174
Naval Asylum, Navy school, 1838, 34
Naval Aviation, beginnings, 167; activities, 1911–1918, 169; Naval Flying Corps, established, 1916, 182; unofficial uniform, 235, 238; device, 243; uniform abolished, 245, 246; fly-

ing uniform reinstated, 247, 249; see also Uniforms, Aviation

Naval Cadets, passed midshipmen, 1883, 174

Naval Constructors, civilian constructors: first frigates, 1794, 21, 22; Joshua Humphreys, "Principal Naval Constructor," 1794, 22; Humphreys, advisor to Secretary Stoddert, 1798-1801, 23, 24; Chief of Bureau of Construction, Equipment and Repair to be a "skilful" naval constructor, 40, 41; pay, 42; relative rank, 51, 126; device, 128; commissioned status, 1866, 158; relative rank, 159, 160; corps abolished, 1940; sleeve insignia, 201; see also Uniforms, Naval Constructors

Naval Militia: authority under the Constitution, 179; Federal support of State Naval Militias, 1891, 180; Navy responsibility for, 181, 182; uniforms for, 232, 234, 238; insignia, 241, 243; uniforms, 247

Naval Personnel, Bureau of: so named, 1942, 173; uniforms, 259, 263; see also Navigation, Bureau of

Naval Reserve: no reserve force in 1861, 49; Medical Reserve, 1912, 179; Dental Reserve, 1913, 179; Naval Reserve Act, 1915, 181, 182

Navigation, Bureau of: created 1862, 49; functions, 50; scientific bureau, 1862, 164, 165; name changed to Personnel, 1942, 173; new uniform instructions, 245; reinstated aviation uniform, 247; uniform, nurses, 260; see also, Bureaus of Naval Personnel, Ordnance and Hydrography, Construction, Equipment and Repair; Equipment and Repair

Navy blue, color, 264, 269

Navy buttons, 59, 64, 74, 96, 200, 225, 249

Navy Department: established, 1798, 23; Board of Navy Commissioners, 1815, 28; duties of the Secretary, 29; personnel, 33; bureau system, 39, 40; additional bureaus, 49; rank structure, 50; uniforms, 55; first uniform instruction, 1802, 60; letter to officers, 1813 uniform, 64; uniform changes, 83; uniforms, 89, 97, 99; changes in administration, 155; rank Civil Engineers, 163; management systems, 164, 165, 167; present organization, 173; responsible for Naval Militia, 1914, 181; manner of issuing uniform regulations, 203; uniformity in dress, 243; aviation dress, 246

Navy Regulations (Government of the Navy): duties of chaplains, 1802, 33; education, 1841, 38; relative rank, 1841, 45, 46; Circular, relative rank, 1871, 160; rank for staff officers, 1918, 163; classes of enlisted personnel, 1885, 174

Navy Strength: vessels, 1800, 24; officers, 25, 27; ships, 1812, 27; officers and men, 1861-1865, 116; ships, 1870, 155

Navy Yards: building sites, 1794,

21; locations, 1800, 24; status, 1815, 29; locations, 1842, 40

Navy Yards and Docks, Bureau of: established, 1842, 39; responsibilities, 40; head of, 41; name changed, 1862, 49; see also Yards and Docks, Bureau of

Noncombatant: authorized, 1794, 21; relative position in Navy, 44; uniform, 59; buttons, 74; coats, 81

Nonregular: temporary commissions, 1917, 238; staff officers, 241; most released 1918, 247; see also Reserve, militia

Office of Detail, assignment of officers, Civil War, 165

Officer Commanding a Squadron; pay established, 1799, 25; clerk for, 33; 1857 called Flag Officers, 47; in 1862 called rear admiral and commodore, 50; insignia, 1802, 64

Officer Strength, 1801, 25, Civil War 116

Officers, Navy; see Assistant Engineer, Assistant Paymaster, Assistant Purser, Boatswain, Captain, Carpenter, Chaplain, Chief Engineer, Civil Engineer, Clerk, Commander, Commodore, "Commodore" (courtesy rank), Dental Corps, Ensign, Flag, Gunner, Hospital Corps, Lieutenant, Lieutenant-Commandant, Lieutenant (junior grade), Lieutenant (Line of Battleships), Master, Master Commandant, Medical Service Corps, Midshipmen, Naval Constructors, Nurse Corps, "Officer Commanding a Squadron," Passed Midshipman, Professor of Mathematics, Purser, Sailing Master, Sailmaker, Secretary, Supply Corps, Surgeon, Surgeon's Mate, Vice Admiral, Wave

Officers, women; see Nurses, Waves

Offices, Navy Department: in 1798, 23; in 1862, 50; of Detail, 165; at present 173

Operations of the Fleet, Aide for, management, Naval Aide System, 165

Ordnance, Bureau of: created, 1862, 49; Construction Board, 1889, 164; arms and armor, 1862, 170; became part of Bureau of Naval Weapons, 1959, 173; see also Ordnance and Hydrography, Bureau of; Naval Weapons, Bureau of

Ordnance and Hydrography, created 1842, 39; duties, 40; Chief of, 41; name changed to Ordnance, 1892, 165; see also Ordnance, Bureau of

Organized Reserve; see Naval Reserve

Overalls, 238

Overcoat, 128, 204, 232, 247, 270

Pantaloons, 79, 81, 104, 111

Passed Assistant Surgeon, rank established 1828, 32; see also Uniforms, Medical Officers; Midshipmen

Passed Midshipman, relative position, Navy, 45; see also Uniforms, Midshipmen

Pay Corps, device, 1863, 127; established, 1871, 165; colored sleeve lace for, 1869, 199; devices, 1869, 201; warrant of-

ficers, 207; name changed to Supply Corps, 1919, 165

Pay Department, rank of Assistant Paymaster authorized, 1861, 49; relative rank of officers, 1863, 51; insignia, 1861, 114; authority of officers, 184

Paymaster: title replaced that of Purser, 1860, 48; relative rank, 1863, 51; device, 1863, 127; relative rank, 159, 160; title changed to Supply Officer, 1919, 165; assigned actual rank, 1899, 163; colored sleeve lace, 1869, 199; relative rank, 1869, 201; clerks for, 204; see also Pursers, Supply Officers

Pennsylvania, battleship, used for aircraft landing, 1911, 167

Pensacola, Florida, early aviation facility, 169

Perry, Captain M. C., captain first Navy steam vessel, 35, prescribed uniforms for engineers, 86, 89

Personnel, Aide-for-Aide System of Naval management, 1909, 165

Petty Officers: authorized 1794, 20; clothing, 59; device, 1841, 94, 96; classes of, 174, 176, 177; rating badges, 192, 200, 205, 208, 216, 220, 221; Naval Militia, 233, 234, 237; Waves, 264, 270; see also Uniforms, Petty Officers

Philadelphia, frigate, stranded Tripoli, 1803, burned, 1804, 25, 26

Porter, Vice Admiral David D, principal assistant to Secretary Borie, 1869, 158, 159, sleeve lace, 222

Preble, Commodore Edward, Mediterranean command, Barbary Wars, 27

President, frigate, 1794, 21

Professors of Mathematics: authorized 1835, 33; duties, 38; shipboard status, 41; awaiting orders, 1846, 42; commissioned status, 1848, 47; relative rank, 1863, 51, 52; corps device, 1863 128; relative rank, 159, 160, 161; corps abolished, 1916, 183, 185; device 1866, 192; relative rank, 1872; colored corps sleeve lace, 1872, 201

Provisions and Clothing, Bureau of: created 1842, 39; duties, 40; bureau reorganization, 1862, 49; name changed to Supplies and Accounts, 1892, 165; see also Supplies and Accounts, Bureau of

Pursers: warrant officers, 1794, 20, 21; commissioned 1812, 27; under Bureau of Provisions and Clothing, 1842, 40; relative rank, 45, 47; title changed to Paymaster, 1860, 48; assistants authorized, 1861, 49; corps device, 79, 93; relative rank, 99; device, 104; relative rank, 111; see also Paymaster, Supply Officers

Raincoat, 270

Rank, 44, 45, 46, 47, 59, 103, 120, 163, 177, 178, 179, 204, 223, 225, 232, 269

Rank devices; see Devices, Rank

Rating badges, 192, 193, 194, 200, 205, 208, 216, 220, 221, 264; see also Petty Officers

Rear Admiral, rank established, 1862, 50, 117; see also Uni-

forms, Rear Admiral
Regular Navy, 233, 238, 243, 244, 245, 249, 250, 263, 269
Regulations; *see* Navy Regulations
Relative rank, 45, 46, 47, 48, 51, 52, 59, 86, 99, 100, 111, 120, 126, 127, 158, 159, 160, 161, 163, 178, 192, 194, 199
Reserve blue, color, 264, 269, 270
Resolutions, Congress, 1826, Survey for Drydocks, 32, 1898, U.S. Auxiliary Naval Force, 180
Resolves, Continental Congress: Nov. 28, 1775, government of the Navy, 22; Nov. 15, 1776, relative rank between Army and Navy, 20
Robeson, George M., Secretary of the Navy: 1871, relative rank, 160; uniform regulations, 1869, 196
Roosevelt, Franklin D., President of the United States, functiions of Chief of Naval Operations, 1934, 169
Sack coat, officers, 131, 188, 189, 200, 203, 204, 205, 207, petty officers, 202, 203, 216
Sailing Master: warrant, 1794, 20; title changed to master, 1837, 34; "in line of promotion," 1837, 34; relative rank, 44, 45, 46, 48
Sailmaker: warrant rank authorized, 1794, 20; pay 22; relative rank, 45; staff officer, 1863, 51, 52; *see also* Uniforms, Sailmaker
Sanger, W.P.S., civil engineer under Board of Navy Commissioners, 1836, 32; "Father of the Civil Engineer Corps," 1867, 158
Schoolmaster, chaplain as, 33, title authorized, 1813, 34
Schools, Navy, 34, 38, 39, 42, 44
Schuyler, Harley and Graham, uniform suppliers, 128
Sea Bees, men of Naval Construction Battalions, 183, 184, 185
Sea Gull, steam dispatch boat, 1823-1825, 35
Seamen, authorized 1794, 20; dress, 1797, 59; first uniform regulation for, 1841, 94, 96; classes of, 176
Sea Officers; *see* Combatant and Line officers
Secretaries: warrant officers, 1835, 33; relative rank, 1863, 51, 160; device, 128; *see also* Uniforms, Secretaries
Secretary of the Navy: head of Navy Department, 1798, 23; military responsibility, 29; Navy Board, assistants to, 34; directed construction of steam vessels, 35; to appoint chief engineers, 38; responsibility for bureaus, 1842, 39; Bancroft, established Naval Academy, 42; gave relative rank to medical officers, 46; relative rank for engineers, 48; Gideon Welles issued order on relative rank, 1863, 51; appointed board to consider transfer of volunteer officers to regular Navy, 1866, 158; Adolph P. Borie, under President Grant, 158, 159; relative rank, 1871,

160; relative rank for civil engineers, 1881, 161; organized Construction Board, 1877, 164; established General Board, 1900, 165; created Naval Aide system, 1909, 165; Aide system abandoned, 1913, 165; creation of Bureau of Naval Weapons, 173; uniform regulations, 1866, 188; General Order No. 90, uniforms and relative rank, 1869, 194, 196; uniform regulations, 1883, 207; uniform regulations, 1885, 208; uniform regulations, 1897, 220; letter on uniform changes, 1899, 221; uniform regulations, 1913, 225; uniform regulations, 1941, 250
Secretary of War, duties concerning naval matters, 1789, 18, 19; Secretary James McHenry issued first Navy uniform instruction, 1797, 56
Service coat, 83, 188, 203, 204, 205, 207, 221, 223, 224, 232, 234, 244, 246, 247, 249, 250, 269, 270
Service dress, 117, 131, 189, 202, 241, 243, 246, 247, 269, 270
Ship construction superintendants, frigates, 1794, list of, 21
Shipped or rated masters' mates, uniform, 114; *see also* Warrant Officers
Ship's Stores, 59; *see also* Slop Stores
Ships, Bureau of (see also Construction, Equipment and Repair; Construction and Repair, Engineering, Bureaus of) problems of divided responsibility, 49; formed by merger of Construction and Repair, and Engineering, 1940, 170; Naval Constructors, 185
Shoulder knots, 205
Shoulder marks, 222, 224, 232, 234, 238, 243, 244, 245, 250, 259, 260, 271
Shoulder Straps, officially introduced in 1830, 83; 93, 97, 99, 107, 108, 110, 113, 117, 120, 124, 126, 130, 131, 189, 201, 204, 205, 220, 222, 224
Sleeve lace, indication of rank, 103, 107, 111, 113, 117, 119, 120, 121, 124, 131, 134, 187, 188, 189, 194, 196, 199, 201, 202, 203, 204, 205, 207, 217, 220, 221, 222, 224, 232, 233, 234, 244, 245, 249, 250, 256, 259, 260, 264, 270
Sleeve lace, warrant officers, 222, 223, 244
Special Dinner dress, 271
Special Full dress, 196, 201, 203, 207, 238, 245, 246
Specialty marks, enlisted, 220, 222, 264
Sprout, Harold and Margaret, *The Rise of American Naval Power*, 1776-1918, 155, 53n, 186n
Staff, 20, 21, 44, 45, 46, 48, 50, 51, 52, 75, 102, 108, 120, 127, 130, 131, 135, 158, 159, 160, 163, 185, 188, 189, 194, 199, 200, 204, 244, 272
Staff Corps; *see* Chaplain, Civil Engineer, Engineer, Hospital, Medical, Medical Service, Naval Constructor, Nurse, Paymaster, Professor of Mathematics and Supply, Corps
Staff officers, first official use, 51;

52, 58, 75, 120, 124, 130, 131, 159, 160, 177, 201
Star, device of the Line; *see* Devices, Line
Star, rank device; *see* Devices, Rank
Steam Engineers: first employment of 1837, 35, 38; status of, 1842, 41; *see also* Engineers
Steam Vessels: *Fulton*, 1814, 34; *Sea Gull*, 1823, 35; *Fulton II*, 1836, 35; *Michigan*, *Mississippi*, *Missouri*, 1839, 38.
Stoddert, Benjamin, first actual Secretary of the Navy, 1798, 23
Straw hats, 97, 99
Submarine officers, uniform, 249
Supplies and Accounts, Bureau of; name given to Provisions and Clothing, 1892, 165; device, 247; women officers assigned to, 264; *see also* Provisions and Clothing, Bureau of
Supply Corps: device, 93; officers addressed as "Pay," 163; so-called, 1919, 165; device, 247; women officers, World War II, 264
Supply Officers, name changed from paymasters, 1919, 165; *see also* Pursers, Paymasters
Surgeon General, Navy, also Chief of the Bureau of Medicine and Surgery, 178
Surgeon of the Fleet, with Fleet, 32; relative rank, 51; insignia, 1847, 99; *see also* Uniforms, Medical Officers; Hospital Surgeons
Surgeons: authorized, 1794, 20; commissioned staff officers, 1794, 21; rank, 33; Barton, W.P.C. first Chief of Medicine and Surgery, 1842, 41; members of Medical Department, 41, 42; instructor at Naval Academy, 1845, 44; relative rank, 1841, 45, 46, 51; device, 127; relative rank, 1869, 159, 160; actual rank, 1899, 163; colored sleeve lace, 1869, 194; device, 1883, 207; colored corps cloth, 207; women surgeons, 1943, 264; *see also* Uniforms, Medical Officers
Surgeon's Mates: authorized, 1794, 20; commissioned staff officers, 21; title changed to Assistant Surgeon, 1828, 32; *see also* Uniforms, Medical Officers
Swords, 58, 74, 117, 118, 246, 247
Temporary officers, Act of Congress, 1861, 49
Thompson, Richard W., Secretary of the Navy, organized board to assist in management, 1877, 164
Todd, Col. Frederick P., Director, West Point Museum, assistance in research, 13
Toucey, Isaac, Secretary of the Navy, relative rank, engineers, 1859, 48, 111
Tracey, Benjamin F., Secretary of the Navy, organized Construction Board, 1889, 164
Tropical uniforms, 97, 99, 188, 250, 270
Trousers, 83, 94, 103, 104, 111, 117, 188, 202, 224, 245, 246, 249, 269
Trousers, gold laced, 103, 104, 111, 188, 202, 245, 246, 269
Undress coat, 1830, 82

Undress uniform, 63, 68, 81, 83, 92, 107, 117, 189, 196, 199, 204, 205; see also Uniforms, undress

Uniform regulations: 1797, 56, 58, 59; 1802, 60, 63, 64; 1813, 64, 65, 68, 69; 1820, 69, 72, 74, 82; 1830, 74, 75, 79, 81, 83, 86, 89; 1841, 89, 92, 93, 94, 96, 97, 99, 100, 101; 1852, 55, 103, 104, 107, 108, 110, 111, 113, 114, 115, 117, 119, 120, 121, 124, 126, 127, 128; 1864, 128, 130, 131, 134, 135; 1866, 187, 188, 189, 192, 193, 194; 1869, 196, 199, 200, 202, 203; 1876, 203, 204, 205; 1883, 207, 208; 1886, 208, 216, 217, 220; 1897, 220, 221; 1899, 221, 222, 223, 224; 1905; 224; 1913, 225, 232, 233, 234, 235, 238, 241, 243, 244, 245, 246; 1922, 246, 249, 250; 1941, 250, 253, 256, 259, 260, 263, 264, 269; 1947, 269, 270; 1951, 270; 1959, 270, 271; changes to, 50, 74, 83, 86, 97, 99, 100, 101, 108, 110, 111, 113, 114, 115, 117, 119, 120, 121, 124, 127, 128, 131, 134, 194, 196, 199, 201, 202, 203, 204, 205, 217, 220, 221, 223, 224, 225, 234, 235, 238, 241, 243, 244, 245, 246, 247, 248, 249, 250, 259, 269, 270

Uniforms: Admiral, 189, 196, 201, 207, 222; Army, 1779, 56; Assistant Engineers (see Engineers); Assistant Paymasters (see Paymasters); Assistant Surgenos (see Medical Officers); Aviation, 225, 235, 238, 241, 243, 245, 247, 249, 250; Blue & buff, 56; Blue & gold, 56, 60, 245, 259; Boatswain (see also Warrant Officers), 59, 65, 69, 74, 81, 92, 101, 104, 107, 108, 110, 128, 130, 188, 204, 207; Carpenter (see also Warrant Officers), 59, 65, 69, 74, 81, 92, 101, 104, 107, 108, 110, 128, 130, 188, 204, 207; Captain, 58, 60, 63, 65, 69, 72, 74, 75, 79, 81, 82, 83, 86, 89, 92, 93, 94, 103, 104, 107, 108, 117, 119, 120, 121, 188, 194, 196; Captain, Five Years Standing, 72; Chaplains, 58, 59, 63, 79, 81, 93, 94, 104, 107, 110, 120, 128, 192, 194, 200, 216, 217, 220, 221, 222, 224, 225, 232, 241, 243, 244, 246, 259; Chief Engineers (see Engineers); Chief Petty Officers (see also Petty Officers), 217, 220, 264; Chief Warrant Officers (see also Warrant Officers), 222, 224, 244; Civil Engineers, 205, 225, 246, 247, 249; Clerks (see also Warrant Officers) 81, 94, 104, 108, 128, 130, 188, 200, 222; Commander (see also Master Commandant), 92, 103, 104, 107, 108, 117, 119, 121, 188, 194, 196; Commodore, 64, 72, 117, 119, 121, 188, 189; Dental Surgeons, 233; Dress, 104, 117; Engineers, 83, 89, 97, 104, 107, 110, 113, 120, 130, 188, 192, 194, 199; Enlisted, 59, 94, 96, 108, 111, 130, 192, 193, 194, 200, 203, 208, 216, 217, 220, 221, 224, 232, 233; Ensign, 119, 120, 121, 124, 128, 196, 205; Evening Dress, 202, 238, 245; Flag Officer (see also Commodore) 64, 72; Full Dress, 68, 92, 117, 188, 199, 200, 202, 217, 245, 246, 271; Gray 259, 264, 270; Green forestry, 225, 241, 243, 245, 249, 250, 270; Gunner (see also Warrant Officers), 59, 65, 69, 74, 92, 101, 104, 107, 108, 110, 128, 130, 188, 204, 207; Hospital Corps, 220; Khaki, 63, 225, 238, 241, 243, 245, 249, 250, 259, 270; Lieutenant, 56, 58, 60, 63, 65, 72, 74, 75, 82, 83, 86, 89, 92, 93, 94, 103, 104, 107, 108, 119, 120, 121, 124, 188, 196; Lieutenant, commandant, 72, 74; Lieutenant commander, 119, 121, 124, 188, 194; Lieutenant, Line of Battleships, 72, 74; Master, 94, 103, 104, 119, 120, 124, 188, 196; Master Commandant, 65, 72, 74, 75, 79, 81, 82, 83, 86, 89; Medical Officers, 58, 63, 65, 68, 74, 79, 83, 86, 92, 99, 100, 104, 107, 108, 110, 111, 113, 120, 194, 199, 201; Mess Dress, 224, 232, 269, 271; Midshipmen, 58, 60, 63, 64, 65, 74, 75, 79, 89, 92, 94, 97, 103, 104, 108, 110, 111, 120, 128, 130, 134, 188, 192, 199, 204; Militia, Naval, 232, 233, 234, 241, 243, 247; National Naval Volunteers, 241, 243; Naval Constructors, 128, 178, 192, 194, 200, 201, 247; Nurses, 250, 253, 256, 260, 269, 270; Paymasters (see also Pursers, Supply Officers), 114, 120, 124, 194, 199, 201; Petty Officers (see also Chief Petty Officers), 59, 94, 96, 108, 130, 192, 193, 200, 202, 203, 205, 208, 216, 217, 220, 221, 234, 264, 270; Professors of Mathematics, 93, 94, 104, 108, 120, 192, 194, 200, 201; Pursers (see also Paymasters, Supply Officers) 59, 63, 68, 74, 79, 92, 93, 94, 99, 100, 104, 107, 108, 110, 111, 113; Rear Admiral, 117, 119, 120, 121, 188, 189, 202; Reserve, 234, 235, 243, 245, 247, 249, 264; Sailmaker (see also Warrant Officers), 59, 65, 69, 74, 81, 92, 101, 104, 107, 108, 110, 128, 130, 188, 204, 207; Sailing Master, 58, 63, 74; Schoolmaster, 81; Secretaries (see also Warrant Officers), 93, 94, 104, 108, 128, 192, 199; Service, 117, 131, 189, 202, 203, 207, 220, 224, 232, 241, 244, 263, 269, 270; Special Full Dress, 202, 238, 245; Summer, 243, 256; Supply Officers, 246; Surgeon's Mates (see Medical Officers); Surgeons (see Medical Officers); Temporary Officers, 117; Tropical, 97, 188, 207, 232, 250; Undress, 63, 68, 81, 82, 83, 92, 107, 117, 189, 196, 199, 204, 205; Vice Admiral, 131, 188, 196, 201; Warrant Officers, 59, 65, 69, 74, 81, 92, 94, 101, 104, 107, 108, 110, 114, 115, 116, 128, 130, 188, 192, 200, 204, 207, 220, 224, 244; Waves, 263, 264, 269, 270; Winter, 92, 241, 243, 250, 256; Women's 241, 253, 256, 260, 263, 264, 269, 270; Working, 82, 200, 201, 224, 232, 238, 246, 247, 249, 263, 264

United States, frigate, 1794, 21, 22

U.S. Army and Navy Journal, 1861, 126

Vera Cruz, Mexico, first use of Naval Aviation in combat, 169

Volunteer Naval Reserve, 182

War Department: organized 1789, 18; responsibility for naval matters, 19; prescribed Navy uniform, 1797, 56; responsible for land militia, 180, 181, 232

Warrant Officers: authorized, 1794, 19, 20; pay increase, 1794, 22; relative rank, 44, 45; carpenters and sailmakers, staff officers, 1863, 51; relative rank, 1863, 52; Hospital Corps, 1898, 177; Chief Warrant Officers, 1889, 178; cap device, 1866, 192, 200; Boatswain and Gunners, Line star on sleeves, 204; cap device, 207, 224; see also Uniforms, Warrant Officers

Washington, General George, issued General Order, uniforms, 1779, 56

Waves, women of the Navy: regular status, 1948, 183; design of uniform, World War II, 263; device, 263, 264, 269, 270

Welles, Gideon, Secretary of the Navy, Civil War: relative rank, 51, 159, 160, 161, 194; Office of Detail, 165; uniforms, 188, 221

Whitney, W. C., uniform regulation, 1886, 208

Winter uniform, Aviation, 241, 249, 270

Working uniforms, 200, 201, 224, 232, 238, 246, 247, 249, 250, 259, 264, 270

Women, Navy, 178, 183, 241, 263, 264, 269; (see also Nurses, Waves, Yeomanettes

Yeomanettes, enlisted women, World War I, 183; uniforms, 241, 263